"Believing that Karl Barth has often ~~been misunderstood by evan~~gelicals, Shao Kai Tseng makes a solid case for taking another look at the Swiss theologian and shows us a way to read him charitably and profitably. If Herman Bavinck engaged and even learned from Kant, Schleiermacher, Hegel, and Feuerbach, the author argues, we can and need to learn from Barth. He's right about that, and one need not agree with every detail of Tseng's revisionary reading of Barth to profit a great deal from it. This is a model of how to read theologians with whom one disagrees."
—**John Bolt**, Jean and Kenneth Baker Professor of Systematic Theology, Emeritus, Calvin Theological Seminary

"Evangelical and Reformed engagement with the theology of Karl Barth continues to develop and mature, and may enter a new era with Shao Kai Tseng's work. He advances the conversation by bringing Barth into dialogue with the voices of Herman Bavinck and Geerhardus Vos and also by probing more deeply than either knee-jerk rejection or slavish acceptance of what Barth offers. This study will prove invaluable not just to those who teach on Barth but to all interested in some of the most pressing concerns of the Christian worldview in the twenty-first century."
—**David Gibson**, Minister, Trinity Church, Aberdeen; author, *Reading the Decree: Exegesis, Election and Christology in Calvin and Barth*

"Karl Barth died more than fifty years ago, but he keeps on being a provocative theologian to new generations. In this book, a fine summary of Barth's Reformed theology, neo-Calvinist theologian Shao Kai Tseng enthusiastically proposes and participates in a conversation with evangelicals about the core value of Barth's theology and theirs, to the benefit of both."
—**George Harinck**, Professor of the History of Neo-Calvinism, Kampen Theological University

"On many points, as Professor Tseng shows, Barth has been misunderstood by friend and foe alike. I know of no other work that, in brief compass, explains Barth's theology with such skill and engages it from a confessional Reformed perspective. Tethered to the primary sources, this work also displays the continuities and discontinuities with post-Barthian scholars—in Asia as well as the West. This is a gem."

—**Michael Horton**, J. Gresham Machen Professor of
    Theology, Westminster Seminary California

"This welcome volume takes ecumenical dialogue to a whole new level when it comes to Karl Barth and the more conservative wing of the Reformed theological tradition. Gone are the wearisome caricatures of the past. Tseng knows how to treat Barth accurately and fairly without losing his critical edge. While many questions remain to be resolved, Tseng narrows the gap by bringing Barth within hailing distance of those who have long opposed him. The nature and function of Holy Scripture, the scope of universal hope, and the urgency of political responsibility—divisive issues in many older Reformed receptions of Barth—are now ripe for creative reconsideration. This is ecumenical theology at its best, and we are greatly in Tseng's debt."

—**George Hunsinger**, McCord Professor of Systematic
    Theology, Princeton Theological Seminary

"As a new-generation Sino-Christian theologian, Shao Kai Tseng has done a great service, not only for his global community of Reformed evangelicals (primarily in the Dutch lineage of Herman Bavinck), but for all others who study the methods of theology. The book is grounded in competent reading of the Barth oeuvre and its reception history, particularly in North America (where Tseng did a great deal of his early theological study) and in the wider Asian context. Tseng's impressive learning, penetrating insight, theological and philosophical vocabulary, and incisive reasoning are complemented by highly intelligible writing. This introductory work is a valuable guide to the sweep of Barthian literature, now in its fifth generation. The refreshing expression of Tseng's theological virtues (faith, hope, love) carries the reader along, including worthy critique of Barth when applicable. The benefit of the book is that theological acuity is at the service of theological practice, and it presents us with a substantial Chinese witness to the rich and enduring contribution of Barth to contemporary theology."

—**Kurt Anders Richardson**, Professor in the Faculty of Theology, McMaster University; Author, *Reading Karl Barth*

"Tseng accomplishes much in this little volume: he provides not only a brief overview of Barth's theology, but also an account of its ongoing global significance, not least in Asia. Above all, Tseng is a confident interpreter who carries out a lively, constructive, evangelical engagement with Barth's theology at a fundamental level."

—**Fred Sanders**, Professor of Theology, Torrey Honors College, Biola University

"Too often, party lines are hastily drawn between these neighboring streams of Reformed theology: do you follow Barth, Reformed orthodoxy, or neo-Calvinism? Resisting this temptation, Tseng offers a charitable presentation and critical engagement of Barth that triangulates admirably between Barth's interpreters, Reformed orthodoxy, and Dutch neo-Calvinism, and in so doing charts a refreshing and eclectic way forward. More dialogues and cross-pollination need to happen between these conversations, and Tseng's book now serves as an invitation to that end."

—**Nathaniel Gray Sutanto**, Assistant Professor of Systematic Theology, Reformed Theological Seminary, DC

Karl

BARTH

GREAT THINKERS

A Series

Series Editor
Nathan D. Shannon

AVAILABLE IN THE GREAT THINKERS SERIES

Thomas Aquinas, by K. Scott Oliphint
Francis Bacon, by David C. Innes
Karl Barth, by Shao Kai Tseng
Richard Dawkins, by Ransom H. Poythress
Gilles Deleuze, by Christopher Watkin
Jacques Derrida, by Christopher Watkin
Michel Foucault, by Christopher Watkin
G. W. F. Hegel, by Shao Kai Tseng
David Hume, by James N. Anderson
Immanuel Kant, by Shao Kai Tseng
Karl Marx, by William D. Dennison
Karl Rahner, by Camden M. Bucey

FORTHCOMING

Alvin Plantinga, by Greg Welty
Plato, by David Talcott
Adam Smith, by Jan van Vliet

Karl

BARTH

Shao Kai Tseng

P&R PUBLISHING

P.O. BOX 817 • PHILLIPSBURG • NEW JERSEY 08865-0817

ISBN: 978-1-62995-887-3 (pbk)
ISBN: 978-1-62995-888-0 (ePub)

Printed in the United States of America

Library of Congress Cataloging-in-Publication Data

Names: Tseng, Shao Kai, 1981- author.
Title: Karl Barth / Shao Kai Tseng.
Description: Phillipsburg, New Jersey : P&R Publishing, [2021] | Series:
  Great thinkers | Includes bibliographical references and index. |
  Summary: "This evangelical reinterpretation and charitable critique of
  Barth's thought, written by a notable Barth scholar, explains his
  writings in their historical context and overviews his impact on
  theology worldwide"-- Provided by publisher.
Identifiers: LCCN 2021028194 | ISBN 9781629958873 (pbk) | ISBN
  9781629958880 (epub) | ISBN 9781629958897 (mobi)
Subjects: LCSH: Barth, Karl, 1886-1968.
Classification: LCC BX4827.B3 T7699 2021 | DDC 230/.044092 [B]--dc23
LC record available at https://lccn.loc.gov/2021028194

To the late J. I. Packer
and in remembrance of
Ah-Gong and Ah-Mah

CONTENTS

SERIES INTRODUCTION

Amid the rise and fall of nations and civilizations, the influence of a few great minds has been profound. Some of these remain relatively obscure even as their thought shapes our world; others have become household names. As we engage our cultural and social contexts as ambassadors and witnesses for Christ, we must identify and test against the Word those thinkers who have so singularly formed the present age.

The Great Thinkers series is designed to meet the need for critically assessing the seminal thoughts of these thinkers. Great Thinkers hosts a colorful roster of authors analyzing primary source material against a background of historical contextual issues, and providing rich theological assessment and response from a Reformed perspective.

Each author was invited to meet a threefold goal, so that each Great Thinkers volume is, first, *academically informed*. The brevity of Great Thinkers volumes sets a premium on each author's command of the subject matter and on the secondary discussions that have shaped each thinker's influence. Our authors identify the most influential features of their thinkers' work and address them with precision and insight. Second, the series maintains a high standard of *biblical and theological faithfulness*. Each volume stands on an epistemic commitment to "the whole counsel of God" (Acts 20:27), and is thereby equipped for fruitful critical engagement. Finally, Great Thinkers texts are *accessible*, not burdened with jargon or unnecessarily difficult vocabulary. The goal is to inform and equip the reader as effectively as possible through clear writing, relevant analysis, and incisive, constructive critique. My hope is that this series will distinguish itself by striking with biblical faithfulness and the riches of the Reformed tradition at the central nerves of culture, cultural history, and intellectual heritage.

Bryce Craig, president of P&R Publishing, deserves hearty thanks for his initiative and encouragement in setting the series in motion and seeing it through. Many thanks as well to P&R's director of academic development, John Hughes, who has assumed, with cool efficiency, nearly every role on the production side of each volume. The Rev. Mark Moser carried much of the burden in the initial design of the series, acquisitions, and editing of the first several volumes. And the expert participation of Amanda Martin, P&R's editorial director, was essential at every turn. I have long admired P&R Publishing's commitment, steadfast now for over eighty-five years, to publishing excellent books promoting biblical understanding and cultural awareness, especially in the area of Christian apologetics. Sincere thanks to P&R, to these fine brothers and sisters, and to several others not mentioned here for the opportunity to serve as editor of the Great Thinkers series.

Nathan D. Shannon
Seoul, Korea

FOREWORD

The towering figure of Karl Barth continues to exert a powerful influence over theological discourse and will continue to do so for at least the foreseeable future. It has been well said that, whatever one's assessment of his theology, Barth cannot be ignored. We cannot detour around him, but must pass through him.

As with all seminal figures, it can seem that there are almost as many interpretations of Barth as there are scholars. Conservatives have historically had serious reservations. While applauding his break with liberalism, they have until recently balked at what they consider, *inter alia*, his weak doctrine of Scripture, his apparently incipient universalism, his redrawing of the doctrine of election, his Christomonism, and his apparent detachment from history.

Many of these reservations arose from some misleading patterns of criticism. Some focused on Barth's work in the immediate years after his break with liberalism, in his *Der Römerbrief* and *Die christliche Dogmatik im Entwurf*. This critical approach was sometimes allied with a preset schematism, consisting of categories regularly imposed on the reading of sources. Moreover, it ignored the evidence of Barth's later growing attention to the Reformed scholastics in *Die kirchliche Dogmatik* and elsewhere. The fact that such criticisms of Barth have been widely regarded as caricatures should have served as a cautionary warning.[1] In this welcome addition to the Great Thinkers series, Dr. Shao Kai Tseng carefully probes the weaknesses of these approaches. While Cornelius Van Til's analysis of Barth has come in for trenchant criticism, Dr. Tseng recognizes that it arose from a careful study of Barth's own writings, which is more than can be said for some other critics, one of whom had not even read Barth, but relied on the reports he had received from those who had.

In recent years a more appreciative, yet critical, approach to Barth has emerged. As the dust of controversy settles, it is easier to recognize the extensive areas of commonality that exist and so to assess where any lasting points of divergence lie. The apostle Paul urges us to "test everything; hold fast what is good" (1 Thess. 5:21). There are things to criticize in all human writings, including our own—especially our own—besides many beneficial insights from those with whom we may strongly disagree. It is not an option to become slavish disciples of another, nor to avoid interaction with those with whom we think we differ. Augustine and Calvin had their faults; we all do. We must press on in the knowledge of God, with careful and discriminating discernment. In this particular endeavor, Dr. Tseng is an excellent guide.

Robert Letham
Professor of Systematic and Historical Theology
Union School of Theology
Fellow in Theology and History, Greystone Theological Institute
Senior Fellow, Newton House, Oxford

1. Thomas F. Torrance, "Review of C. van Til, *The New Modernism*," *Evangelical Quarterly* 19, no. 2 (1947): 144–49.

PREFACE

By the wonders of providential contingency, I experienced the loss of loved ones while writing the three volumes that I have contributed to the present series. It is in the present volume, however, that I finally get to discuss the article of faith that lies at the heart of Christian hope, namely, the resurrection of Jesus Christ, through which the work of justification has been accomplished once and for all (Rom. 4:25).

My maternal grandmother passed away in the same week I submitted the full manuscript. All five of her children were led to faith in Christ by God's providential care. She always wanted to go to church with her children, but was prevented from doing so by my grandfather's opposition to the faith. He finally yielded to the grace of God on his deathbed, where he was converted and baptized. I was overwhelmed at my grandfather's memorial service, during which water was sprinkled on my grandmother's living body in the name of the Father, the Son, and the Holy Spirit.

Another person dear to me who passed away when I was writing the manuscript for the present volume was my beloved teacher J. I. Packer. I learned from him many treasured truths. He taught me, contrary to the strain of evangelicalism handed down from Carl Henry, that biblical authority and inerrancy is a starting point in the faith-seeking-understanding process, rather than an intellectualistic position provable apart from the biblical revelation of God in Jesus Christ. I also learned from him that Christ's work of propitiation lies at the heart of the gospel. These positions are highlighted in the third chapter of the present volume.

I used to quarrel with Dr. Packer on the impassibility of God in the classroom. He would tell his students that this doctrine originated in Hellenistic philosophy and has no place in the Bible. I was able to stand my ground by setting forth the biblical and theological rationale behind the doctrine of impassibility. Many evangelical seminary students are equipped to do that. Few evangelicals, professional theologians included, I suspect, however, are capable of defending impassibility against the onslaught of modern criticisms.

It was in fact my Barthian teacher, George Hunsinger, who assured me that the classic doctrine of impassibility is not the result of what Adolf von Harnack famously called the "Hellenization" of early Christianity, and that this ancient doctrine, if understood in light of the *regula fidei* set forth at Nicaea, Constantinople, Ephesus, and Chalcedon, is defensible against the criticisms of modern theologians from Schleiermacher to Moltmann. Professor Hunsinger taught me more than just how to read Barth, and how to do so with charity. He drilled into my head the classical Reformed doctrine of union with Christ. In the pedagogical process, he would read to his students passages from the works of Richard Gaffin. In his course on the doctrine of justification, Professor Hunsinger presented Barth's doctrine of ontological union with Christ as a theological option, and the classical Reformed doctrine of union with Christ through faith as a *sine qua non* for what Luther called the *articulus stantis vel cadentis ecclesiae.*

When Professor Hunsinger repudiated the penal-substitutionary view of the atonement in the classroom, I stood my ground as an evangelical. Yet, when he insisted with Calvin against Osiander that the cultic aspect of justification must always be accompanied by the forensic, I had a hunch that he was not altogether opposed to the historic Protestant doctrine of penal substitution. Indeed, Professor Hunsinger argues in an excursus on the notion of "merciful substitution" in his recently published commentary on Philippians that "salvation in Christ, for Paul, is . . . a merciful event with a forensic aspect. It is a matter of 'merciful substitution' with secondary penal elements as opposed to 'penal substitution' with secondary merciful elements."[1]

Professor Hunsinger's proposal is especially significant for possible dialogue between evangelicals and Barthians in the future: "God is a God of mercy from beginning to end. He is never a vengeful Father. He does not need to be 'appeased' in order to be made merciful. He is already merciful. He needs only to carry out his mercy without compromising his righteousness, which is precisely what he does in the vicarious death of Christ (Rom. 3:25–26)."[2]

While Dr. Packer always insisted on the vindictatory justice of God, he also taught his students, with reference to John Owen's *Dissertation on Divine Justice,* that God's wrath, jealousy, and vengeance are functions of his holiness, rather than the other way around. Owen relinquished his earlier supralapsarianism and adopted an infralapsarian position in the *Dissertation,* said Dr. Packer, precisely because he wanted to ensure that God's punitive justice is contingent upon the prospect of humanity's

---

1. George Hunsinger, *Philippians* (Grand Rapids: Brazos, 2020), 186.
2. Hunsinger, *Philippians,* 186.

sin in God's eternal counsels. Punitive justice, in other words, is only an expression of God's holiness, and holiness includes both mercy and righteousness. Dr. Packer would have at least agreed with Professor Hunsinger that God's "mercy and righteousness are one in the atoning blood of Christ."[3]

The similarities and differences between evangelicals and Barthians, partly represented by the views of Professors Hunsinger and Packer on the atonement, have always motivated me to reflect further in the faith-seeking-understanding vocation. One of my goals in writing the present volume is to convince evangelical readers that once we suspend what we think we already know about Barth and begin to read his writings charitably, with a rule of interpretation of the text from the text itself, we may find ourselves in a position where we can learn many things from Barth and Barthians. I have no intention of converting the evangelical reader to Barthianism or the Barthian reader to evangelicalism. I am simply calling evangelicals and Barthians to mutually edifying engagement and dialogue.

I remain committed to historic Reformed orthodoxy as a neo-Calvinist of Herman Bavinck's lineage. It is precisely from this theological position that I find among Barthian colleagues and mentors powerful allies against theologians, including ones who self-identify as conservative evangelicals, who propose to relinquish the historic orthodoxy of the church on the basis of modernistic assumptions.

Knowing God as the immutable one in the essence of the Father, the Son, and the Holy Spirit, and as the eternal Word who became human without ceasing to be God—knowing the Father who is in the Son as "the only true God" and knowing "Jesus Christ whom [he has] sent": "this is eternal life" (John 17:3). This is the central message that the present volume, with all the

3. Hunsinger, *Philippians*, 187.

academic considerations of Barth and evangelicalism, is trying to communicate. It is with the hope that stands or falls with this biblical truth proclaimed in and by the church that I remember in this volume the loved ones who have gone to be with the Lord.

Shao Kai Tseng
15 February 2021, Shanghai

ACKNOWLEDGMENTS

This volume is most significantly shaped by the influences of two masters who taught me, namely, the late Professor J. I. Packer and Professor George Hunsinger. Their names occupy most of preface and repeatedly appear at important junctures throughout this volume.

Professor John Fesko helped me enthusiastically with my endeavors to bring Barth into dialogue with Reformed orthodoxy when I was a doctoral student, and in this book I continue to rely on his research for the same purpose. Professor William Edgar contacted me when the present volume was under way and gave me an opportunity to interact with the ongoing scholarship on Barth at Westminster Theological Seminary, Philadelphia.

Professor Paul Molnar has been for many years a source of encouragement and academic guidance in my work on Barth. Professor Hans Boersma, notwithstanding the changes in his own convictions, encouraged me to explore theological traditions other than my own in a charitable fashion, while remaining faithful to what he, in the Dutch spirit, likes to call "historic Calvinism." My former mentors at Oxford, including Professor Markus

Bockmuehl, Dr. Timothy Bradshaw, Professor Paul Fiddes, Professor George Pattison, Professor Joel Rasmussen, Professor Benno van den Toren, and Professor Johannes Zachhuber, gave me the academic foundations on which the present work is built, especially in the area of modern Christian thought and culture.

Mark Jones keeps me straight confessionally. Reading his written works and listening to his weekly sermons online have strengthened my faith and reminded me of the true meaning of my vocation as an academic theologian. My friends from the circle of neo-Calvinism studies, including James Eglinton, Bruce Pass, Nathaniel Gray Sutanto, and Ximian Xu, as well as Cory Brock and others with whom I have a newly developing friendship, have set for me excellent examples of Christian scholarship. Their works have provided me with the theological framework within which to bring Barth into conversation with the historic Reformed tradition.

Nate Shannon, editor of the present series, has been exceptionally reassuring when I was uncertain about the possible reception of my work on Barth among conservative Reformed evangelicals. John Hughes, academic project manager at P&R, has been most helpful and pleasant to work with, as usual. Jim Scott, copyeditor of the present volume as well as the one on Hegel, went out of his way to provide me with research materials needed for the revisions that he most helpfully suggested.

I thank God for the loving family that he has given me. My parents never hide from their children their personal struggles in the faith, and from them I have learned the practical meaning of the *articulus stantis vel cadentis ecclesiae*. My wife, Jasmine, has always insisted on predestinarian and Christological supralapsarianism for the simple reason that I subscribe to infralapsarianism: she challenges me on such topics so that I will not grow excessively confident in my own theological position. Even though I think I have the upper hand in the ongoing debate, I have not yet managed to convert her to the infralapsarian camp. She and our canine son, Bobo, cheered me up and encouraged me to press on with my work when unfavorable circumstances arose during the composition of the present volume. These loved ones have, however indirectly and implicitly, shaped my work in academic theology to an incalculable extent, and I would like to take this opportunity to acknowledge them.

March 2021
Hangzhou, China

ABBREVIATIONS OF WORKS BY BARTH

Anselm	*Anselm: Fides Quaerens Intellectum: Anselm's Proof of the Existence of God in the Context of His Theological Scheme*, trans. Ian Robertson (London: SCM, 1960)
CD	*Church Dogmatics*, ed. G. W. Bromiley and T. F. Torrance, trans. G. W. Bromiley, 4 vols. in 12 parts (I/1–IV/4) (Edinburgh: T&T Clark, 1956–75)
Gottes Gnadenwahl	*Gottes Gnadenwahl* (Munich: Chr. Kaiser, 1936), translation mine (unpublished)
KD	*Die kirchliche Dogmatik*. 4 vols. in 12 parts (I/1–IV/4) (Zurich: Theologischer Verlag Zürich, 1980)
Romans II	*The Epistle to the Romans*, trans. Edwyn Hoskyns (1922; London: Oxford University Press, 1933)

1

WHY BARTH MATTERS TODAY

*"Quite properly men speak of Karl Barth as the most influential
theologian of our time. We must therefore seek to understand him."*
—*Cornelius Van Til, 1962*[1]

Barth's Undiminished Influence
on Protestant Theology

Karl Barth (1886–1968) was undoubtedly the most influential
theologian of his generation. A native of Basel, Switzerland, he
rose to fame across German academia with his ballyhooed commentary on Romans in 1919. The reputation that accompanied
the work earned him, *inter alia*, a professorship at the prestigious
Georg August University of Göttingen in 1921, but this was
only the beginning of his illustrious career. By the mid-1920s,
his name was known across Europe, and by the 1930s, leading
intellectuals in Asia, including the famed founders of the Kyoto

---

1. Cornelius Van Til, *Christianity and Barthianism* (Philadelphia: Presbyterian and
Reformed, 1962), 1.

School of Philosophy, began to interact with his works. His visit to America in 1962 was of such cultural significance that his portrait was featured on the front cover of the April 20 issue of *Time* magazine that year.

In the early 1990s, however, as Professor Carl Trueman recounts, it seemed to many Anglophone evangelicals that "Barth had probably had his day."[2] Professor Trueman paints a vivid picture of a certain evangelical impression at the time: "The Barthian bomb had detonated in the playground of the theologians, but now the noise and dust had died down and the children had returned to playing their traditional games."[3]

In broader academic theology beyond evangelicalism, it seemed to many onlookers in the 1990s that Barth's influence had finally been eclipsed by theologians of a later generation, most notably Jürgen Moltmann (born 1926) and Wolfhart Pannenberg (1928–2014). In fact, Moltmann and Pannenberg were both heavily influenced by Barth, which means that the three biggest names in twentieth-century Protestant theology were Barth and two Germans influenced by him.

One popular misperception, which obscured Barth's influence, has been that the theological approach of which these theologians are representative "marked a return to precisely the questions of history that Barth had dismissed as theologically wrong-headed."[4] Part and parcel of this misperception is the popular misunderstanding that "the historicity of the resurrection," among other historical truth-claims of the Bible, is deemed "irrelevant" in Barth's theology.[5]

There has indeed been a tendency among both followers

---

2. Carl Trueman, "Foreword," in *Engaging with Barth: Contemporary Evangelical Critiques*, ed. David Gibson and Daniel Strange (Nottingham: Apollos, 2008), 14.

3. Trueman, "Foreword," 14.

4. Trueman, "Foreword," 14.

5. Trueman, "Foreword," 14.

and opponents of Barth to interpret him along ahistorical lines. This tendency, more often than not, is based on an interpretive framework that portrays the development of his theology as the unfolding of the eternity-time dialectic of his early thought. As Barth worked out this dialectic—so purport such ahistorical readings—the vertical dimension (the self-disclosure of the transcendent God from above) of his thought gradually outgrew the horizontal (God's eschatological immanence proleptically present in history). Such readings, like certain "historicized" interpretations, often fail to recognize the substantive discontinuities between the allegedly (neo-)Kantian and/or Kierkegaardian origins of Barth's early theology and the later stages of his intellectual development.

This is basically the case with Pannenberg's reading of Barth as an ahistorical or anti-historical thinker. As Pannenberg sees it, the ahistorical nature of the Trinitarian form of Barth's theology in the *Church Dogmatics* was developed on the basis of the same eternity-time dialectic—a largely Kierkegaardian one, in Pannenberg's view—set forth in *Romans* II.[6] The same tendency to understand the later Barth in the light of his early dialectic undergirds Van Til's ahistorical reading as well: "One must look back to the *Christian Dogmatics* of 1927 and even to the commentary on Romans . . . in order to trace the development of

---

6. See Wolfhart Pannenberg, *Systematic Theology*, trans. Geoffrey Bromiley, 3 vols. (Grand Rapids: Eerdmans, 2009), 3:536–37. Pannenberg recognizes that in Barth's *Church Dogmatics* (henceforth *CD*), the eschatological focus of his early theology fades into the background. As Pannenberg sees it, however, the "eschatological mood" of the early Barth was only "taken up into a Christological orientation to the unity between God and us in Jesus Christ" in *CD* (*Systematic Theology*, 3:537). Barth's early view of the "dialectical turning of judgment into grace," according to Pannenberg, is retained in the later Barth. Pannenberg offers concentrated and extensive treatment of Barth's intellectual biography against the background of modern German Protestant theology in *Problemsgeschichte der neueren evangelischen Theologie in Deutschland: Von Schleiermacher bis zu Barth und Tillich* (Göttingen: Vandenhoeck & Ruprecht, 1997).

Barth's thinking. But in the *Church Dogmatics* we have the ripe fruition of a long lifetime of arduous reflection and research."[7]

As we shall see in chapter 2, this intellectual-biographical view of Barth is fundamentally misguided and academically out-dated. Van Til, together with the publishing of G. C. Berkouwer's *Triumph of Grace* in 1956, has made ahistorical interpretations of Barth popular among Anglophone evangelicals.[8] As a result of such misinterpretations, any resurgence of interest in the questions of history that Barth had allegedly dismissed would be perceived as a sign of the obsolescence of his theology. The fact is, however, that Moltmann and Pannenberg were both sig-nificantly informed by Barth despite their criticisms of him.

To understand Moltmann's and Pannenberg's critical reliance on Barth, we must begin with a little philosophical-historical background. The characteristically modern interest in history that Moltmann and Pannenberg exhibit first arose in the gen-eration of post-Kantian idealists like Johann Gottlieb Fichte (1762–1814), Friedrich Schelling (1775–1854), and G. W. F. Hegel (1770–1831).[9] The strong process-historical tendencies in Moltmann and Pannenberg are admittedly indebted primarily to Hegel. According to Hegel, history is the dialectical process by which spirit actualizes itself and becomes God at the con-summation of history. It is through Hegelian-historicist lenses that the characteristically modern questions of history become

7. Van Til, *Christianity and Barthianism*, 2.

8. See Gerrit Berkouwer, *The Triumph of Grace in the Theology of Karl Barth*, trans. Harry Boer (London: Paternoster, 1956). Berkouwer thinks that Barth only pays lip service to "the open situation" of the futurity of God's act in the mature, Christo-centric phase of his doctrine of election (p. 296). This misreading is still influential among evangelicals today. See, for example, Oliver Crisp, "Karl Barth and Jonathan Edwards on Reprobation (and Hell)," in *Engaging with Barth*, 319. This ahistorical reading of Barth has led many to the conclusion that Barth is an incipient universalist, a myth that we will debunk in chapter 2.

9. See Karl Ameriks, *Kant and the Historical Turn* (Oxford: Oxford University Press, 2006).

important in Moltmann and Pannenberg. (Historicism, simply put, is a label for philosophical views that see history as purposeful activity.)

What sets Moltmann and Pannenberg apart from Hegel—as well as the process ontologies of Alfred North Whitehead (1861–1947) and Charles Hartshorne (1897–2000), for that matter—is primarily their explicit reliance on Barth's understanding of history as an *ad extra* vehicle through which God is said to be self-determined in one way or another (God qua God, in the cases of Moltmann and Pannenberg; God-for-us without ceasing to be God-in-and-for-himself, in Barth's case), rather than a process in which God and world occurrences are essentially merged into one another. Moltmann and Pannenberg are indeed opposed to Barth's insistence on divine immutability in their contention that God's act is identical to his being, but they also emphasize the ontological distinction between the history of creation and the development of God's being. For Moltmann and Pannenberg, God acts on the basis of creaturely history to determine his own essence as God.

Moltmann's express insistence on God's "qualitative transcendence" beyond creation—as opposed to a merely "quantitative transcendence"—is what both Moltmann and Pannenberg inherited from Barth.[10] Without this Barthian dimension to their theological infrastructure, Moltmann and Pannenberg would only represent a return to the historicism of nineteenth-century panentheism (the view that the universe is contained within the being of God) or pantheism (the immediate identification of God with nature), and there would have been nothing characteristically twentieth-century about them.

Pannenberg, in particular, is known for having adopted what

---

10. Jürgen Moltmann, *Der lebendige Gott und die Fülle des Lebens: Auch ein Beitrag zur gegenwärtigen Atheismusdebatte* (Gütersloh: Gütersloher Verlagshaus, 2014), 27, 42.

he understands to be Barth's notion of the ontological determination of nature and history "from above" (*von oben*), which Pannenberg calls the "vertical" dimension of historical revelation.[11] That Pannenberg's theology is significantly informed by his (mis)reading of Barth is hardly surprising, given the fact that Pannenberg once left Germany to study with Barth in Basel, Switzerland. Pannenberg's *Systematic Theology* is, of course, known for its severe criticisms of what he sees as Barth's dismissal of the relevance of nature and history to theology, but Pannenberg's "reconstruction of Christian eschatology" is also admittedly indebted to the early Barth's "focusing of primitive Christian expectation of the kingdom of God on the reality of God himself, whose immanence for us and the world means judgment as well as salvation."[12]

Moltmann's criticism of Barth, like Pannenberg's, has often been misunderstood as a simple abandonment of the Barthian paradigm. I cannot put it better than my friend Hong Liang, Professor Moltmann's ultimate *Doktorsohn* ("doctoral son") and a Barth scholar well-regarded in Germanic and Sinophone academia: "The most misleading" way of "understanding the mode of relationship between Moltmann and Barth" is "to see Moltmann as a 'post-Barthian' theologian," if "the simple 'post-'" is taken to signify an "abolition" of the "intellectual continuity between the two."[13] True enough, it has been reported that Moltmann occasionally describes himself colloquially as "post-Barthian," but the way this term is often applied to him is highly problematic. Hong explains:

11. Pannenberg developed this view early on in his career. See Wolfhart Pannenberg, ed., *Revelation as History* (London: Macmillan, 1969).

12. Pannenberg, *Systematic Theology*, 3:537.

13. Hong Liang [洪亮], *Six Studies in the Theology of Karl Barth and Jürgen Moltmann* [巴特與莫特曼神學管窺] (Hong Kong: VW Link [德慧文化], 2020), 141. Translation mine here and henceforth.

This [the post-Barthian label] is correct only in a chronological sense. . . . This understanding [of a post-Barthian
Moltmann] downplays at once the intellectual force of the
influence of Barth's theology down to our day, as well as
Moltmann's own insights and creativity. . . . In many respects,
Moltmann has inherited some of the basic characteristics of
Barth's theology. In terms of traditional affiliation, they are
both representatives of twentieth-century covenant theology: they both appeal to . . . some covenant-theological framework to break free of historical positivism in their respective
views of history. In terms of their critical relationships to
nineteenth-century theology, they are completely united in
their approaches, in that they both treat the act of God in history—rather than humanity's religious self-consciousness—
as the starting-point of theology. . . . In terms of formal theological method, they both appeal to one doctrinal locus to
regulate all other loci: for Barth it is Christology, and for
Moltmann, eschatology.[14]

Hong reports that "Moltmann often says he had two intellectual 'fathers'—Bonhoeffer and Barth."[15] It is true that Bonhoeffer,
whom Moltmann never met, inspired him to pursue the theology of a suffering God and provided him with an understanding
of nature that moved away from Barth's antagonism towards
natural theology. It is also true that Moltmann's discovery of
left-Hegelianism lent him some intellectual tools needed for his
eschatological reconstruction of Protestant theology.

We must acknowledge, however, that Moltmann was in many
ways building on Barth in this attempt. Barth's doctrine of election, among other aspects of his theology, remains admittedly

14. Hong, *Six Studies*, 141.
15. Hong, *Six Studies*, 140.

one of the most important sources of inspiration for Moltmann. This is evinced by Professor Daniel Migliore's dedication of his edited volume on Barth to Professor Moltmann, which begins with a chapter on Barth's doctrine of predestination by Moltmann.[16]

In the United States, Robert Jenson (1930–2017) developed a theological approach that echoes Moltmann and Pannenberg. Jenson's indebtedness to Barth is much better acknowledged than in the cases of Moltmann and Pannenberg. It is explicitly stated in Jenson's celebrated early work, *God after God: The God of the Past and the God of the Future, Seen in the Work of Karl Barth* (1969).[17] Unlike Pannenberg and Moltmann, who criticize Barth for having driven too great a wedge between time and eternity, Jenson claims Barth as an ally by reading into Barth a Christocentric ontology in which God's eternity is fully historicized and rendered identical with events in time. That Jenson has been appreciated as an influential voice, misleading as it might be, on Barth's thought is demonstrated partly by the fact that Colin Gunton (1941–2003), one of Britain's foremost Barthian theologians, wrote his doctoral thesis on Barth and Hartshorne under Jenson's supervision at Oxford.

Contrary to popular perception, then, the rise of the historical-eschatological approach to theology, represented by Moltmann, Pannenberg, and Jenson, did not mark the obsolescence of Barth's theology at all. It was, rather, a revisionist reconstruction of the theological edifice that Barth had built. Even one entire generation thereafter, theologians who assumed this approach continued to be inspired by and wrestle with Barth. The widely influential *The Creative Suffering of God* (1988), by the British theologian Paul Fiddes (born 1947), is a

---

16. Daniel Migliore, ed., *Reading the Gospels with Karl Barth* (Grand Rapids: Eerdmans, 2017).

17. Robert Jenson, *God after God* (Minneapolis: Fortress, 2010).

classic example.[18] Barth has remained one of the most important sources of inspiration, and has continued to present some of
the most significant challenges to be overcome, in contemporary
Protestant theology.

Barth's Influence across the Theological Spectrum

The influence of Barth's thought is detectable across the
theological spectrum. Receptions of Barth, of course, vary from
one theological circle to another. One brand of theology positively indebted to Barth—and even explicitly Barthian in some
individual cases—is postliberalism, a label derived from George
Lindbeck's *The Nature of Doctrine: Religion and Theology in a
Postliberal Age*.[19] Leading representatives of postliberal theology
include Hans Frei (1922–88), George Lindbeck (1923–2018),
Stanley Hauerwas (born 1940), George Hunsinger (born 1945),
and William Placher (1948–2008), among others.[20] Because of
postliberalism's affinities with classical Protestantism, evangelical
theologians like Gabriel Fackre have suggested it as an alternative
for evangelicals dissatisfied with the kind of propositional revelation espoused by the likes of Carl Henry and Robert Reymond,
which significantly downplays the traditional notion of God's
archetype-ectype revelation through redemptive history as an
indirect and mediated revelation of God's essence. (Professor
Michael Horton has made a similar observation—see chapter 3).

Also known as "narrative theology" because of its accentua-
tion of the narrative aspect of the Christian faith, postliberalism

18. Paul Fiddes, *The Creative Suffering of God* (Oxford: Oxford University Press,
1988).

19. George Lindbeck, *The Nature of Doctrine: Religion and Theology in a Postliberal
Age* (Louisville: Westminster John Knox, 1984).

20. See George Hunsinger, "Postliberal Theology," in *The Cambridge Companion
to Postmodern Theology*, ed. Kevin Vanhoozer (Cambridge: Cambridge University
Press, 2003), 42–57.

adopts a basically Barthian view of revelation as the grand history of God and humankind in Jesus Christ, narrated in Scripture and attested to by the historic and ongoing proclamations of the church. (We will discuss Barth's formulation of the Word of God revealed, written, and proclaimed in chapter 2.) The relationship of the propositional truth-claims of Christian dogmatics to this grand narrative is likened to the relationship between grammar and language. Human language has a logical structure, and grammar is our attempt to articulate this structure. It is the rationality of language in its everyday actuality that gives rise to grammar, not the other way around. Similarly, Christian dogmatics is regulated by the history of God and humanity in Christ, as narrated by the biblical witness. While we should strive to make our dogmatic truth-claims as consistent as possible, the finite human mind is never capable of fully systematizing this grand narrative in propositional terms. It is important to note that the largely Barthian formulations of the relations between church dogmas, biblical narratives, and the stories of ecclesial witnesses vary from one postliberal theologian to another.

George Hunsinger, recipient of the prestigious Karl Barth Prize (2010), draws on Barth's insights with what might be called a "traditionalist" interpretation (see chapter 2)—one that best exemplifies close and charitable readings of the text by assuming its basic coherence and literal perspicuity. Where Barth's theology does not sufficiently honor the teachings of Scripture, Professor Hunsinger would often prefer to follow, say, Luther or Calvin.[21] His political radicalism and endorsement of democratic socialism may not appeal to mainline evangelicals, but some important aspects of his political involvement, such as the National Religious Campaign Against Torture that he founded in 2006,

21. For example, George Hunsinger, "A Tale of Two Simultaneities: Justification and Sanctification in Calvin and Barth," in *Conversing with Barth*, ed. John McDowell and Mike Higton (Aldershot, UK: Ashgate, 2004), 86.

set good examples for evangelicals committed to the doctrine of natural rights as one grounded in and integral to the Christian doctrine of creation. Those familiar with Professor Hunsinger's writings would easily recognize that these political activities arise out of his engagement with Barth. His commitment to ecclesial orthodoxy—especially the dogmatic boundaries delimited at "Nicaea, Constantinople, Ephesus and Chalcedon"—in his biblical expositions and his high view of traditional Protestant doctrines have drawn him close to evangelical students and colleagues.[22] His express affinities with views endorsed by Professor Richard Gaffin and familiarity with historic Reformed doctrine have been warmly acknowledged by Professor Michael Horton.[23]

Hans Frei, Professor Hunsinger's doctoral supervisor at Yale University, also drew on Barth in explicit ways. Barth's break with liberal theology against the background of the First World War and his subsequent theological defiance of the Third Reich were especially significant to Frei, not least because of Frei's identity as a Jewish refugee from Germany. Frei's doctoral dissertation at Yale on the early Barth's doctrine of revelation, in which he made a distinction between the "dialectical" and "analogical" phases of Barth's theology, was a product, not only of intellectual inquiry, but also of personal struggles in the Christian faith.[24] Frei's interpretation of Barth as a theologian who largely stood in line with ecclesial orthodoxy remains influential in Anglo-American scholarship to this day.

Lindbeck's theological hermeneutics are also significantly informed by Barth's treatment of the textuality of the Christian

22. See George Hunsinger, *Philippians* (Grand Rapids: Brazos, 2020), xvii–xviii.
23. See George Hunsinger, *Disruptive Grace* (Grand Rapids: Eerdmans, 2000), 338–60, cited by Michael Horton, "A Stony Jar: The Legacy of Karl Barth for Evangelical Theology," in *Engaging with Barth*, 378.
24. Hans Frei, "The Doctrine of Revelation in the Thought of Karl Barth, 1909–1922" (Ph.D. diss., Yale University, 1956), 194.

tradition.[25] He introduced to narrative theology Ludwig Wittgenstein's (1889–1951) notion of "grammar" as the internal logic that underlies a system of thought. Of course, Lindbeck consciously avoided the reduction of Christian theology to a language game. The Catholic theologian David Tracy aptly describes "Lindbeck's substantive theological position" as "a methodologically sophisticated version of Barthian confessionalism. The hands may be the hands of Wittgenstein and Geertz but the voice is the voice of Karl Barth."[26]

Of course, not all postliberals apply Barth's theology in traditionalist or confessionalist ways. Hauerwas's project can be seen as reconstructionistic and revisionistic, both in its relation to Barth and to ecclesial dogmas. If Barth's political theology is essentially soteriological (that is, Christological), then Hauerwas's soteriology is essentially political. Hauerwas builds on Barth's motif of Christ's ontological triumph over evil to reconstruct a new political soteriology. Salvation is defined by Hauerwas as "God's work to restore all creation to the Lordship of Christ."[27] Salvation as such is "about the defeat of powers that presume to rule outside God's providential care."[28] The church triumphs over the powers represented by Rome by reenacting through martyrdom the accomplished reality of Christ's victory on the cross.[29] In Hauerwas, then, the Barthian distinction without separation between biblical witness and ecclesial witness is much more blurred than in Hunsinger's version of postliberal theology, and the regulating function of church dogmas is much weaker.

25. See George Lindbeck, "Barth and Textuality," *Theology Today* 43 (1986): 361–76.
26. David Tracy, "Lindbeck's New Program for Theology: A Reflection," *The Thomist* 49 (1985): 465, cited by Howland Sanks, "David Tracy's Theological Project: An Overview and Some Implications," *Theological Studies* 54 (1993): 725.
27. Stanley Hauerwas, *After Christendom?* (Nashville: Abingdon, 1991), 37.
28. Hauerwas, *After Christendom?*, 37.
29. Hauerwas, *After Christendom?*, 38.

Another brand of twentieth-century theology that interacted closely with Barth is *nouvelle théologie*, a Catholic theological movement that directly contributed to the development of narrative theology. The first generation of theologians associated with this movement included Henri de Lubac (1896–1991), Yves Congar (1904–95), Karl Rahner (1904–84), Jean Daniélou (1905–74), Hans Urs von Balthasar (1905–88), Henri Bouillard (1908–81), and others. Joseph Ratzinger (Pope Benedict XVI, born 1927) and Hans Küng (born 1928) pertain to the second generation. Much as postliberals were antagonistic towards what they deemed to be dogmatic over-systematization, *nouvelle* theologians reacted against the neo-scholasticism that dominated Catholic theology in the aftermath of the First Vatican Council (1869–70).[30]

The Trinitarian shape of Rahner's theology, developed against the background of nineteenth-century German philosophy, is so strikingly similar to Barth's, that comparisons have often been made between the two.[31] The Catholic Barth scholar Paul Molnar points out that many modern theologians, including Moltmann, Pannenberg, and Eberhard Jüngel (born 1934), have come under the influences of both Barth and Rahner. Rahner identifies the immanent Trinity with the economic, but Professor Molnar rightly stresses that Barth draws a clear distinction between God's immutably triune essence and his Trinitarian acts *ad extra*.[32]

30. For more information on the developments leading to and following after the First Vatican Council, see my "Church," in *The Oxford Handbook of Nineteenth-Century Christian Thought*, ed. Joel Rasmussen, Judith Wolfe, and Johannes Zachhuber (Oxford: Oxford University Press, 2017), 621–24.

31. For instance, Bruce Marshall, *Christology in Conflict: The Identity of a Saviour in Rahner and Barth* (Oxford: Blackwell, 1987). See James Buckley, "Barth and Rahner," in *The Wiley-Blackwell Companion to Karl Barth*, ed. George Hunsinger and Keith Johnson (Oxford: Wiley-Blackwell, 2020), 607–17.

32. See Paul Molnar, "The Function of the Immanent Trinity in Karl Barth: Implications for Today," *Scottish Journal of Theology* 42 (1989): 367–99.

Ratzinger first became familiar with Barth's thought upon reading Küng's doctoral thesis on Barth's doctrine of justification in the late 1950s. In 1967, Ratzinger visited Basel, where he met Barth in person. During the Basel visit, Ratzinger attended Barth's colloquium on the Dogmatic Constitution on Divine Revelation (*Dei verbum*) from the Second Vatican Council (1962–65), a council in which the influence of *nouvelle théologie* was strongly felt. According to the report of Eberhard Busch (born 1937), hailed by some as the "prince of Barth studies," who served as Barth's academic assistant at the time, the exchange between Barth and Ratzinger demonstrated both mutual respect and some fundamental disagreements.[33]

Among the Teutonic *nouvelle* theologians, the two who interacted most closely with Barth were his Swiss compatriots, Balthasar and Küng. Küng, recipient of the 1992 Karl Barth Prize, wrote his doctoral thesis on Barth's doctrine of justification, with an interpretation approved by Barth himself.[34] It should be noted, however, that Barth was often generous in giving approvals, but the interpretations of which he approved were not always entirely correct.[35]

Many have referred to Barth and Balthasar as the "two stars of Basel," though the latter was actually not a native Basler. Balthasar's *The Theology of Karl Barth* (1951) set the first dominant intellectual-biographical paradigm of Barth studies, one that lasted for decades and was strengthened in Anglo-American scholarship by Frei and T. F. Torrance (1913–2007), only to be challenged by German-speaking scholars in the 1980s; it

33. See Eberhard Busch, *Meine Zeit mit Karl Barth* (Göttingen: Vandenhoeck & Ruprecht, 2011), 229–35.

34. Hans Küng, *Justification: The Doctrine of Karl Barth and a Catholic Reflection* (Philadelphia: Westminster, 1981).

35. This is partly suggested in Trevor Hart, "Barth and Küng on Justification: 'Imaginary Differences'?" *Irish Theological Quarterly* 59 (1993): 94–113.

was superseded by the paradigm proposed by Professor Bruce McCormack, another Barth Prize recipient, in 1995.[36] More will be said about the different paradigms of Barth studies and the continuing importance of some of Balthasar's insights in chapter 2. Suffice it now to note that apart from being a constructive theologian in his own right, Balthasar was also a lifelong Barth scholar, who drew critically on Barth's theology. In his appraisal of Barth's take on the analogy of faith, Balthasar makes a quint-essentially Catholic assertion against Barth, that "the spontaneity of human knowing belongs to its very nature, which has not been destroyed by sin."[37] In many ways, then, Barth was a mirror in which Balthasar sought to better understand his own Catholic identity.[38]

Bouillard's work on Barth is less known in the Anglophone world than Balthasar's and Küng's. Upon his visit to America in 1962, however, Barth told the journalists from *Time* magazine that "the best critical work on his works . . . has been done by such Catholic thinkers as French Jesuit Henri Bouillard and Father Hans Urs von Balthasar of Basel."[39] After being discharged from the Jesuit school of Fourvière in 1950 for his associations with *nouvelle théologie*, Bouillard launched a large-scale research project on Barth, resulting in a second dissertation, which was defended in the presence of the Swiss theologian himself. The dissertation was published in two volumes in 1957, marking a significant event in Francophone Barth studies and the Catholic reception of Barth.[40]

36. Hans Urs von Balthasar, *The Theology of Karl Barth*, trans. Edward Oakes (San Francisco: Ignatius, 1992).

37. Balthasar, *Theology of Karl Barth*, 160.

38. For Balthasar's agreements and disagreements with Barth on the problem of analogy, see Hans Boersma, *Nouvelle Théologie and Sacramental Ontology* (Oxford: Oxford University Press, 2009), 131–34.

39. Karl Barth, "Witness to an Ancient Truth," *Time* 89, no. 16 (April 20, 1962): 59.

40. Henri Bouillard, *Karl Barth*, 2 vols. (Paris: Aubier, 1957).

Barth's influence on Catholic theology has in fact continued
into our own day. Professor Molnar's name has been mentioned
above. David Tracy (born 1939) is another instance, yet of a very
different nature. His attempt at a modern Catholic treatment of
the problem of analogy shows that this is a subject in which Barth
is a figure that no one after him can bypass.[41] In his application
of the notion of analogical imagination, Tracy identifies three
paradigms of Christian responses to contemporary situations,
one of which is that of "proclamation," represented by Barth.[42]
Tracy does not adopt any Barthian paradigm, nor does he try to
refute it or overcome its challenges. Rather, his project is one that
brings a plurality of theological paradigms into conversation. In
this sense, Tracy may be seen as having incorporated Barthian
thinking into his own program as a conversation partner.

In contrast to Barth's more positive reception in Catholicism,
he is often regarded negatively in the Eastern Orthodox communion, not least because of his harsh criticisms of the Orthodox
notion of *theosis* (deification). Orthodox scholars tend to see
Barth as an obstacle to be overcome in ecumenical dialogues
between Protestantism and Orthodoxy.[43] If the Orthodox scholar
Paul Gavrilyuk is right that Barth is misguided in "making *theosis* guilty by association" with theological views showing traits
of "ebionite Christology," then there may yet be something in
what Barth positively states that is worth the consideration of
Orthodox theologians.[44] This explains why Professor Hunsinger
would recommend Gavrilyuk's writings to his students, and why
Gavrilyuk later came to endorse Professor Hunsinger's work on

41. See David Tracy, *The Analogical Imagination: Christian Theology and the Culture of Pluralism* (New York: Crossroad, 1981).

42. See Sanks, "David Tracy's Theological Project," 717.

43. Paul Gavrilyuk, "The Retrieval of Deification: How a Once-Despised Archaism Became an Ecumenical Desideratum," *Modern Theology* 25 (2009): 647–59.

44. Gavrilyuk, "Retrieval of Deification," 648.

Barth.[45] In fact, Barth has often been chosen as a representative of twentieth-century Protestant theology in ecumenical dialogues with recent Orthodox theologians such as John Zizioulas (born 1931).[46]

The Reception of Barth around the World

The foregoing discussions on Barth's influence across the theological spectrum alluded to the geographical scale of his impact. Aside from the Teutonic names already mentioned, Michael Beintker, Wolf Krötke, Christoph Schwöbel, Ingrid Spieckermann, Günter Thomas, Christiane Tietz, Michael Weinrich, Michael Welker, and a host of other prominent theologians in the German-speaking world have relied on Barth, wrestled with him, and/or propagated his thought in one way or another. The same may be said of an array of luminaries in British theology from past to present: Nigel Biggar, Paul Fiddes, David Ford, Colin Gunton, Trevor Hart, T. F. Torrance, Graham Ward, John Webster, and Rowan Williams, among others. In North America: James Buckley, Hans Frei, Stanley Hauerwas, George Hunsinger, Robert Jenson, George Lindbeck, Bruce Marshall, Bruce McCormack, Daniel Migliore, William Placher, Katherine Sonderegger, Kathryn Tanner, Ronald Thiemann, Miroslav Volf (an American-based Croatian), John Howard Yoder, and many others.

Barth's name was known across Reformed Hungary and Transylvania by the 1930s, and his 1936 trip to those places was a major event among the seminaries and churches there. In the Netherlands, Barthian theologians like Theodoor L. Haitjema

45. George Hunsinger, *Reading Barth with Charity* (Grand Rapids: Baker Academic, 2015).

46. For instance, Paul Collins, *Trinitarian Theology, West and East: Karl Barth, the Cappadocian Fathers, and John Zizioulas* (Oxford: Oxford University Press, 2001).

(1888–1972) began to emerge as a considerable force in academia and the churches in the 1920s. Hendrikus Berkhof (1914–95) incorporated the insights of Schleiermacher and offered a highly secularized and admittedly heterodox reconstruction of Barthian theology a generation later. Barth was in fact reputed to be a possible friend of conservative Dutch Calvinism in the early 1920s. In 1926, however, the Barthians began to attack neo-Calvinism, and by the 1930s, "the Barthians" had become "the most serious opponents of neo-Calvinism."[47] The relationship between the Barthians and Dutch Calvinists worsened when Barth himself entered the fight in 1951, attacking the latter as "men of stupid, cold and stony hearts to whom we need not listen."[48] After reading Berkouwer's *Triumph of Grace*, however, Barth issued an apology for "the fierce attack which [he] made on Dutch neo-Calvinists *in globo*," and commended Berkouwer's serious work on his theology despite critical interpretations therein that Barth deemed incorrect.[49] At the time, Barth was still appalled by the "fundamentalists" among Dutch and Dutch-American neo-Calvinists, famously calling them "butchers and cannibals."[50] When he finally met Cornelius Van Til in person during his 1962 visit to America, he took the initiative to shake hands with Van Til. This was later followed up with a personal letter that Van Til wrote to Barth with good will, which Van Til undersigned by jokingly referring to himself as *"ein Menschfresser* [a cannibal]."[51] In fact, the course of events in the Netherlands

47. George Harinck, "How Can an Elephant Understand a Whale and Vice Versa?," in *Karl Barth and American Evangelicalism*, ed. Bruce McCormack and Clifford Anderson (Grand Rapids: Eerdmans, 2011), 19, 28.

48. *CD* III/4, xiii.

49. *CD* IV/2, xii.

50. *CD* IV/2, xii.

51. Cornelius Van Til letter to Karl Barth, December 21, 1965, Van Til Papers, Montgomery Library, Westminster Theological Seminary, Philadelphia, cited by Harinck, "Elephant," 41.

significantly shaped the reception of Barth, not only in America, but also, and to a larger extent, in South Africa.[52]

In Latin American liberation theology, of which the Peruvian Catholic theologian Gustavo Gutiérrez (born 1928) is among the best-known founders, Barthianism is often taken to represent an imperialistic bondage from which theology must be liberated. In *A Theology of Liberation* (1971), for example, Gutiérrez relies on Moltmann to criticize what he sees as Barth's eschatological affirmation of eternity and negation of history.[53] Meanwhile, however, Gutiérrez also credits Barth—with a somewhat deconstructionist reading—for having laid the foundations for "Christian anthropocentrism," which lies at the heart of liberation theology.[54]

Liberation theologians in the United States have also engaged with Barth in significant ways. His socialist leanings and his personal support for Martin Luther King Jr. during his visit to America have led some Black liberation theologians to claim him as a theological ally of James Cone (1938–2018). That Barth continues to inspire and challenge liberation theology in the United States and beyond is evident in Rubén Rosario Rodríguez's *Dogmatics after Babel* (2018), a work that seeks to break through the purported impasse between the theologies of revelation and of culture, represented respectively by Barth and Paul Tillich (1886–1965).[55]

Barth's influence in East Asia is perhaps not as well known to Anglophone readers, with the exception of Korea. Compared to academics from other Asian countries, Korean scholars tend

---

52. John De Gruchy, "Reflections on 'Doing Theology' in South Africa after Sixty Years in Conversation with Barth," *Stellenbosch Theological Journal* 5 (2019): 11–28.

53. Gustavo Gutiérrez, *A Theology of Liberation* (New York: Orbis, 2012), 93.

54. Gutiérrez, *Theology of Liberation*, 6.

55. Rubén Rosario Rodríguez, *Dogmatics after Babel: Beyond Theologies of Word and Culture* (Louisville: Westminster John Knox, 2018).

to be more active in Anglophone academia. Meehyung Chung, the first woman to be awarded the Karl Barth Prize (2006), is among the most celebrated Barth scholars in Asia. Well published in English, German, and Korean, Chung is an important voice in the areas of feminist theology and political theology in the West, as well as in her native Korea. The name Sung Wook Chung, a native Korean evangelical Barth scholar who is well known and well published in the English-speaking world, may perhaps be more familiar to evangelical readers. There has indeed been a long-standing tradition of Barth scholarship and constructive Barthian theology in Korea.[56] Korean is one of the few languages into which the *Church Dogmatics* has been translated in its entirety.

Academic theology in Sinophone Christianity has not enjoyed the same level of success as that in Korean Christianity, due to various historical, cultural, sociopolitical, and theological factors. The twentieth century saw two generations of blossoming Chinese revivalists whose influence, as far as the number of converts is concerned, easily matched that of Billy Graham or Charles Finney. Few Chinese theologians of the early twentieth century, however, left behind legacies that continue to inspire later generations. Many historians of Sinophone Christianity have commented that Tzu-ch'en Chao (趙紫宸, 1888–1979) was probably the only one worthy of this description.

Originally trained in sociology at Vanderbilt University, Chao's early theology was an attempt at the indigenization of Christianity by combining Confucianism with a kind of moral theology reminiscent of Ritschlian liberalism. The Second World War forced Chao to rethink this liberalism. It was in the theologies of Barth and Paul Tillich (1886–1965) that Chao found

---

56. See Young-Gwan Kim, *Karl Barth's Reception in Korea* (New York: Peter Lang, 2003).

the core materials for the transformation of his theology. Chao's *Barth's Religious Thought* (1939) represents one of the earliest Asian attempts at interpreting Barth.[57]

Under the overall pietistic and separatist mood that dominated mainline Chinese Christianity up to the 1970s (i.e., the Jerusalem-Athens type of separation), however, pursuits of academic theology were highly discouraged among believers. This meant that Chao's work on Barth would be met with overall neglect or even belligerent disapproval in Chinese Christianity for decades.

The acceptance of academic theology among mainline Chinese churches in the 1970s was partly a result of the endeavors of a group of Chinese church leaders who attended Westminster Theological Seminary in the 1960s, most notably the late Jonathan Chao (趙天恩, 1938–2004). Their efforts contributed to the founding in 1975 of the China Graduate School of Theology (CGST) in Hong Kong. A generation of elite students from CGST and other seminaries in Hong Kong were then encouraged to study abroad for higher degrees in theology. The United Kingdom was unsurprisingly the favorite destination because of colonial connections at the time.

Three of Hong Kong's foremost theologians are representative of that generation: Carver Yu (余達心, born 1949), Milton Wan (溫偉耀, born 1952), and the late Arnold Yeung (楊牧谷, 1945–2002). Together, they reflect Barth's influence on Sinophone theology, directly or indirectly, through British academia in the 1980s. Yu's 1981 doctoral dissertation at Oxford is indirectly informed by Barth, as it relies heavily on the theological method of Barth's venerated Scottish pupil, T. F. Torrance.[58]

57. Tzu-ch'en Chao [趙紫宸], *Barth's Religious Thought* [巴德的宗教思想] (Shanghai: Youth Association Press [青年協會書局], 1939).

58. See Carver Yu, "The Contrast of Two Ontological Models as a Clue to Indigenous Theology" (D.Phil. diss., University of Oxford, 1981).

Wan earned his doctorate from Oxford in 1984 with a thesis comparing the theological anthropologies of Barth and Tillich.[59]

Unlike Wan and Yu, Yeung was never closely connected to the CGST circle, and yet he was clearly an academic theologian characteristic of that generation in Hong Kong. He studied with none other than T. F. Torrance at Edinburgh before proceeding to Cambridge for a doctorate, which he earned in 1981. Yeung's *Theology of Reconciliation and Church Renewal*, to my mind, remains the most philosophically sophisticated work of constructive theology in the Chinese language to date.[60] This is an opus that builds on Barth's doctrine of reconciliation in the *Church Dogmatics*, with a theological method derived from T. F. Torrance, to address indigenous issues in Hong Kong and broader Chinese culture.

In mainland China, academic theology began to emerge in the 1980s as an initiative related to the Open and Reform program. Chinese scholars were initially concerned with the role of Christianity in the economic and social success of Western democracies. This eventually grew into an interest in Christianity itself in its theological, historical, ecclesiastical, ecumenical, philosophical, (inter-)cultural, social, and interreligious dimensions. In the late 1980s, the so-called Sino-Christian theological movement (漢語神學運動) began to take shape, with the intention of establishing an interdisciplinary model of Christian studies situated in a distinctively Sinophone context. The intellectual forerunners of this movement were mostly scholars from mainland China, most notably Liu Xiaofeng (刘小枫, born 1956) and He Guanghu (何光沪, born 1950).

The theological dimension of the Sino-Christian theological movement in its earliest stages was dominated by Liu, who later

---

59. Milton Wan, "Authentic Humanity in the Theology of Paul Tillich and Karl Barth" (D.Phil. diss., University of Oxford, 1984).

60. See Arnold Yeung [楊牧谷], *Theology of Reconciliation and Church Renewal* [復和神學與教會更新] (Hong Kong: Seed Press [種籽出版], 1987).

dissociated himself from the movement. Liu studied in Barth's hometown, Basel, and earned his doctorate in Christian theology from the University in 1993, with a dissertation on the German philosopher Max Scheler (1874–1928). The early Liu drew on a number of sources, but his theological paradigm was basically Barthian. Under his influence, Sino-Christian theology took on a strongly Barthian tone in the early stages of its development, with T. F. Torrance as one of the most frequently mentioned figures in attempts to define Sino-Christian Theology.[61] Liu's later abandonment of Barthianism and Sino-Christian theology in favor of a Nietzschean approach to Chinese culture represents a significant challenge to certain Sino-Christian theologians today.[62]

Sino-Christian theology today has become a broad umbrella covering a wide variety of academic projects, ranging from the study of the Nestorian mission to China in the late fifth century to the study of the phenomenology of Jean-Luc Marion. The movement encompasses proponents of a wide range of doctrinal convictions—Catholic, Orthodox, Lutheran, Reformed, Anglican, Methodist, Baptist, liberal, neo-orthodox, postliberal, evangelical, neo-Calvinist, etc. Still, Barth is among the most frequently discussed theologians in Sino-Christian publications, along with Augustine and Thomas Aquinas. The 2019 volume of the *Yearbook of Chinese Theology*, a special edition that focuses on Barth and Sino-Christian theology, attests to the scale of his influence on Sinophone theology in recent decades.[63]

One strain of linguistically Sinophone theology that developed relatively independently of Chinese Christianity was

61. See Guanghu He [何光滬] and Daniel Yeung [楊熙楠], eds., *Sino-Christian Theology Reader* [漢語神學讀本], 2 vols. (Hong Kong: Logos and Pneuma [道風], 2009).

62. See Thomas Qu, "After Nietzsche: How Could We Do Sino-Christian Theology Today?," *Logos and Pneuma* 50 (2019): 155–82.

63. See Thomas Qu and Paulos Huang, eds., *Yearbook of Chinese Theology 2019* (Leiden: Brill, 2019).

Formosan Presbyterianism. In the 1960s, two theologians rose to international prominence from my native Taiwan. Choan-Seng Song (宋泉盛, born 1929), a leading representative of contemporary Asian theology, earned his Ph.D. at Union Theological Seminary with a dissertation on Barth and Tillich (1964).[64] Song interacted closely with liberation theology and saw the impasse between the theologies represented by Barth and Tillich as one to be overcome from a new starting point in the liberation of indigenous cultures from (post-)colonial influence. Cambridge-trained pastor and theologian Shoki Coe (黃彰輝, 1914–88), Song's close friend and colleague in the Presbyterian Church of Taiwan, espoused a more traditional theology that had won the approval of the likes of T. F. Torrance. So deeply informed by Barth was Coe's thought that Song famously dubbed it a "theology in Babylonian bondage" awaiting liberating indigenization.

This strain of traditionalist Barthian influence has proved pastorally relevant in Taiwanese Presbyterianism up to our day. The works of contemporary Taiwanese Presbyterian theologian Hong-Hsin Lin (林鴻信, born 1955), who earned the first of his two doctorates from Tübingen under Moltmann's supervision, reached out to a broader Chinese readership beyond Taiwanese Presbyterianism in the 1990s, and is one of the most sought-after speakers among Mandarin churches worldwide today. As a non-Barthian evangelical, Lin draws on Barth's insights in significant ways. With his two-volume *Systematic Theology* (2017) spanning nearly two thousand pages, he has been recognized as one of the most authoritative voices for Protestantism in Sinophone academia.[65]

64. Choan-Seng Song, "The Relation of Divine Revelation and Man's Religion in the Theologies of Karl Barth and Paul Tillich" (Ph.D. diss., Union Theological Seminary, 1964).

65. See Hong-Hsin Lin [林鴻信], *Systematic Theology* [系統神學], 2 vols. (Taipei: Campus [校園], 2017).

The introductions of Barth's theology to Japan and mainland China were almost concurrent. Unlike what happened in China, however, Barth's theology quickly took root in Japan and burgeoned without a break. By the 1950s, he had gained such a following in Japan that he felt obliged to openly address Japanese Christians to remind them not to follow him, but to follow Christ. His message was occasioned by the celebration of his seventieth birthday in 1956. In February that year, Barth received a letter from the editors of *Gospel and World* (福音と世界), the most influential and widely read periodical among the "twenty million Christians in Japan" at the time, informing him that they were "planning a special edition with various articles on Barth and his theology in the May 1956 issue for his seventieth birthday."[66]

Barth wrote in reply to his "dear Japanese friends":

Make as little exhibition of my name as possible! Because there is only *one* interesting name, while the elevation of all other names can only lead to false commitments and stir up bland jealousy and impenitence among others. Do not take from me a single sentence untested either, but rather measure each of them by the only true Word of God, which is the judge and supreme teacher of us all![67]

Barth's fame in Japan was partly owed to Yoshio Inoue (井上 良雄, 1907–2003), one of the aforementioned editors of *Gospel and World*. Inoue was himself a leading Japanese constructive theologian—there is even a small academic field dedicated to the study of his thought.[68] He translated the fourth volume of the

66. Barth, *Offene Briefe 1945–1968*, in *Gesamtausgabe* V.15 (Zurich: Theologischer Verlag Zürich, 1984), 370. Translation mine here and henceforth.

67. Barth, *Offene Briefe 1945–1968*, 375.

68. See Eiichi Amemiya [雨宮栄一], Keiji Ogawa [小川圭治], and Heita Mori [森平太], eds., *Yoshio Inoue Studies* [井上良雄研究] (Tokyo: Protestant Press [新

Church Dogmatics in 1959–88.[69] The other three volumes were translated by Masayoshi Yoshinaga (吉永 正義, born 1925).[70] In 1986, the Karl Barth Society of Japan was founded under the leadership of one of Inuoue's followers, Keiji Ogawa (小川 圭治, 1927–2012).

Partly due to the efforts of Inoue and his colleagues and pupils, including Yoshinaga, Ogawa, Eiichi Amemiya (雨宮 栄一, 1927–2019), Hiroshi Murakami (村上 伸, born 1930), and others, the study of Barth in Japan has been more advanced than in Anglophone scholarship in certain areas, most notably political theology. Well before Barth's *Evangelium und Gesetz* ("Gospel and Law," 1935), *Rechtfertigung und Recht* ("Justification and Justice," 1938), and *Christengemeinde und Bürgergemeinde* ("The Christian Community and the Civil Community," 1946) became available in English in 1960, Inoue had recognized their significance for Barth's political theology.[71] Inoue translated *Evangelium und Gesetz* into Japanese in 1952, followed in 1954 by the translation of the two other pieces with Kazuo Hasumi (蓮見和男, born 1925).[72]

Barth's political theology and the political implications of his theological method have been profoundly influential and polarizing in Japanese theology and philosophy. This has to do with

教出版社], 2006).

69. Karl Barth, *The Doctrine of Reconciliation* (*Church Dogmatics*) [和解論（教会教義学）], trans. Yoshio Inoue (Tokyo: Protestant Press, 1959–88).

70. Karl Barth, *The Doctrine of the Word of God* (*Church Dogmatics*) [神の言葉（教会教義学）], trans. Masayoshi Yoshinaga (Tokyo: Protestant Press, 1975–77); *The Doctrine of God* (*Church Dogmatics*) [神論（教会教義学）], trans. Masayoshi Yoshinaga (Tokyo: Protestant Press, 1978–83); *The Doctrine of Creation* (*Church Dogmatics*) [創造論（教会教義学）], trans. Masayoshi Yoshinaga (Tokyo: Protestant Press, 1980–85).

71. Karl Barth, *Community, State, and Church: Three Essays*, trans. A. M. Hall and G. Ronald Howe (Garden City, NY: Doubleday, 1960).

72. Karl Barth, *Gospel and Law* [福音と律法], trans. Yoshio Inoue (Tokyo: Protestant Press, 1952); Karl Barth, *Church and State* [教会と国家], ed. and trans. Yoshio Inoue and Kazuo Hasumi (Tokyo: Protestant Press, 1954).

the political situation in Japan during and after the Second World War. Both left-wing liberals and right-wing militarists tried to find support in his writings. Inoue undoubtedly stood in line with the spirit of the Confessing Church in Germany. In 1935, he was accused of having violated the Peace Preservation Laws, enacted in Imperial Japan for the suppression of left-wing resistance, though no charges were pressed in the end.

If Inoue exemplifies the Barthian spirit of resistance, then the famed Kyoto School of Philosophy, which actively supported Japan's militarist regime during the war, would be an example of the opposite. That Kitaro Nishida (西田 幾多朗, 1870–1945), founder of the school, was intellectually indebted to Barth in his construction of the concept of God has long been a well-acknowledged fact among German-speaking scholars, but it was not until around 2010 that Anglophone scholars began to explore Nishida's appropriation of Barth's theology.[73] Hajime Tanabe (田辺 元, 1885–1962), Nishida's pupil and cofounder of the Kyoto School, also drew critically on Barth's dialectical method for the construction of his early philosophy of the "logic of species" (種の論理).[74] The wartime Kyoto School appealed eclectically to Barth's insights to support an ideology of which he would never have approved.

Towards the end of the war, Tanabe became critical of Japanese militarism and nationalism. He developed a philosophy of guilt and repentance, and coined the term "metanoetics" (懺悔道) to describe this philosophy. Tanabe's postwar philosophy drew on a number of sources, including Christianity, Buddhism, and Kantianism. Barth was one of Tanabe's significant dialogue

---

73. Curtis Rigsby, "Nishida on God, Barth and Christianity," *Asian Philosophy* 19 (2009): 119–57.

74. Chin-Ping Liao [廖欽彬], "Tanabe Hajime's Religious Philosophy [田邊元的宗教哲學]," *NCCU Philosophical Journal* [國立政治大學哲學學報] 32 (2014): 57–91.

partners during this period. Tanabe, like Kitamori, was critical of what he saw as a lack of focus on history in Barth's theology, but often pointed to Barth's thought and life for inspiration to illuminate the "path of repentance," or "metanoesis."[75]

Katsumi Takizawa (滝沢 克己, 1909–84), a leading Japanese philosopher and theologian of Inoue's generation, was directly influenced by both Nishida and Barth. He began his academic career as a philosophy student. His early essay on the development of Nishida's philosophy won the approval of the master himself, and with Nishida's personal recommendation, Takizawa traveled to Germany for advanced studies in 1933, where he eventually became a student of Barth at the University of Bonn. Takizawa wrote an outstanding student essay under Barth's guidance, which was subsequently published in the prominent *Evangelische Theologie* in 1935.[76] The famed "Immanuel Philosophy" that Takizawa later developed was critically indebted to both Barth and Nishida.

Kazoh Kitamori (北森 嘉蔵, 1916–98), yet another Kyoto-trained thinker, is one of the Japanese theologians best known in the West. Rooted in the Lutheran tradition, he studied under Tanabe in the Literature Department at Kyoto University, where he received a Ph.D. in Literature in 1962. Kitamori developed a *theologia doloris* made famous in the West partly by Moltmann's reliance thereupon in the celebrated *The Crucified God* (1972). Like *The Crucified God*, the 1975 Spanish translation of Kitamori's *Theology of the Pain of God* (神の痛みの神学, first published in Japanese in 1946) has provided a source of inspiration for Latino theology.[77]

75. Yu-Kwan Ng [吳汝鈞], *Phenomenology of Pure Vitality: Second Volume* [純粹力動現象學：續篇] (Taipei: Commercial Press [台灣商務], 2008), 244–46.
76. Katsumi Takizawa, "Über die Möglichkeit des Glaubens," *Evangelische Theologie* 2 (1935): 376–402.
77. Leopoldo Sánchez, "What Does Japan Have to Do with Either Latin America

The thrust of Kitamori's *theologia doloris* is that "the cross is in no sense an external act of God, but an act within himself."[78] Pain—a concept that Kitamori develops in the context of Japanese Bushido—is essential to God's being as the living God. The pain that God suffers is not an abstract essence in his eternal substantiality, but rather his concrete act in temporal history. Any theology that denies the pain of God as such is, on Kitamori's view, guilty of docetism.[79]

Kitamori is known for his sporadic and yet harsh attacks on Barth in *Theology of the Pain of God*. These criticisms are densely focused as one self-contained piece in Kitamori's own foreword to the 1972 German translation of the work. The foreword begins with a dismissal of the ecumenism espoused by the Barthian theologian Keiji Ogawa as one that sets forth an "abstract universality" rather than a "concrete universality."[80] Kitamori then proceeds to criticize Barth's notion of "the First Commandment as a theological axiom," set forth in the 1930s, which he deems legalistic.[81] Echoing Luther's *theologia crucis*, Kitamori contends that the cross is the only axiom for Christian theology, apart from which all theologizing inevitably leads to abstractions.

What readers of Kitamori often miss is his critically positive appraisal of Barth in the fifth edition of *Theology of the Pain of God*, the edition translated into English, German, and Spanish. Kitamori credits Barth for having become "aware of his own abstraction" and attempting to replace it with "concrete truth"

---

or U.S. Hispanics? Reading Kazoh Kitamori's 'Theology of the Pain of God' from a Latino Perspective," *Missio Apostolica* 12 (2004): 36–47.

78. Kazoh Kitamori, *Theology of the Pain of God* (Eugene, OR: Wipf and Stock, 2005), 45.

79. Kitamori, *Theology of the Pain of God*, 35.

80. Kazoh Kitamori, *Theologie des Schmerzes Gottes*, trans. Tsuneaki Kato and Paul Schneiss (Göttingen: Vandenhoeck & Ruprecht, 1972), 9. Translation mine here and henceforth.

81. Kitamori, *Theologie des Schmerzes Gottes*, 10.

in *The Humanity of God* (1956), and for making Christology not only the content of, but also the prolegomenon to, theology.[82] As Kitamori sees it, however, Barth failed to follow through with this intention. Kitamori's criticisms of Barth in the fifth edition of *Theology of the Pain of God*, then, are in some sense aimed at completing the Christological project that Barth had initiated, though the Kyoto theologian was of course not nearly as intellectually indebted to Barth as Moltmann was.

Barth's reception in China, Hong Kong, Japan, and Taiwan might be little known to Anglophone readers for various reasons. This serves to remind us that in our assessment of the depth and extent of a thinker's influence, it is important to look beyond our own cultural and linguistic confines. As Anglophone evangelicals, we should be especially careful about the Anglo-American tendency to overlook the rest of the world, coupled with a certain isolationist ethos within evangelicalism that we have been trying to overcome since the inception of the neo-evangelical movement. In a word, Barth is in fact much more significant than most Anglophone evangelicals used to imagine in the 1990s and early 2000s.

Barth and Evangelical Theology Today

After about a decade of overall indifference, Anglo-American evangelical engagements with Barth and Barthianism(s) began to intensify in the 2000s, as the 2019 *Blackwell Companion to Karl Barth* indicates. The list of contributors reveals the presence of evangelical scholars in contemporary Barth studies: David Gibson, Ryan Glomsrud, Nathan Hieb, Matt Jenson, and myself, to name but the ones carrying clear-cut evangelical identities. My friend JinHyok Kim is a Korean evangelical with Barthian

82. Kitamori, *Theologie des Schmerzes Gottes*, 12, 21.

leanings. Keith L. Johnson (not to be confused with Keith E. Johnson), co-editor of the *Companion* and leading American Barth scholar today, has also been associated with traditionally evangelical institutions; he is Professor of Theology at Wheaton College and an InterVarsity Press author. One evangelical expert on Barth not included in the *Companion* is Sung Wook Chung, whose 2006 edited volume on Barth and evangelical theology continues to provide a good glimpse of the diverse receptions of Barth in contemporary evangelical theology.[83]

In addition to evangelicals involved in the secondary literature on Barth, there have also been those who have tried to incorporate his insights into constructive evangelical theology. As an alumnus of Regent College, I think immediately of Professor Ross Hastings and Professor Archie Spencer.

G. W. Bromiley (1915–2009), lead translator and coeditor of Barth's *Church Dogmatics* in English, is perhaps the best-known example of an evangelical attempting to incorporate Barth's theology. Bromiley himself held to a normative evangelical view of biblical inspiration.[84] He finds Barth's formulation of the humanity of Scripture illuminating and argues that "it is not really necessary to insist on errors in the Bible," as Barth does, "to maintain its true humanity."[85] Bromiley attempted to eclectically and critically appropriate Barth's insights without compromising what was in his day the basic evangelical consensus on biblical revelation.

Jack Rogers and Donald McKim, by contrast, departed from the normative evangelical understanding of the verbal inspiration of Scripture, and located themselves at some midway point between what they considered to be Barthian "neo-orthodoxy"

---

83. Sung Wook Chung, ed., *Karl Barth and Evangelical Theology: Convergences and Divergences* (Grand Rapids: Baker Academic, 2006).

84. See Geoffrey Bromiley, "Karl Barth's Doctrine of Inspiration," *Journal of the Transactions of the Victoria Institute* 87 (1955): 66–80.

85. Bromiley, "Karl Barth's Doctrine of Inspiration," 80.

and conservative evangelicalism.[86] The Rogers-McKim reinterpretation of the history of Protestant doctrine remains influential in some evangelical circles today.

Kurt Anders Richardson's *Reading Karl Barth* suggests ways in which Barth can provide new directions for North American theology, evangelicalism included. Unlike Bromiley, Professor Richardson does not try to reconcile Barth's doctrine of the Word of God with evangelical or Roman Catholic norms on biblical infallibility.[87] Rather, he moves beyond the battle on biblical authority and finds in Barth's notion of union with Christ a point of convergence between Barthianism and evangelicalism, suggesting that Barth's pneumatological formulation of the *unio* and the presence of Christ be taken seriously in evangelical theology as a starting point in its theological method.[88]

Kevin Diller has suggested that Barth and Alvin Plantinga, a leading contemporary American philosopher and the famed proponent of "Reformed epistemology," in fact provide a unified response to the epistemological challenges characteristic of the modern era.[89] Especially noteworthy is Diller's observation on how the two thinkers approach natural theology in similar ways.[90] Instead of rejecting natural theology wholesale, Barth and Plantinga only deny its status as *praeambula fidei*. They both treat the doctrine of faith as properly basic and proceed from the starting point of the properly basic truths of faith to interpret sensible

86. See Jack Rogers and Donald McKim, *The Authority and Interpretation of the Bible* (San Francisco: Harper & Row, 1979).

87. Kurt Anders Richardson, *Reading Karl Barth: New Directions for North American Theology* (Grand Rapids: Baker, 2004), 105–6.

88. Kurt Anders Richardson, "*Christus Praesens*: Barth's Radically Realist Christology and Its Necessity for Theological Method," in *Barth and Evangelical Theology*, 136–48. Also see Richardson, *Reading Karl Barth*, 83–87.

89. Kevin Diller, *Theology's Epistemological Dilemma: How Karl Barth and Alvin Plantinga Provide a Unified Response* (Downers Grove, IL: IVP Academic, 2014).

90. Diller, *Theology's Epistemological Dilemma*, 179–96.

reality. This agreement between Barth and Plantinga is in fact reflective of some significant similarities between Barth and the modern Dutch Reformed tradition, which we shall see in the next two chapters.

John Bolt, a famed proponent of neo-Calvinism and the editor of Herman Bavinck's four-volume *Reformed Dogmatics* in English, draws critically on Barth in the spirit of Reformed eclecticism.[91] Chung's brief comment that Bolt attempts to "integrate Barth's theology into evangelical theological construction" can be misleading.[92] Bolt tries only to integrate elements of Barth's theology selectively. He comments that "even for a theologian as problematic as Barth, there are for evangelicals useful insights and some salutary lessons to be learned from exploring Barth's eschatology."[93] Bolt is right in his description of Barth's Christocentric ontology as one in which creation is rendered ontologically dependent on redemption.[94] Bolt's criticism that this ontology blurs "the Creator/creation distinction," however, is in my view misguided (see chapter 2).[95]

Despite this interpretational difference, I am in agreement with Bolt's eclectic approach to Barth. If Calvin could gain positive insights from Osiander, and if Edwards was allowed to adopt elements of John Locke's philosophy, then why should evangelicals reject Barth altogether?

In any case, Barth is not a theologian whom evangelical theologians today can simply bypass. Professor Trueman was certainly right when he wrote in 2008 that "positive reception of Barth by evangelicals continues apace," and that "interacting

91. See John Bolt, "Exploring Barth's Eschatology: A Salutary Exercise for Evangelicals," in *Barth and Evangelical Theology*, 209–35.
92. Sung Wook Chung, "Foreword," in *Barth and Evangelical Theology*, xx.
93. Bolt, "Exploring Barth's Eschatology," 211.
94. Bolt, "Exploring Barth's Eschatology," 216–17.
95. Bolt, "Exploring Barth's Eschatology," 217.

with Barth as a great mind wrestling with serious issues is surely of tremendous help."[96] Regarding the characteristically modern problems that Barth struggled with, I am in cordial agreement with Professor Trueman that "Bavinck . . . offers a more helpful resource" for evangelicals.[97] Professor Hunsinger, too, suggests that "the views of Abraham Kuyper and Herman Bavinck" can lead to "fruitful evangelical dialogue" with Barthians and postliberals.[98] I will add the name of Geerhardus Vos to this list—with some sense of urgency.

In chapter 3, I resort specifically to Bavinck and Vos, along with the historic Reformed theology on which they relied, in my engagement with Barth from an evangelical and confessionally Reformed perspective. As we resort to Bavinck and Vos, we should also be reminded of their Reformed eclecticism. The eclectic spirit of neo-Calvinism—also discernable in older Reformed theologians from Calvin to Jonathan Edwards— means that we should not take Barth to be "helpful," as Professor Trueman has insinuated, primarily or even only at those points where we disagree with him, where we are "forced to wrestle most passionately" in such a way that our "own thought is clarified and strengthened."[99] Just as Bavinck draws positively from Kant, Hegel, Schleiermacher, and even Feuerbach, and as Edwards critically adopts aspects of Lockean philosophy, there is much that we can positively learn from Barth, much more so than from the philosophers with whom both Barth and Bavinck wrestled.[100] To achieve a critically and selectively fruitful engage-

---

96. Trueman, "Foreword," 15.

97. Trueman, "Foreword," 15. See Cory Brock, *Orthodox Yet Modern: Herman Bavinck's Use of Friedrich Schleiermacher* (Bellingham, WA: Lexham Press, 2020).

98. Hunsinger, *Disruptive Grace*, 340.

99. Trueman, "Foreword," 15.

100. See Cory Brock and Nathaniel Gray Sutanto, "Herman Bavinck's Reformed Eclecticism: On Catholicity, Consciousness, and Theological Epistemology," *Scottish Journal of Theology* 70 (2017): 310–32.

ment with Barth, however, we must first establish a fair interpretation of his writings that honors his texts and pays heed to his intellectual-biographical and intellectual-historical context, and examine certain evangelical myths about him, a task we now take on in chapter 2.

2

A SUMMARY OF
BARTH'S THEOLOGY

Why Do We Need a
Reinterpretation of Barth Today?

Before I first started reading Barth, I heard many things about
him from evangelical mentors. I was given a copy of Cornelius
Van Til's *Christianity and Barthianism* during my sophomore year
in college, and I read it carefully in preparation for seminary. The
first time I actually read Barth's own writings was in a J. I. Packer
seminar on the atonement. The experience was rather difficult,
because I could hardly make sense of the text at hand within the
interpretive framework that I had inherited. In my bewilderment,
I was struck by the humility that Dr. Packer exemplified during
the session on Barth, when he said to a student who challenged
his interpretation: "I am no Barth scholar, and I admit that I may
well be wrong about him."

Such humility, I believe, is a necessary starting point for
any genuinely Christian scholarship. All too often, when we tra-
verse the path, which I once trod, of discovering contradictions

between what we have been taught about Barth and what he explicitly states in the text, we all too easily explain this away by assuming that he does not mean what he writes, or that he is guilty of smuggling the presuppositions of modern philosophy into Christianity by disguising it under the cloak of orthodox terms and phrases. Such assumptions led to misinterpretations of Barth on the part of early evangelical and Reformed critics like Cornelius Val Til, Carl Henry, Gordon Clark, Fred Klooster, Francis Schaeffer, Klaas Schilder, and, to a lesser extent, G. C. Berkouwer.

Interestingly, neo-Calvinists like Herman Bavinck and Herman Dooyeweerd have also been accused of similar offenses in certain theological circles—think of the all-too-familiar "two Bavincks" thesis.[1] Van Til, too, has been accused of adulterating traditional doctrine with modern philosophy because of his frequent use of Kantian and Hegelian terms—the allegation came most notably from J. Oliver Buswell in the 1940s and 1950s. Even today, some conservative Reformed theologians still think that Van Til's presuppositionalism is essentially German idealism in the guise of confessional Reformed theology.[2] If we think that Bavinck, Dooyeweerd, and Van Til have been misunderstood because of insufficient knowledge of their intellectual backgrounds on the part of their critics—or if we are at least open to that possibility—why should we not also suspend for the moment the assumptions we have inherited about Barth and attempt to interpret him afresh?[3]

---

1. See Jan Veenhof, *Revelatie en inspiratie* (Amsterdam: Buijten & Schipperheijn, 1968).

2. E.g., John Fesko, *Reformed Apologetics: Retrieving the Classical Reformed Approach to Defending the Faith* (Grand Rapids: Baker, 2019).

3. Professor Fesko's fine work serves as an important reminder for us to return to our roots in classical Reformed theology. I have long benefited from his writings on the lapsarian controversy and the *pactum salutis*. His assessment of modern Reformed theologians like Van Til, however, is not as impressive as his presentation

In any case, an evangelical reinterpretation of Barth is needed today, not simply because our predecessors largely misinterpreted him. More importantly, the noble example of Van Til requires us to reread Barth in our own generation. His treatment of Barth is in fact admirable in a number of ways, and worthy of our emulation today, notwithstanding fundamental mistakes in his interpretation.

First, Van Til took Barth seriously, read Barth in the original German before English translations were even available, and paid close attention to fine details of Barth's text. Due to the limitations on his time, Van Til did not have at hand adequate secondary scholarship on Barth or reliable resources on Immanuel Kant (1724–1804), Friedrich Schleiermacher (1768–1834), G. W. F. Hegel (1770–1831), Søren Kierkegaard (1813–55), Wilhelm Herrmann (1846–1922), Adolf von Harnack (1851–1930), Hermann Cohen (1842–1918), and other thinkers who influenced Barth. Professor George Harinck has also suggested that despite Van Til's Dutch roots and his expertise in continental philosophy, he lacked sufficient knowledge of the contemporary cultural and intellectual milieu in continental Europe.[4]

In fact, Van Til's antagonism towards Barth was largely shaped by contention between neo-Calvinists and Barthians in the Netherlands, which arose in the late 1920s and 1930s. Van

---

of Reformed orthodoxy. For one thing, when he uses the term "German idealism," he does not demonstrate knowledge of the differences between Kantianism (which is transcendentally idealistic and empirically realistic) and post-Kantian idealism (which is thoroughly idealistic—though thorough idealism and thorough materialism are two sides of the same coin). "German idealism" usually refers to the latter, and yet Professor Fesko uses the expression almost synonymously with Kant's transcendental idealism. Curiously, Hegel's name is mentioned only three times in the book—a striking omission for any possible interpretation of Van Til and presuppositionalism. See Fesko, *Reformed Apologetics*, 101, 104, 144.

4. George Harinck, "How Can an Elephant Understand a Whale and Vice Versa?," in *Karl Barth and American Evangelicalism*, ed. Bruce McCormack and Clifford Anderson (Grand Rapids: Eerdmans, 2011), 13–41.

Til came to adopt the view espoused by Klaas Schilder (1890–1952), but still, he did try to read Barth for himself.[5] Before Van Til came to his own assessment of Barth, he wanted to meet Barth in person to listen to what Barth had to say for himself, and actually tried to do so in the summer of 1927, though the personal encounter did not take place until 1962.[6]

Van Til came to a formed opinion about Barth in the 1930s and set forth his view systematically in *The New Modernism* (1946). As I point out in the Kant volume of the present series, Van Til's portrayal of Barth as a worshipper of Kant in this book was based on a newly rising Anglo-American paradigm in Kant scholarship, which culminated in, and became dominant through, P. F. Strawson's *The Bounds of Sense* (1966).[7] This reading of Kant was foreign to continental Europeans, and could not have been Barth's understanding of Kant. Strawson's interpretation of Kant is now outdated, not least because of its blatant distortion of the primary texts in an attempt to secure Kant's continuing relevance against the rise of analytic philosophy. Yet this was the most advanced model in Kant scholarship in Van Til's time. In *Christianity and Barthianism* (1962), Van Til's assessments of Barth in *The New Modernism* are, in Van Til's own words, "established" even "more firmly."[8] It is Van Til's opinion that Barth never quite left behind his Kantian roots in his later theology. The obvious problem here is that if Van Til's interpretation of Kant is fundamentally wrong, his reading of Kant into Barth cannot be fundamentally right.

None of this, however, is to Van Til's discredit, as far as his

5. Harinck, "Elephant," 23.

6. See Harinck, "Elephant," 20.

7. See Shao Kai Tseng, *Immanuel Kant* (Phillipsburg, NJ: P&R, 2020), 32. See also Cornelius Van Til, *The New Modernism* (Philadelphia: Presbyterian and Reformed, 1946), 25.

8. Van Til, *Christianity and Barthianism* (Philadelphia: Presbyterian and Reformed, 1962), vii.

personal example as a scholar is concerned. He was constrained by the limitations on his time. "He should be commended," I wrote in my Kant volume, "for having followed the pioneers of Kant studies to the frontiers" and not having simply submitted "to the authority of his predecessors, such as Bavinck."[9] Similarly, Van Til tried his best to read Barth for himself, instead of forming his judgments of Barth by hearsay. It was not without independent and critical inquiry that Van Til finally came to adopt Schilder's view of Barth.

It ill becomes those who embrace Van Til's work, then, to refuse to disagree with his interpretations of Kant, Barth, or any other thinker for that matter, saying, "We don't need to read Barth for ourselves, because Van Til has already done it for us." (I heard this in person from a well-known Van Tilian, a seminary professor no less!). It would be regrettable if Van Tilianism in particular and evangelicalism in general deteriorate into such epistemic and academic authoritarianism and anti-intellectualism.

Second, despite the characteristically belligerent tone of his writing, Van Til was in fact sincere when he wrote that "in reading it [the *Church Dogmatics*] one's admiration for Barth knows no bounds."[10] When Barth visited the United States in 1962, Van Til was eager to meet him in person—which he already intended to do in 1927. An opportunity arose when Barth delivered the Warfield Lectures at Princeton Theological Seminary, but the seminary turned down Van Til's request to meet with Barth. Van Til traveled to Princeton anyway and caught up with Barth in the hallway. In a personal letter to Barth dated December 21, 1965, Van Til wrote: "When at last I did come near to you in the hallway and somebody called your attention to my presence and you graciously shook hands with me, saying: 'You said some bad

9. Tseng, *Immanuel Kant*, 2.
10. Van Til, *Christianity and Barthianism*, 1–2.

things about me but I forgive you, I forgive you,' I was too over-whelmed to reply. . . ."[11]

In this letter, Van Til assured Barth:

> The main thing I want to say is that I have always admired you greatly. . . . The fact that my views differed from your published writings and that I tried to say why, did not, in the least, detract from my esteem for you personally. And I never did say that you were the 'greatest heretic' of all time. . . . I have never, never judged of your personal faith in this Christ [of Scripture]. . . . If, and so far as I have, in spite of this, mis-understood and misrepresented your views I beg for your forgiveness for Christ's sake.[12]

Unless there is any reason to doubt Van Til's sincerity and integ-rity in this letter, I can see no legitimate reason for his followers and theological allies to insist that he never misunderstood or misrepresented Barth, when Van Til himself was humbly open to this possibility.

If we wish to engage with Barth fruitfully, then, I suggest that we take two necessary steps. First, when we seek to understand Barth's theology, let us remember the personal respect that Van Til had for Barth, and his desire to get to know Barth personally. Van Til's polemical tone may have come across as hostile, but hostility was really not his intent, nor should it be ours. One simple reason is that hostility impairs our judgment and unavoidably blinds us from our own assumptions and possible biases. Second, let us for the moment suspend what we think we already know about Barth, in order to come to a fair and objective reappraisal of his theology.

11. Cornelius Van Til letter to Karl Barth, December 21, 1965, Van Til Papers, Montgomery Library, Westminster Theological Seminary, Philadelphia, cited by Harinck, "Elephant," 41.
12. Van Til letter to Barth, December 21, 1965, Van Til Papers.

To these ends, I have arranged the theological topics of the second main part of this chapter in the form of a series of "myth busters." Before we proceed, however, it would be helpful for us to obtain a hermeneutical kit by exploring some basic motifs guiding Barth's theology and by establishing a basic understanding of his intellectual biography.

A Brief Intellectual Biography

Given the complexity of Barth's theology and the sheer expanse of the *Church Dogmatics*—twelve part-volumes in total—a comprehensive summary of his thought would be unrealistic for the present volume. A book that guided me through the labyrinth of Barth's thought more decisively than any other when I first began to wrestle with his writings was Professor George Hunsinger's *How To Read Karl Barth* (1991).[13] Especially helpful to me were the first two chapters, which offer four basic theological motifs underlying Barth's writings as a whole, followed by two further motifs. They provide the reader with a hermeneutical key with which to unlock his difficult text. In what follows, I will discuss the four basic motifs that Professor Hunsinger identifies in his first chapter against the background of new developments in Barth studies. Before presenting these motifs, however, it would help to introduce briefly the intellectual-biographical framework underlying my analyses.

1. Barth's early theology was significantly shaped by his neo-Kantian training in Marburg during his student years. His break from liberalism and his Marburg teachers in 1914 prompted him to look for a new theological starting point, and Kierkegaardian dialectics revolving around the "infinite qualitative difference"

13. George Hunsinger, *How to Read Karl Barth* (Oxford: Oxford University Press, 1991).

between eternity and time was his major source of inspiration in *Romans* I (1919) and II (1922).[14] During this period, Barth's eternity-time dialectic was significantly informed by Kierkegaard's adaptation of Kant's noumena-phenomena distinction, but it was not a neo-Kantian "*Realdialektik*," a rarely employed term that has no systematic usage in Barth's writings.[15]

2. Barth's appointment as Professor of Reformed Theology at the University of Göttingen in 1921 required him to study historic Reformed orthodoxy in preparation for his lectures. Although his reading of the Reformed classics was largely informed by the biased historiographies of Heinrich Heppe and Alexander Schweizer, he did grasp the characteristically Reformed rendition of Chalcedonian Christology, fully expressed in the 1924 lectures on Reformed dogmatics, popularly known in Anglophone scholarship as "The Göttingen Dogmatics." With the incarnation as the objective side of revelation and the soteric work of the Holy Spirit as the subjective side, Barth reformulated the "dialectic of veiling and unveiling" in a distinctively Reformed way:

> Barth did not need Kant any longer once he discovered the ancient anhypostatic-enhypostatic Christology in . . . 1924 and began to absorb the lessons of the traditionally Reformed understanding of the *indirect* relation of the two natures in Christ to each other (as mediated through the 'person of the union'). . . . So after 1924, the claim that revelation is indirect was no longer a Kantian claim; it was a distinctively Reformed claim.[16]

14. *Pace* Bruce McCormack, *Karl Barth's Critically Realistic Dialectical Theology* (Oxford: Clarendon Press, 1995), 236. See Sean Turchin, "Kierkegaard's Echo in the Early Theology of Karl Barth," *Kierkegaard Studies Yearbook* 2012, no. 1 (2012): 323–36.

15. See Sigurd Baark, *The Affirmations of Reason: On Karl Barth's Speculative Theology* (Cham, Switzerland: Palgrave Macmillan, 2018), 15.

16. Bruce McCormack, "Afterword: Reflections on Van Til's Critique of Barth," in

3. The previous phase that began in 1924 would last through Barth's appointment in Münster until he wrote *Anselm* (published in 1931) in Bonn. *Anselm* did not occasion a shift from dialectic to analogy.[17] However, *Anselm* did mark the maturation of Barth's faith-seeking-understanding program, characterized by the originally idealist method of reflective after-thinking (*Nachdenken*).[18] Barth reacted against both the neo-Kantian (positivist) and the post-Kantian idealist (metaphysical) approaches to theology by adopting a mode of theological reflection that takes as its starting point the immutable subjectivity of the triune God in the processes of revelation and salvation. Between 1931 and 1936, however, Barth was still reluctant to describe God as being-in-act, for fear of falling into the errors of Hegel, Schleiermacher, and other post-Kantian idealists. Instead, he would only speak of a revelation-in-act, as he did in the previous period.

4. Barth's basically Anselmian program of *credo ut intelligam* led him to abandon the *Christian Dogmatics* (*Die christliche Dogmatik im Entwurf*, 1927) that he began while at Münster. He started his dogmatic endeavor afresh in the *Church Dogmatics*. Barth's "use of the reflection structure to secure God's subjectivity, sovereignty, selfhood and personality" was the "new approach in the *Church Dogmatics* of 1932."[19] This approach was aimed at overcoming the challenges of the two major strands of neo-Protestant theology, namely, neo-Kantian positivism (e.g., Ritschl, Herrmann, Harnack, and Kaftan) and metaphysical historicism (e.g., Hegel, Schelling, Schleiermacher, and Troeltsch).

5. The Anselmian approach culminated in 1936 when Barth,

Barth and American Evangelicalism, ed. McCormack and Anderson, 372.

17. Rightly McCormack against Hans Urs von Balthasar. See McCormack, *Barth's Dialectical Theology*, 421–41.

18. Pace McCormack, *Barth's Dialectical Theology*. See Baark, *The Affirmations of Reason*.

19. Rightly Jürgen Moltmann, *The Trinity and the Kingdom* (Minneapolis: Fortress, 1993), 142.

inspired by a lecture on election delivered by his friend Pierre Maury at the *Congrès international de théologie calviniste* in Geneva, reformulated his doctrine of election by identifying election with the incarnation. This Christocentric reorientation of the doctrine of election was first set forth in *Gottes Gnadenwahl* [God's gracious election] (1936). For the first time in his career, Barth came to describe our knowledge of God in terms of his being-in-act, though the precise terminology was not yet developed. The formulation of God's primary and secondary absoluteness in terms of his love and freedom in *CD* II/1 and the identification of Jesus Christ with the electing God in II/2 were both grounded in *Gottes Gnadenwahl*. In *CD* II/1–2, Barth developed a more robust and precise vocabulary to express the doctrine developed in 1936, but there was no substantial development or difference between *Gottes Gnadenwahl* and *CD* II/2.[20] In particular, his identification of Jesus Christ with the electing God in *CD* II/2 was already in place in *Gottes Gnadenwahl*, and although Barth spelled it out more clearly in *CD* II/2, he did not present a substantially new theological ontology in the later work.[21]

"How to Read Karl Barth": Four Theological Motifs

The foregoing intellectual biography involves a number of debates central to contemporary Barth studies. I freely admit that my reading is aligned with the "traditionalist" school in opposition to the "revisionist." My previous monograph, written and published almost concurrently with Sigurd Baark's (2018, cited

20. *Pace* Bruce McCormack and Matthias Gockel. See Bruce McCormack, "The Actuality of God: Karl Barth in Conversation with Open Theism," in *Engaging the Doctrine of God*, ed. Bruce McCormack (Grand Rapids: Baker Academic, 2008), 213; Matthias Gockel, *Barth and Schleiermacher on the Doctrine of Election* (Oxford: Oxford University Press, 2006), 167.

21. *Pace* Bruce McCormack, "Seek God Where He May Be Found: A Response to Edwin van Driel," *Scottish Journal of Theology* 60 (2007): 64.

above), sets forth a reading of Barth in light of his adaptation of the Western theological tradition that resonates with Baark's interpretation of the role of *Anselm* in Barth's intellectual development.[22] It is within the framework of this previous study and in light of Baark's arguments that I proceed here to present the theological motifs identified by Professor Hunsinger in *How to Read Karl Barth*.

1. Actualism. Actualism is a motif that undergirds Barth's thought as a whole, even before his break with liberal theology in 1914. "It is present whenever Barth speaks, as he constantly does, in the language of occurrence, happening, event, history, decisions, and act."[23] Barth's theology is actualistic in that it "might well be described as a theology of active relations."[24] In his mature writings, actualism is expressed centrally by the notion of "being-in-act" (*Sein in der Tat*).

Barth's actualistic ontology came to full-blown expression in *CD* II/1–2, where he identifies the triune God as the archetypal being-in-act (*Urbild*), and Jesus Christ the ectype (*Abbild/Nachbild*). This archetype-ectype analogy is presented in *CD* III/2 as an "*analogia relationis*," whereby Barth speaks of the essence of the human being-in-act as a determination from above (*von oben*) by Jesus Christ, who, as the ectype in the analogy, is the very *imago Dei*.

Contrary to popular evangelical belief, Barth adamantly defends the immutability of God's triune essence revealed in Jesus Christ.[25] Barth, like Augustine in the famous *De Trinitate*, books 8–9, considers the biblical proclamation, "God is love"

---

22. Shao Kai Tseng, *Barth's Ontology of Sin and Grace* (London: Routledge, 2019).

23. Hunsinger, *How to Read Karl Barth*, 30.

24. Hunsinger, *How to Read Karl Barth*, 30.

25. See Baark, *Affirmations of Reason*, 255. Also see Shao Kai Tseng, "Barth on Actualistic Ontology," in *The Wiley-Blackwell Companion to Karl Barth*, ed. George Hunsinger and Keith Johnson (Oxford: Wiley-Blackwell, 2020), 739–51.

(1 John 4:16). Love is intrinsic to God's essential being: he loves necessarily and immutably. Yet, at the same time, Scripture everywhere attests to God's freedom both in and for himself (*potentia absoluta*) and in relation to us (*potentia ordinata*).[26] How, then, are we to make sense of the truth, revealed in Jesus Christ, that God loves freely, and is free in the love that is essential to his being?

In answering this question, Barth appropriates Augustine's insight that love is of a subject that loves, an object that is loved, and the very act of love. God's love is free in the primary sense that the Holy Trinity *is* love *a se*: he does not need an *ad extra* object to realize his prospective essence as love. In and for himself, God *is* love. Within God's eternal triune essence is an immutable object of love, which Barth calls God's "primary objectivity."[27]

Rejecting the Hegelian view that God needs an *ad extra* object to actualize his essence, Barth insists that the "freedom of God . . . , his primary absoluteness . . . has its truth and reality in the inner trinitarian life of the Father with the Son by the Holy Spirit."[28] The Hegelian term "absolute" here denotes a subject's being in-and-for-itself (*an-und-für-sich*), which involves the subject's self-objectification and act of self-acknowledgment. Hegel also appeals to Augustine's subject-object-act triad in the construal of a logical trinity, but Hegel's trinity becomes absolute only by the historical process of self-determination through self-alienation and reconciliation.

Barth insists against Hegel that God's loving essence is immutable: this essence *is* the triune God's eternal being in the act of love, and as such it is complete in and for itself from and to all eternity, prior to and apart from any *ad extra* act of love. In

---

26. Barth adopted this Reformed scholastic language while in Göttingen, and continued to employ the terms in the *Church Dogmatics*. E.g., *CD* I/1, 37.

27. *CD* II/1, 317.

28. *CD* II/1, 317.

a word, God is love in perfect freedom and is perfectly free in his immutable love, in the primary sense of *aseity* and *unconditionedness*, such that "even if there were no such relationship [between God and the creature in Jesus Christ], *even if there were no other outside of him, he would still be love.*"[29]

According to the orthodox Western doctrine of God's unknowability *per essentiam*, however, God's essence must be mediated to us through sensible means. As we shall see in chapter 3, Herman Bavinck and Barth agree on this particular point, insisting on God's essential unknowability and the indirect (i.e., mediate) nature of revelation. There is nothing Kantian in agreeing with Kant on this point, because Kant is in agreement with historic Protestantism in the first place. For Bavinck, "Kant is perfectly correct when he says that our knowledge does not extend farther than our experience."[30]

The problem then arises: how are we to speak legitimately of God's immutable essence, when our knowledge is confined to the mutable realm of sensible experience? Barth acknowledges that our "human mutability" means that we can only perceive God's "act" in historical actuality.[31] But does this not lead to the Hegelian and Schleiermacherian proposal to reduce God's essence to historical activity and process?

Against post-Kantian idealism, Barth insists that we can and "have to gaze upon God's immutability in human mutability."[32] God's immutable essence is indirectly (i.e., mediately) knowable to us, because God *became* human without ceasing to *be* God. With a starting point in faith, we know that he who *became* flesh *is* God, and so by faith and "only by faith can we speak about

29. CD II/2, 6 (italics added).
30. Herman Bavinck, *Reformed Dogmatics*, ed. John Bolt, trans. John Vriend, 4 vols. (Grand Rapids: Baker, 2003–8), 2:50.
31. *Gottes Gnadenwahl*, 48.
32. *Gottes Gnadenwahl*, 48.

God's immutability and faithfulness and identity," the identity between God-in-and-for-himself and God-for-us.[33]

God-in-and-for-himself became God-for-us without ceasing to be God-in-and-for-himself, and this is precisely the secondary sense in which God is love in freedom and free in his love. In addition to—but not in place of—the notion of God's primary freedom as aseity and unconditionedness, Barth states that God's love is free in the secondary sense that God freely binds himself to covenantal relationship with the creature without altering his essence. God remains perfectly free in this *ad extra* self-binding in a way that corresponds perfectly to God's essence *ad intra*.

Note that Barth, like Augustine and Kant, is opposed to the voluntaristic view of freedom as license: "There is no caprice [*Willkür*] about the freedom of God."[34] Freedom in the secondary sense, according to Barth, consists in the *perfect correspondence* between inner essence and *ad extra* activities. Barth's actualism differs from that of Hegel and Schleiermacher on one side (post-Kantian idealism) and that of Hermann Cohen (neo-Kantianism) on the other, precisely in that Barth speaks of God as being-*in*-act rather than being-*as*-act.[35] Being-*in*-act pre-

---

33. *Gottes Gnadenwahl*, 48.

34. *CD* II/1, 318.

35. Although on the odd occasion Barth refers to God *as* act or event, he does not in those places depart from his basic conception of God as being-in-act. The context shows that what he means to emphasize there is simply that God is the living God. See *CD* II/1, 263–64; IV/3, 47. Professor McCormack claims that Barth derived his actualism from Cohen: "For Hermann Cohen . . . , the human simply *is* the sum total of his or her lifetime of knowing activities. Expressed more expansively: the human is what he or she does. It was but a short step from here to reflection upon the divine nature as actualistic—a point which Barth would begin to ground christologically just two and a half years after publishing his second *Romans*." This imposition of Cohen's actualism on Barth inevitably distorts Barth's text. It has no way of satisfactorily explaining Barth's insistence on God's primary absoluteness. See Bruce McCormack, *Orthodox and Modern: Studies in the Theology of Karl Barth* (Grand Rapids: Baker Academic, 2008), 12. Against McCormack's post-neo-Kantian interpretation, I offer a post-idealist reading in "Barth on Actualistic Ontology."

supposes a dynamic essence that is complete in itself, prior to *ad extra* decisions and acts.

The covenantal relationship between God and humankind in Christ "is a relation *ad extra*, undoubtedly; for both the man and the people represented in him are creatures and not God."[36] It is, to be sure, "a relation in which God is self-determined, so that the determination belongs no less to him than all that he is in and for himself."[37]

The term *Bestimmung* here is obviously used in a Hegelian rather than (neo-)Kantian sense. This is evident in Barth's use of the Hegelian vocabulary of God's being "in and for himself" in conjunction with "determination." In Hegel, "determination" is the process by which a thing becomes rationally defined and definite through its history of interacting with objects other than and different from itself. Self-determination is the process by which a being is determined by its own essence, which Hegel defines as what a thing has in it to ultimately become.

Barth insists against Hegel that God is essentially triune, and this essence is determinate *a se* in his primary absoluteness: God does not need an object other than himself to determine himself as absolute. When he adopts the Hegelian language of *Bestimmung* to describe God, then, he has in mind an un-Hegelian

36. *CD* II/2, 7.
37. *CD* II/2, 7. It is characteristic of revisionists to appeal to Barth's talk of God's self-determination to contend that election is, as Matthias Gockel writes, "a constitutive or necessary aspect of God's being" ("How to Read Karl Barth with Charity: A Critical Reply to George Hunsinger," *Modern Theology* 32 [2016]: 260). This contention, again, shows a striking neglect of Barth's reactions against Hegelian idealism. Their equation of "determination" with ontological "constitution" does not even square with revisionism's own post-neo-Kantian interpretive framework. Kant's use of the term "determination" (*Bestimmung*) is largely in line with that of Gottfried Wilhelm Leibniz (1646–1716) and Christian Wolf (1679–1750). Determinacy, in Leibniz, Wolf, and Kant, refers to the reasoned state of a definite thing in which it is known as *that* thing and *not* something else. By no means does "determination" denote "constitution" (*Konstitution* or *Beschaffenheit*) in (neo-)Kantian terminology.

notion of God's essence that is perfect in itself, and whatever is added to this essence in the process of self-determination does not alter God's being ontologically.[38] Contrary to popular evangelical readings of Barth, what God self-determines, according to Barth, is God's existential being (*Sein*)—his being-for-us *ad extra*—rather than his triune essence (*Wesen*).

God's act of binding himself to covenant with humankind is perfectly free on his part, but his freedom is not the "caprice of a tyrant."[39] His will corresponds perfectly to his essence, which is, according to Barth, "entirely self-sufficient" as the intra-Trinitarian act of love.[40] So the secondary sense in which God is love in freedom and free in his love is this: God is free in loving us, for when he determines himself as God-for-us, he is not forced to cease to be what he is essentially, but rather opens himself up in an overflow (*Überfluß*), as it were, of his essence in the *ad extra* act of election in Christ.

God's primary absoluteness is the ground upon which he can be freely *pro nobis*. As Eberhard Jüngel puts it, "God can be the God of humanity without being defined as God by his relation to humanity. . . . God's being-for-us does not define God's being."[41] Jürgen Moltmann, too, observes that God's will, "Barth argues, determines his nature," but "God's nature also determine[s] his will."[42] God "chooses that which corresponds to his nature," and God's being-for-us is self-determined by God's gracious election,

---

38. So George Hunsinger, *Reading Barth with Charity: A Hermeneutical Proposal* (Grand Rapids: Baker Academic, 2015), 139–42; cf. 127–36.

39. *CD* II/2, 43.

40. *CD* II/2, 10.

41. Eberhard Jüngel, *God's Being Is in Becoming: The Trinitarian Being of God in the Theology of Karl Barth*, trans. John Webster (Grand Rapids: Eerdmans, 2001), 119–20.

42. Jürgen Moltmann, "The Election of Grace: Barth on the Doctrine of Predestination," in *Reading the Gospels with Barth*, ed. Daniel Migliore (Grand Rapids: Eerdmans, 2017), 7.

while this very act "is in conformity with his essential nature," writes Moltmann. "So we cannot proceed solely from God's will if we want to understand his essential nature; we must also start from God's essential nature if we want to know his will."[43] Thus Barth says, God "is the same even in himself, even before and after and over his works, and without them. . . . They are nothing without him. But he is who he is without them."[44]

When Barth applies the Christocentric form of his actualistic ontology to anthropology and the doctrine of creation, he tells us that no creature can be determinate in-and-for-itself, for only God is absolute and immutable in his unsublatable (i.e., unnegatable) subjectivity. The human being-in-act is dialectically determined from above (*von oben*) by God's gracious election in Christ and from below (*von unten*) by the history of Adamic sin.

The determination from above constitutes human essence and nature, and it is the unalterable substance of the human being. Because the determination from below has been *a priori* (*zum Vornherein*) overcome by election in Christ, sin is an ontological impossibility for humankind.

Here we see again, then, that Barth's actualistic anthropology does not exclude the category of nature and essence as something already complete prior to the subject's *ad extra* activity and history. The human being in the act of sin is not ontologically determined by his own sinful activities. Barth's notion of being-in-act must not be misconstrued as a neo-Kantian or post-Kantian or post-neo-Kantian or neo-idealist being-as-act, otherwise his notion of the ontological impossibility of sin would become quite meaningless.[45]

What permits the human being-in-act to after-think God's

43. Moltmann, "Election of Grace," 7.
44. CD II/1, 260.
45. I offer a fuller account of Barth's theological and anthropological ontologies in "Barth on Actualistic Ontology," 739–51.

works analogically with a starting point in faith in his triune essence is God's *becoming* human: in Jesus Christ we grasp by faith the fullness of the immutable Godhead and come to understand that God *became* human without ceasing to *be* God. It is this process of flesh-*becoming* that reveals to us God's eternal *being*-in-act as Father, Son, and Holy Spirit in the dynamic fellowship of eternal and immutable love.

2. Particularism. Like actualism, particularism is not a rigid mode of theologizing. The programmatic aspect of Barth's theology is always governed by its concrete content. He never begins with a general program to be imposed on the particulars of his theological content. Rather, the general program is always derived from the particulars of the Christian faith.

"Programmatically," particularism describes Barth's "concerted attempt always to move from the particular to the general rather than from the general to the particular."[46] After the Christocentric reorientation of his doctrine of election in 1936, Barth's particularism was guided, in John Webster's words, by "an almost ruthless particularity, a concentration of the imagination on one point and one point only: the name of Jesus, his absolute specific as 'this one,' the first and the last and the most simple thing."[47]

Barth's particularism is partly aimed at tackling the one-and-many problem, one of the oldest themes in the history of Western philosophy. Traditionally, particulars are usually considered to be concrete, while universals are intelligible by the method of abstraction. Barth agrees with Hegel that God's truth is to be sought *concretely* rather than *abstractly*. For Hegel, *concretion* denotes the unification of the particular with the universal, which is the same as the actualization of the universal in a determinate particular. While consummate concretion is an eschatological event

---

46. Hunsinger, *How to Read Karl Barth*, 32.
47. John Webster, *Karl Barth* (London: Continuum, 2004), 62.

of which we can know only by reflecting on historical phenomena, Hegel believes that the *concrete universal* as the consummate essentiality of historical reality can be reflected through particular things in the here and now. Through the concrete universal (i.e., God as absolute spirit who is yet to come), we can establish a systematic worldview in which all particulars are consummately identical with, and thus revelatory of, universal divinity.

Barth's language of concretion (a classic instance of which is found in *CD* II/1, 602),[48] partly borrowed from Hegel, is used in place of the Kantian concept of the "ideal" of pure reason. Hegel's notion of the concrete is similar to Kant's notion of an ideal, which designates the manifestation of a universal idea in a particular being. Strictly speaking, God is for Kant the only ideal of pure reason. Barth's choice to adopt Hegelian instead of (neo-) Kantian vocabulary has profound implications for his struggles with Hegel and post-Kantian idealism. When Hegel proposes to unveil reflectively the concrete universal through historical particularities, the underlying assumption is that an abstractly universal subject becomes concrete only through historical progress. God does not become fully God—concretely determined as the absolute—until he completes the historical processes of self-objectification and self-reconciliation. However concrete, God as such is reduced to a universal concept of the absolute that is comprehensible to human reason.

The all-encompassing notion of "the absolute" (*das Absolute*), in the grammar of an adjectival noun (German) or nominal adjective (English), suggests a subject-predicate reversal characteristic of Hegelian philosophy. Theologians of the classical Western tradition are accustomed to the predication "God is absolute." Hegel's rejection of substantialist thinking (i.e., the kind of thinking in which "becoming" is determined by "being")

48. See Hunsinger, *How to Read Karl Barth*, 32.

entails a reversal of the terms: "the absolute is God" (i.e., the being of God is determined by the process of becoming absolute). Because "absolute" is originally an adjective, it remains abstract (i.e., unactual and nonexistent) without corresponding subjects that it predicates. Indeed, Hegel frequently uses "absolute" as an adjective to describe subjects such as "spirit," but spirit remains abstract until it evolves into "absolute spirit" through the process of a subjective-objective-absolute triad. In order to avoid abstraction (i.e., positing a subjectless predicate or unpredicated subject), then, Hegel must assert an ultimate identity between the adjectival noun and all the subjects it predicates in attributing ontological priority to the predicate.

The Hegelian program is highly problematic for Barth. When we say, "God is love," and proceed with Hegel from the starting point of particular phenomena of this-worldly love, we end up conjuring up a universal idea of God defined by creaturely predications.

Against Hegel, Barth insists that subject-predicate relations must never be confused or reversed in predications involving "God is." Barth's particularism means that he "does not first ask about what might be true or meaningful on general grounds and then move to fit theological statements into that framework."[49] Predications involving "God is" require us to bear in mind what Baark calls the unsublatable subjectivity of God.

The predication "God is being," for instance, must never be reversed. "It is not being in an ascribed simplicity and pure actuality which is God, but God who is being. We do not believe in and pray to being, but to God who is being."[50] To make the predicate ontologically prior to the subject—which is to make "becoming" the essential constitution of "being"—would be to

49. Hunsinger, *How to Read Karl Barth*, 32.
50. CD II/1, 564.

repeat Hegel's error. Barth declares, with a nod to Feuerbach, that "Hegel's living God . . . is actually the living man."[51]

Whereas Hegel proposes to understand the whole of reality through the lens of a concrete universal, then, Barth sides with Schleiermacher in insisting upon a theological method that focuses ruthlessly on particularity. The early Schleiermacher already asserted that the infinitude of the universe is to be found in the "smallest part of the particular," for "the realm of intuition is so infinite precisely because of this independent particularity."[52] In his magnum opus, *The Christian Faith*, the particularity of his theological starting point is narrowed down to "no other individual life than that of the Redeemer."[53]

Well before Barth's Christocentric revision of his doctrine of election in 1936, however, he was already aware that Schleiermacher's particularism would inevitably lead to a dissolution of particularity in universal world-occurrence. The problem with Schleiermacher, as Barth puts it in *Gottes Gnadenwahl*, is that he frames the particularity of Christ in a "systematics of human history that can certainly not be described as anything other than a speculative worldview."[54]

The idealist term "worldview" (*Weltanschauung*) is perhaps better translated as "world intuition." The term "intuition," simply stated, means "immediate cognition." Kant stated that the human intellect is incapable of intuiting things in themselves: intellectual intuition belongs to God alone. Schleiermacher sought to establish the possibility of a Christian worldview

51. Karl Barth, *Protestant Theology in the Nineteenth Century*, trans. Brian Cozens and John Bowden (London: SCM, 2001), 405.

52. Friedrich Schleiermacher, *On Religion: Speeches to Its Cultured Despisers*, ed. and trans. Richard Crouter (Cambridge: Cambridge University Press, 1996), 27.

53. Friedrich Schleiermacher, *The Christian Faith: A New Translation and Critical Edition*, trans. Terrence Tice, Catherine Kelsey, and Edwina Lawler (Louisville: Westminster John Knox, 2016), 751.

54. *Gottes Gnadenwahl*, 25.

by suggesting that every intuition is associated with a feeling (*Gefühl*). The feeling of absolute dependence and of the need for redemption allows us to intuit divine realities. Salvation is to be found in Christ alone, says Schleiermacher, for this soteric feeling is supremely and originally manifested in the man Jesus alone and actualized in the believer by the Holy Spirit. The redeemed elect, endowed with the life of Christ, can feel the infinite God by intuiting individual moods of religiosity in this world. On Barth's reading, the particularity of Christ that Schleiermacher fought so hard to maintain is inevitably dissolved by the notion of world intuition in "statements about an ultimate and general overcoming of judgment by grace, about a gradual and finally triumphant restoration of all things."[55]

Barth's mature doctrine of election is aimed at overcoming Schleiermacher's difficulties. Many commentators have missed the fact that when Barth formulated the doctrine of an election of *all* in *Christ* in 1936, the word "all" stands for the universality of sinful world history shut up in disobedience, and "Christ" is the particular in whom this sinful universality is sublated (i.e., negated). Without emphasizing the reprobation that *Christ* suffered particularly in our stead, any doctrine asserting the election of *all*, according to Barth, would be dissolved into the generalization of abstract universals.

Abstract universality belongs not to Christ, but to Adam: "When we speak of Adam's sin, we speak of the sin of us all. The name Adam tells what the actuality of us all is."[56] Abstract universality can only describe the prison of disobedience into which God has concluded us all (Rom. 11:32). "The name Christ," however, "does not speak of 'all' in this sense."[57]

The name Christ spells particularity. "Already in the name

55. *Gottes Gnadenwahl*, 25.
56. *Gottes Gnadenwahl*, 45.
57. *Gottes Gnadenwahl*, 45.

lies the particularity: this man, the Anointed, Christ! It is concerned with the selectivity of election [*Auswahl*] here."[58] God did
not elect us all *simpliciter*. God elected this one man out of the
mass of perdition, and us *in* and *with* him.

"Election refers to the call out of the *universality* of *all*, and
so it refers to movement and event," namely, the movement and
event whereby the pathway from crucifixion to resurrection is
traversed.[59] The notion of a *simpliciter* election of *all* is tantamount to an apocatastasis in which particularity is dissolved.

The election of *all* (universality) in *Christ* (particularity), by
contrast, is a process in which the particularity of Christ as God's
elect sublates the universality of the prison of disobedience. This
leaves no room for any universalistic understanding of election:
"'God has shut up all under disobedience, whereupon He might
have mercy upon all' (Rom. 11:32). All: that is to say without the
shadow of a doubt from the meaning and the context: all, upon
whom He wills to and shall have mercy in Jesus Christ—thus
there is no room for the speculation of an eternal apocatastasis."[60]

Still, the question remains as to whether this doctrine of the
election of all in Christ implies that all will be saved at his Second
Coming. This is a point that we will return to when we discuss
Barth's allegedly universalistic doctrine of election below.

3. Objectivism. The motif of objectivism describes Barth's
conviction that the event of Jesus Christ is an objective one that
occurred *extra nos*—outside the subjective sphere of our knowledge and experience. This motif "has two important aspects. The
one concerns knowledge of God, the other, salvation in Christ."[61]

Once again, Barth's epistemological objectivism is primarily
aimed at overcoming the challenges of post-Kantian idealism.

58. *Gottes Gnadenwahl*, 45–46.
59. *Gottes Gnadenwahl*, 46 (italics added).
60. *Gottes Gnadenwahl*, 27.
61. Hunsinger, *How to Read Karl Barth*, 35.

He resorts to Ludwig Feuerbach and David Friedrich Strauss, two followers of Hegel and Schleiermacher, to demonstrate the ultimately materialistic implications of German idealism. Feuerbach, in particular, famously deduced from Hegelian and Schleiermacherian premises the "anthropological" essence of theology and "idolatrous" essence of the Christian religion.

Feuerbach's reasoning can be summed up as follows. Hegel says that all subjects are defined by predicates; a subject without predicates is abstract and empty. Schleiermacher says that each finite individual is a partial manifestation of the infinite. But if Hegel is right, then the concept of God would be defined in terms of creaturely predications. For example, in the predication "God is love," "God" is defined by particular acts of love in this world. And if Schleiermacher is right, then the God we worship would be nothing but the infinitude of our own nature freed from individual limitations. Christianity would be, then, nothing more than a projection of the human image unto a pseudo-object that we conjure up as God (idolatry), and theology would be nothing more than the study of human nature (anthropology).

In a rather famous statement, Barth stresses that "proper theology begins just at the point where the difficulties disclosed by Strauss and Feuerbach are seen and then laughed at."[62] This laughter comes only when the objectivity of our knowledge of God is established against the theological turn to the subject in post-Kantian idealism.

In his Christocentric reorientation of the doctrine of election, the epistemological and soteriological aspects of Barth's objectivism are united as a function of election and incarnation. One significant implication of Barth's Christocentric doctrine is that humankind's salvation is entirely determined in Christ from above, and no factor from below can alter this objective

---

62. Barth, *Protestant Theology in the Nineteenth Century*, 554.

reality. The immanent history of Jesus Christ from his birth to his ascension to his Second Coming, as attested in Scripture, is here described as the objective basis of our knowledge of God's act and essence, as well as our salvation from the history of sin. Scripture, too, is now described as an objective witness, the validity of which no longer depends on the subjective responses of the reader. This is a point that we will further discuss below under the rubric of Barth's allegedly subjectivist view of Scripture's becoming the Word of God.

4. Personalism. I like to use "relationalism" synonymously with "personalism" to describe Barth's thought, and I take it to be a spinoff from the motif of actualism. Personalism serves to caution against unilateral emphases on his soteriological objectivism. Readers like G. C. Berkouwer have asserted that "the question of the universality of the triumph of grace confronts us squarely with Barth's doctrine of election."[63] According to Berkouwer, if Christ's triumph over sin, evil, and death is said to be an objective reality accomplished *a priori* (*zum Vornherein*), ontologically determinative of all creatures from above, then the existential realities of faith and lack of faith would be meaningless with respect to the final outcomes of our lives and histories.[64]

Recall, however, that Barth is emphatic on the immutably relational nature of God's triune essence. God's inward essence is an endless encounter of persons. This essence is the archetype of a relationship *ad extra*, namely, the God-human relationship in the person and history of Jesus Christ. In *CD* III/2, Barth identifies Christ as the very image of God in human creatures. "The term 'image'" refers to "a correspondence and similarity between the two relationships," namely, "the relationship within the being of God on the one side" and "between the being of God and that

63. G. C. Berkouwer, *The Triumph of Grace in the Theology of Karl Barth*, trans. Harry Boer (London: Paternoster, 1956), 262.
64. Berkouwer, *Triumph of Grace*, 296.

of man on the other."[65] This is "not . . . an *analogia entis* [analogy of being]," but an "*analogia relationis* [analogy of relations]" that "consists in the fact that the freedom in which God posits" himself as the triune God "is the same freedom as that in which he is the Creator of man, in which man may be his creature, and in which the Creator-creature relationship is established by the Creator."[66]

"In this [covenantal] relationship *ad extra*, God *repeats* a relationship proper to himself in his inner divine essence."[67] The human essence is determined by this relationship in Jesus Christ, and in this sense humankind is described as having been made in God's image.[68] As Father, Son, and Holy Spirit are *for* one another, and as the one triune God is *for us*, "it is the essence of this man [created by God], to be for God."[69]

The repetition of the interpersonal relationships does not stop at the point of the incarnation, however. Because human essence is the determination of the human being by the particular relationship between God and the man Jesus, the actualization of our ontological relationship with God *completely* hinges upon the present-tense reenactment or actualization of Christ's grace *extra nos* (objectivism) by the renewing work of the Holy Spirit *in nobis* (actualism). That is, what Christ accomplished in his finished and perfect work of salvation there and then, the Holy Spirit repeats in our personal encounters with God *in Christo* here and now in a secondary and dependent form (personalism).

65. *CD* III/2, 220.
66. *CD* III/2, 220.
67. *CD* III/2, 218 rev. (italics added).
68. Millard Erickson erroneously describes Barth's relational view of the *imago Dei* as "antisubstantialist" by setting up a false opposition between substantialism and relationalism. See Millard Erickson, *Christian Theology* (Grand Rapids: Baker Academic, 2013), 520–30. This assessment is oblivious to the fact that Barth's relationalist definition of the *imago Dei* is in fact an actualistic rendition of Augustine's *vestigium trinitatis*. As we saw, Barth's actualism is not at all "antisubstantialist." See my *Barth's Ontology*, 57–59.
69. *CD* III/2, 71.

In the *perfect tense* of the one and inseparable triune economy *pro nobis*, our essence is a God-given covenantal relationship in Jesus Christ that cannot be altered by existential realities from below. In the *present* and *future tenses*, which are distinct and ontically necessary aspects of one and the same triune economy, of the historical reenactment of God's work by the Holy Spirit *in nobis*, our essence is the personal relationship that we are to enjoy in Christ consummately, which is distinct, albeit inseparable, from what we already *are* in him.

The question remains as to whether our personal relationship with God, which evangelicalism has so emphasized since the times of Jonathan Edwards and John Wesley, at present will have any bearing on our status at the Last Judgment. Barth's answer is in fact in the affirmative, but in a way that differs significantly from traditional evangelicalism. This is a point that we will discuss in more detail later.

Rereading Barth against Popular Myths

Having introduced the major motifs underlying Barth's theology, we now turn to a rereading thereof against myths that are popular in evangelicalism and beyond. I have listed below ten commonly held myths about him and his thought. Some of them are sustainable, but debated in contemporary scholarship; some are partly true; some are unhelpfully confusing, though not necessarily false; and some are simply false.

1. "Barth was a neo-orthodox theologian." The "neo-orthodox" label on Barth involves many complications. Because the term is often used without disambiguation, it tends to lead to confusion rather than clarification.

"Neo-orthodoxy" is sometimes used as an alternative label for an alleged theological school or movement known as "dialectical theology" or "theology of crisis," purportedly led by Barth,

Eduard Thurneysen (1888–1973), Friedrich Gogarten (1887–1967), Emil Brunner (1889–1966), and others. Barth denies that there ever was such a school or movement, and emphasizes in the preface to *CD* I/1 that his dogmatics does not represent this group of theologians.[70]

In the German context, the "neo-orthodox" label was initially coined to describe the aforementioned dialectical theologians. Both supporters and opponents of these theologians used the label to highlight their supposed enmity towards modern theology and higher criticism in favor of premodern orthodoxy.[71] Barth himself reports in the preface to *Romans* II that he was "blamed" by some and "praised" by others for his purportedly "Biblicist" approach to Scripture.[72] His high view of the Reformers, Reformed orthodoxy, and classical theologians like Anselm in the 1920s and 1930s led to the charge of neo-orthodoxy from the liberal camp, by which he was considered "a theological reactionary who wanted to overthrow the fruits of scientific theology acquired since the 1780s . . . in order to return to the theology of a former age."[73] When used in this sense, the term "neo-orthodox" certainly fails to recognize the modern characteristics of Barth's theology.

In Anglo-American evangelicalism, by contrast, the accent of the term "neo-orthodoxy" tends to fall on the "neo" rather than the "orthodox." Neo-orthodoxy is considered to be in line with liberal theology in its acceptance of higher criticism and denial of biblical inerrancy. Jack Rogers defines neo-orthodoxy as "a return to the Bible, through the insights of the sixteenth-century Reformers, but without abandoning the critical scholarly study of Scripture developed by liberalism."[74] God's revelation, accord-

---

70. *CD* I/1, xv.
71. See McCormack, *Barth's Dialectical Theology*, 25.
72. *Romans* II, 11.
73. McCormack, *Barth's Dialectical Theology*, 25.
74. Jack Rogers, "Biblical Authority and Confessional Change," *Journal of*

ing to the neo-orthodoxy defined by Rogers and Donald McKim, is indeed infallible, but Scripture is only a fallible witness to Christ, who is the true revelation.[75] This allegedly Barthian view of Scripture is rejected by mainline evangelicals in the *Chicago Statement on Biblical Inerrancy* (Article III).

So, while German theologians who label Barth as "neo-orthodox" usually do so with the understanding that he was opposed to higher criticism and modern scientific theology, Anglo-American evangelicals use the same term to highlight his continuities with the liberal tradition. Used either way, the "neo-orthodox" label gives rise to misunderstandings that distract us from the complexity of Barth's theological vocabulary.

One further complication arises when revisionist Barthians blame Hans Frei and T. F. Torrance, among others, for having advanced a certain neo-orthodox reading of Barth in "Anglo-American" theology on the basis of Balthasar's intellectual-biographical paradigm on Barth.[76] Revisionism usually uses the term "neo-orthodox" with the German emphases outlined above. Accordingly, this neo-orthodox reading posits a radical revolution in Barth's 1931 book on Anselm that marks a return to historic orthodoxy, thus construing "a Barth stripped of his dialectical origins" (referring to the dubious neo-Kantian *"Realdialektik"* that revisionism often imposes on Barth).[77] Revisionism often accuses traditionalist readers, who align Barth with the classical theologians, of trying to bring back "the neo-orthodox Barth."

In this context, "neo-orthodox" implies a simplistic return to premodern orthodoxy, as if modernity never happened. The post-Kantian Barth reconstructed by revisionism reacts to Kant's

Presbyterian History 58 (1981): 135.

75. Jack Rogers and Donald McKim, *The Authority and Interpretation of the Bible* (San Francisco: Harper & Row, 19799).

76. McCormack, *Barth's Dialectical Theology*, 4, 24.

77. McCormack, 24.

challenge by drawing on the insights of post-Kantian idealists like Schleiermacher. The result of this construal is a neo-idealist Barth who, like Hegel and Schleiermacher, denies the immutability of God's triune essence.

As we have seen, however, Barth's traditionalistic adherence to classic Trinitarian ontology is by no means neo-orthodox. The traditionalist Barth is thoroughly modern in that this Barth confronts not only the problems to which Kant and Barth's neo-Kantian teachers gave rise, but also the challenges of post-Kantian idealism represented chiefly by Hegel and Schleiermacher.[78] I like to call the intellectual-biographical interpretation proposed by Baark and myself "post-idealist": the post-idealist Barth who insists on God's immutable essence as unsublatable subjectivity is by no means neo-orthodox in the sense of neglecting the fruits and challenges of modern scientific theology.

2. "Barth teaches that 'the Bible is merely a witness to revelation,' and that the Bible 'becomes revelation in encounter' and 'depends on the responses of men for its validity' (*Chicago Statement on Biblical Inerrancy*, **Article III)."**

To understand Barth's doctrine of Scripture, we might begin with a famous story about him. "Jesus loves me, this I know, for the Bible tells me so," Barth reportedly said during his visit to America in 1962, in reply to a student in Chicago or Richmond (or both) who asked him to sum up his theology in a pithy statement. The story has been confirmed by eyewitness reports from both Chicago and Richmond, and the details of the reports vary. The truthfulness of their attestation, of course, can hardly be subjected to the scrutiny of modern historical sciences. Despite the ambiguous and uncertain nature of the witness, however, we can believe in its basic truthfulness, because we can discern no deceptive intent in the reporters, and, more importantly, because

78. See my "Barth on Actualistic Ontology."

this is something that Barth certainly would have said, given what we know about him. And even if he never said it, the story is still helpful for our attempt to understand him.

Such is also the nature of the Bible as the Word of God in written form, which bears witness to Jesus Christ, the eternal Word of God revealed in history—our very temporal history to be sure. (Barth speaks of the Word of God in three forms as revealed in Jesus Christ, written in Scripture, and proclaimed in the church.) The Bible, however, differs from any other witness in that God was providentially present in a special way during the authorial and redactional processes in the formation of the biblical canon.

So, does Barth say that the Bible *is not* the Word of God in its own essence, and *becomes* revelation only in act and encounter? Does he believe that the validity of the written Word of God depends on the responses of the reader? This is certainly one common and plausible way of understanding Barth. This reading is accepted by many on both the evangelical and Barthian sides.[79] It is, as we saw, the reason why many evangelicals attach the "neo-orthodox" label to Barth.

After all, Barth does explicitly state in *CD* I/1 that "the Bible . . . becomes God's Word" when "God's action on man has become an event . . . , and the Bible has grasped at man."[80] The identity between Scripture and revelation, says Barth, is not immanent: "their union is really an event."[81] So, "in the statement

79. E.g., Kevin Vanhoozer, "A Person of the Book? Barth on Biblical Authority and Interpretation," in *Karl Barth and Evangelical Theology*, ed. Sung Wook Chung (Grand Rapids: Baker, 2006), 72; Bruce McCormack, "The Being of Holy Scripture Is in Becoming," in *Evangelicals and Scripture: Tradition, Authority and Hermeneutics*, ed. Vincent Bacote, Laura Miguelez, and Dennis Okholm (Downers Grove, IL: IVP Academic, 2004), 66, cited by Ximian Xu, "Karl Barth's Ontology of Holy Scripture Revisited," *Scottish Journal of Theology* 74 (2021): 27.

80. *CD* I/1, 109.

81. *CD* I/1, 113.

that the Bible is God's Word the little word 'is' refers to its being in this becoming. It does not become God's Word because we accord it faith but in the fact that it becomes revelation to us."[82]

To conclude from such passages that, for Barth, the validity of Scripture as revelation depends on the response of the reader, however, gives rise to a number of problems. First, in *CD* I/1, Barth still defines election as the temporal event in which God gives faith to the sinner, and the event in which the Bible becomes the Word of God to this or that reader is the event of his or her election. With the Christocentric revision of his doctrine of election in 1936, however, Barth no longer sees the validity of revelation as dependent on the event of faith. Why, then, did Barth show no sign of revoking his formulation of the being-in-becoming of Scripture as revelation in the later volumes of *CD*, when he expressly changed his mind on a number of other points?

Another problem with the aforementioned interpretation of Barth's doctrine of Scripture is that it does not square with his own exegetical practices. Although he does claim that Scripture is humanly fallible in theory, it is a well-known fact that he never pinpointed any specific error or contradiction in Scripture. To be sure, he does take liberty with biblical texts at times, reading into them his own theological formulations by bypassing the perspicuous meanings of the texts *ad litteram*. Still, there is in Barth a clear hierarchy in the *regula fidei*: the theologian's proclamation must conform to the church's dogmas, and the church's dogmas must conform to Scripture. The biblical canon, for Barth, is a stable standard with a supremely regulative function in the church that is valid at all times during and ever since its formation, and this objective validity does not depend on the reader's faith or lack of faith. As Barth himself puts it, the Word

---

82. *CD* I/1, 110.

of God "in its writtenness as 'Bible' . . . must be distinguished from and given precedence over the purely spiritual and oral life of ecclesial tradition."[83]

The neo-Calvinist scholar Ximian Xu's recent piece on Barth's ontology of Scripture sheds light on these problems.[84] Relying on my "nomenclatural study" of Barth's ontological language, Xu points out that Barth speaks of both the *Wesen* and the *Sein* of Scripture. *Wesen* is a term Barth adopts from traditional Western theology to denote essential being, while *Sein/Dasein* is a modern philosophical term that denotes existential being. *Sein/Dasein* becomes determinate through act and event, but *Wesen* is something already complete, either in and for itself (as in the case of God) or determined *a priori* (*zum Vornherein*) by God's act from above (as in the case of creatures).

With a careful examination of Barth's use of these terms in context, Xu concludes that "for Barth Holy Scripture *is* the Word of God insofar as the *Wesen* of Scripture is the witness of Jesus Christ, the one eternal Word of God; meanwhile, Holy Scripture *becomes* the Word of God insofar as the *Sein* of Scripture is the human expression of the Word of God."[85] In its essential being, Scripture is determined as the Word of God as a divinely written attestation to the history of Jesus Christ; in its existential being, Scripture becomes the Word of God only in the event of faith, in which a noetic union of the human word with divine revelation occurs.

This is not to say that Scripture is *essentially* God's Word in a hypostatic sense: even Reformed orthodoxy would distinguish between *Verbum Dei essentiale* and *Verbum Dei scriptum*, identifying Christ as *essentially* divine as the second person of the Godhead and Scripture as *originally* divine as God's work *ad*

83. *CD* I/1, 106.
84. Xu, "Barth's Ontology of Scripture," 28–33.
85. Xu, "Barth's Ontology of Scripture," 38.

extra. When Barth speaks of the *Wesen* of Scripture, he is referring only to what Scripture is in itself, prior to the event of being read.

Now, what sets Scripture apart from the church's proclamation is not just their different places in the hierarchy of the three forms of the Word of God. There is an essential difference between Scripture and proclamation. Scripture is *originally* the Word of God and *existentially* becomes so in the event of faith. Proclamation, by contrast, is always an existential event; in its *Wesen* it is nothing more than a human word.

Xu points to the second section of *CD* §19, titled "Scripture as the Word of God," where Barth contends that the Bible in its essence is "more than" a human word.[86] Barth writes: "In general, therefore, the witness of Holy Scripture to itself consists simply *in its essence* [*Wesen*] *as the witness of Jesus Christ.* And the knowledge of the truth of this self-witness, the knowledge of its unique authority, stands or falls with the knowledge that Jesus Christ is the incarnate Son."[87] I would add here that for Barth, Scripture is not only a human word attesting to Christ. In its essence it *is* the written Word of God that attests to its own authority ("self-witness") in its *essentially being* the "witness of Jesus Christ." Thus Barth: "We believe in and with the Church that Holy Scripture *has* the priority over all other writings and authorities, even those of the Church. We believe in and with the Church that Holy Scripture as the *original* and legitimate witness of divine revelation *is itself* the Word of God."[88] Barth adds:

> The [words] "has" and "is" speak about a divine disposing, action and decision, to which when we make these statements we have on the one hand to look back as something which has

86. Xu, "Barth's Ontology of Scripture," 35.
87. *CD* I/2, 485 and *KD* I/2, 538, cited by Xu, "Barth's Ontology of Scripture," 35. Revised translation and italics by Xu.
88. *CD* I/2, 502 (italics added).

already taken place, and on the other to look forward as something which has yet to do so. . . . If we say: the Bible has this priority, it is the Word of God, we must first replace the "has" by a "had" and "will have," and the "is" by a "was" and "will be." It is only as expounded in this way that the two words correspond to what we can actually know and say: we who are not in a position to carry through that divine disposing, action and decision or to handle them as though they were ours.[89]

Here we see Barth's actualism at work in his doctrine of Scripture. His notion of "being-in-act," rather than "being-as-act," as we saw, is such that God *has acted* (perfect tense) in such a way that he *acts* (present tense) and *will act* (future tense) in correspondence to what he already accomplished there and then. God's present and future acts are anchored in his perfectly accomplished work. This means that the Bible cannot *become* God's Word *to us* through God's "disposition, action and decision" here and now, unless it *was* already God's Word "originally" (*ursprünglich*). Scripture's *becoming* God's Word must correspond to Scripture's *originally being* the Word of God.[90]

This interpretation of Barth's doctrine of Scripture is superior to the more popular one, in that it is consistent with his own formulation of the noetic and ontic aspects of revelation in *Anselm*, which partly occasioned the substitution of the *Christian Dogmatics* with the *Church Dogmatics* (see the intellectual biography above). In *Anselm*, Barth distinguishes between "ontic *ratio*" and "noetic *ratio*." The latter *ratio* (reason or rationality) is "noetic" in that it is the "knowing *ratio* of the human faculty of making concepts and judgments"; the former, by contrast, is

---

89. *CD* I/2, 502.

90. *Pace* Katherine Sonderegger's exposition of the same passage in "The Doctrine of Inspiration and the Reliability of Scripture," in *Thy Word Is Truth: Barth on Scripture*, ed. George Hunsinger (Grand Rapids: Eerdmans, 2012), 21–22.

"peculiar to the object of faith."[91] Understanding (*intellectam*) is attained when the believer's noetic *ratio* conforms to the ontic *ratio* of God's revelation.

Barth further distinguishes between two ontic *rationes*. *Ratio veritatis* is "identical with . . . the divine Word consubstantial with the Father. It is the *ratio* of God."[92] Following the orthodoxy of the Western tradition, Barth denies the possibility of direct human knowledge of God *per essentiam*, and so the *ratio veritatis* can be given to human knowledge only through *ratio fidei*, which is the Word of God as the object of faith (Barth, unlike Van Til, uses "direct" and "immediate" synonymously).

On this view, Scripture as ontic *ratio is* ontically the Word of God. In the event of faith, it noetically *becomes* the Word of God as the object of faith *to the believer*. The ontic validity and being of Scripture as the Word of God, then, does not depend on the response of the reader for Barth. Scripture carries a supremely regulative function in the faith of the church, precisely because it is ontically the Word of God, regardless of the reader's noetic responses. Revelation as an event becomes complete in both the perfect and present tenses, when the noetic *ratio* conforms to the ontic.

3. "The historicity of Christ's resurrection is irrelevant for Barth." This myth about Barth is simply false. Again, it misses the actualistic character of Barth's Christocentric ontology. The "time of Jesus Christ" of which Barth speaks, which he identifies as God's time for us, is fully and truly eternal as it is fully and truly historical. He is unequivocal on this point:

> The Gospels distinguish the life of Jesus from myths proclaiming timeless truth by underlining, though not overstressing,

91. *Anselm*, 45.
92. *Anselm*, 45.

the temporal limitations to which Jesus was subject. Palestine, Galilee and Jerusalem are the indispensable background to his life, giving him a concrete relationship to His contemporary social environment and a definite place in history (Luke 2:1f.; 3:1f.). The inclusion of Pontius Pilate in the creed means, *inter alia*, that the Church wished to pinpoint the death of Jesus as an event in time.[93]

Barth speaks of the history of Christ's birth up to his passion as having taken place in the "first history," in which the whole Adamic race is included.[94] "Easter history" is the "second history," through which eternity breaks into our time.[95] This "second history," too, has to have taken place in our time: it is "the history of the forty days between His resurrection and ascension."[96] In this Easter history, the resurrected Jesus was "the One whom at this time His disciples had heard, and seen with their eyes, and looked upon, and their hands had handled (1 John 1:1)."[97]

Barth is emphatic that "the Easter history and Easter time" really took place "in the sphere of history and time no less than in the case of the words and acts and even the death of Jesus."[98] Christ's resurrection is "not just a timeless idea."[99] It is, rather, the temporal and historical "prism" of "the time of the forty days," through which the promise of eternal life can be concretely known by human beings in time.[100] Without Easter as the in-breaking of eternity, history would be void of meaning and purpose. "It was by this specific memory, and not by a timeless and nonhistorical

93. *CD* III/2, 441.
94. *CD* III/2, 441.
95. *CD* III/2, 441–42.
96. *CD* III/2, 441.
97. *CD* III/2, 442.
98. *CD* III/2, 442.
99. *CD* III/2, 442.
100. *CD* III/2, 442.

truth, that the apostles and the Churches they founded lived in all the relations between Jesus and them and them and Jesus."[101]

This is precisely the reason why it was "so important" for the evangelists to "emphasize and underline the concrete objectivity of the history attested" in "the Easter stories."[102] Barth is at pains to stress the historical objectivity and reality of Christ's resurrection as a concrete event in the sensible world. "If Jesus is not risen—bodily, visibly, audibly, perceptibly, in the same concrete sense in which He died, as the [Gospel] texts themselves have it—if He is not also risen, then our preaching and our faith are vain and futile."[103]

I see no ambiguity in Barth's statement that "Easter . . . is the concretely historical event of the self-manifestation of Jesus after His death."[104] Surely it is an event in the history of Jesus Christ, and as such it is unlike any ordinary event in our history as Adamic history. However, this event has to have taken place in our history and our time, in order to make it "possible for us to recognize" the "reconciliation" that has taken place "in His history."[105] If Easter is to be revelatory at all, it has to be an "event in which this [the incarnate] Word becomes an effective Word spoken to men."[106] Easter as such "is the event in which it can be, and actually is, known among men, in the sphere of human acceptance and experience and thought."[107] For Barth, the possibility of human knowledge of God stands or falls with the historicity of Christ's resurrection, and it is a far-fetched myth to say that he undermines the historicity of this event in the plain sense of the term "historicity."

101. *CD* III/2, 442.
102. *CD* IV/1, 351.
103. *CD* IV/1, 351–52.
104. *CD* IV/2, 146.
105. *CD* IV/2, 146.
106. *CD* IV/2, 146.
107. *CD* IV/2, 146.

4. "But Barth undermines the very notion of 'history' as understood by the average historian." In fact, even Van Til acknowledges that, for Barth, "God and man *must* participate in a common history."[108] Van Til concurs that, for Barth, "the resurrection is physical and historical."[109] However, says Van Til, "this is true only in the sense that, though it is primarily *Geschichte*, it is *also* an innerworldly something."[110]

Here Van Til is relying on the problematic hermeneutical key of the *Geschichte-Historie* distinction that he reads into Barth. According to Van Til, Barth means by *Geschichte* what really happens in the revelational time of Jesus Christ, in which God becomes present to us in act and encounter, while *Historie* denotes "history as the past, history as studied by the average historian, whether Christian or non-Christian."[111] Van Til believes that, for Barth, "the resurrection must primarily be *Geschichte* and only secondarily *Historie*."[112] The resurrection as such, according to Van Til's take on Barth, cannot be "directly identified with anything in *Historie*."[113] Van Til's misunderstanding partly arises from his imposition of his own distinction between "direct" and "immediate" on Barth's vocabulary, in which the two terms are in fact synonymous. When Barth speaks of the historical objectivity of Christ's resurrection, claims Van Til, he has in mind the reality of the event in *Geschichte*, for nothing in *Historie* can provide any "truly objective basis for the believer's faith."[114]

This reading of Barth is highly problematic, not least because he never contrasts *Geschichte* and *Historie* in his writings. It is true that he gives these terms different definitions, but there

108. Van Til, *Christianity and Barthianism*, 104.
109. Van Til, *Christianity and Barthianism*, 25.
110. Van Til, *Christianity and Barthianism*, 25 (italics original).
111. Van Til, *Christianity and Barthianism*, 8–9.
112. Van Til, *Christianity and Barthianism*, 25.
113. Van Til, *Christianity and Barthianism*, 25.
114. Van Til, *Christianity and Barthianism*, 25.

is no systematic dichotomy between them. The German word *Geschichte*, from the verb *geschehen* ("to happen"), also means "story." For Barth, *Geschichte* simply denotes what has happened, and it is best translated as "history."

Barth speaks of three kinds of *Geschichte*. The first is the history of God-in-and-for-himself, which is the eternal occurrence of God's triune *opera ad intra*. The essential history of God's immutable being-in-act is not immediately knowable to creatures within Adamic world history (*Weltgeschichte*), which is the history accessible to our thoughts and experiences. The third *Geschichte* is the history of Jesus Christ, which is the history of God-for-us, in which God the Son takes our Adamic history to be his own without ceasing to be the fullness of God-in-and-for-himself in the triune Godhead. Christ's history is the inward basis of world history, and world history is the stage on which Christ's history is enacted. The distinction, yet inseparable union, between world history and Christ's history is especially important for Barth's doctrine of reconciliation in *CD* IV.[115]

Now, by *Historie*, Barth refers specifically to *modern* historiography. However, he does not mean, as Van Til puts it, "the facts of the world as the neutral historian sees them."[116] Van Til himself knew very well that there can be no such thing as "neutral" historiography. He should have agreed with Barth, then, that there can be *objectivity*, but no *neutrality*, in human dealings with historical facts. An objective interpretation of history is one that corresponds to historical truth. Van Til and Barth would in fact agree that only God's knowledge of history is entirely objective, and our historical knowledge can indirectly participate in this objectivity only through faith in historical revelation. Historians, of course,

---

115. I offer a detailed exposition of Barth's distinction between *Weltgeschichte* and the *Geschichte* of Christ from *CD* IV/1 in *Karl Barth's Infralapsarian Theology* (Downers Grove, IL: IVP Academic, 2016), 265–69.

116. Van Til, *Christianity and Barthianism*, 14.

must strive for objectivity. However, no historian can ever be neutral in the sense of being without presuppositions, and the presuppositions with which we interpret historical data are ultimately theological. Without faith in revelation—that is, without the right theology—no historiography can be genuinely objective.

When Barth uses the word *Historie* in the sense of modern historiography, he has in mind the historical consciousness characterizing post-Kantian modernity and the historical-critical sciences to which it gave rise. The term *Historie* as such often connotes the biases and hubris of the modern historian. Hans Frei points out that Barth's refusal to interpret Scripture as *Historie* is intended as a criticism of historical criticism.[117] Frei explains that by *Historie*, Barth means *"that which can be historically proven*—that is to say, empirical history, history to which our fact questions are relevant. . . . It's that kind of history: 'What's the evidence for that?' that Barth speaks of . . . , that which can be historically proven."*[118]

Modern historians like Leopold von Ranke (1795–1886) prided themselves in being able to interpret spatio-temporal phenomena and events objectively without the aid of revelation. Hermann Gunkel (1862–1932) betrays a characteristically modern historical-critical bias against revelation when he asserts that the biblical authors were "incapable of objectively interpreting their experiences."[119]

When Barth speaks of the "historical objectivity" of the resurrection, what he means is that the Easter narratives in the Gospels objectively interpret the experiences of the disciples who reported the events. It is the critical historian, in Barth's view,

117. Hans Frei, "Scripture as Realistic Narrative: Karl Barth as Critic of Historical Criticism," in *Thy Word Is Truth*, 49–63.

118. Frei, "Scripture as Realistic Narrative," 56.

119. Hermann Gunkel, *Genesis*, trans. Mark Biddle (Macon: Mercer University Press, 1997), vii.

whose modern *Historie* is incapable of objectively interpreting the Easter event—or any event in world history, for that matter.

Barth is especially opposed to the Bultmannian bias "that an event alleged to have happened in time can be accepted as historical only if it can be proved to be a 'historical fact'" on the assumptions of "modern historical scholarship."[120] He blames the historical positivism espoused by the "Marburg Kantians" for having brought about the hubris of the modern historian.[121] According to them, reports of past events can be accepted as genuinely historical only if they can be scientifically verified on the basis of naturalistic assumptions.

Against Bultmann's identification of the biblical narratives as mythology (historically incredible tales aimed at conveying timeless truths), then, Barth resorts to the literary genre of *saga* to describe biblical reports of God's participation in the creaturely realm. He is not using the term "saga" in the generally accepted sense of a literary "form which, using intuition and imagination, has to take up historical narration at the point where events are no longer susceptible as such to historical proof."[122] Although biblical saga also fits this general description, "within this genre biblical saga is a special instance which cannot be compared with others but has to be seen and understood in and for itself."[123]

Recall that when Barth uses the Hegelian term "in and for itself" (the basic definition of "the absolute") in the framework of his actualism, he has in mind an essence that is already complete within the subject prior to acts and events external to the subject itself. Strictly speaking, only the triune God is absolute, but Barth sometimes ventures to apply this description to Scripture as the Word of God. Scripture is essentially an accomplished work of

120. CD III/2, 446.
121. CD III/2, 447.
122. CD IV/1, 508.
123. CD IV/1, 508.

God in history, such that in biblical saga "intuition and imagination are used but in order to give prophetic witness to *what has taken place* by virtue of the Word of God in the (historical or pre-historical) sphere where there can be no historical proof."[124]

The Easter narrative in the historical sphere (where there are written eyewitness reports) and the creation narrative in the prehistorical sphere (where there was no human witness present at the event) are described as "saga," not because they are mere figments of human imagination, but because they report historical truths that are beyond historical-scientific proof. That these events must have really happened in our history and our time cannot be demonstrated by modern historical criticism. Rather, this necessity is revealed to us by the fact that they are events in the history of Jesus Christ, attested to us in Scripture as God's very own work.

The history of Jesus Christ as God's time for us, according to Barth, is the inward basis of world history, and world history is the outward basis of the history of God-for-us *in Christo*. For this very reason, we cannot objectively understand the meaning of world history apart from the history of Christ. Yet, the converse is also true. Apart from world history, which God the Son has assumed as his own, there can be no history of God-for-us to which our creaturely knowledge is accessible. The resurrection that happened in our time *is* the resurrection that happened in God's time for us, just as the mother of the Nazarene is properly called the *Theotokos*. Far from denying the importance of ordinary history, then, Barth is emphatic that there can be no effective revelation apart from objective reports of events that occurred in our temporal sphere. His often dismissive remarks about *Historie* are only meant to challenge the naturalistic, positivist, and/or objectivist biases of modern historical criticism.

124. CD IV/1, 508 (italics added).

5. "Barth holds that nothing historical can be directly revelational, and that revelation is necessarily indirect." This description of Barth is not incorrect per se, but the way it is usually understood reflects a widespread evangelical misunderstanding to which Van Til, among others, gave rise. It is often in this sense, as we saw, that evangelicals label Barth as "neo-orthodox." A striking passage found in Van Til's influential 1954 article on Barth illuminates this view:

> In the act of God's revelation nothing is simply past or simply future. Nor is anything simply present. The idea of the present does not refer to a date on the calendar. If it did there would, after all, be direct revelation. If it did then the witness to revelation would, after all, be identical with revelation. For any past or present or future point in the ordinary historical sense (*bloss historisch, K.D.,* I. 2, p. 558) we must substitute the notion of the divine present (*göttliche Präsens, idem*).[125]

It is true that Barth rejects any notion of direct human knowledge of God, but this rejection carries two important implications that Van Til has missed. First, Barth agrees with Van Til and historic Protestantism that God is unknowable *per essentiam*: there can be no immediate human knowledge of God's essence. Truths about God's essential being are mediated to us through his self-revelation in history. "For our vision and understanding, the knowledge of Jesus Christ in His pure form [as preincarnate Son in God's triune essence] is an indirect knowledge."[126] Because the revealed God (*Deus revelatus*) and the hidden God (*Deus absconditus*) are one, however, our knowledge of Christ in his pure form, though indirect, is true. From 1924 onward, it

125. Cornelius Van Til, "Has Karl Barth Become Orthodox?," *Westminster Theological Journal* 16 (1954): 138.

126. *CD* IV/3, 389.

is primarily in this sense that Barth describes revelation as indirect. <u>What he means is that creatures cannot obtain unmediated knowledge of God's essence.</u>

ˋ   Second, when in *CD* I/1–2 Barth asserted that nothing in history is directly identical to revelation, he had not yet developed the Christocentric doctrine of election that governed all aspects of his later theology. In the 1936 *Gottes Gnadenwahl*, however, he contended, for the first time in his career, that Christ's birth in creaturely history is directly identical to God's eternal self-determination to become God-for-us: "[Incarnation] is election! And this is completely directly and immediately [*ganz direkt und unmittelbar*] what our election is."[127]

Revelation of God's essence, of course, is still described as indirect in that it is mediated through the union of Christ's two natures, rather than an immediate verbal unveiling of God *per essentiam*. What is remarkable here is that the truly and fully historical person of Christ is now directly identified with God's eternal act *ad extra* of determining himself to be God-for-us. That is, in *Gottes Gnadenwahl* Barth begins to recognize world history as an anhypostatic-enhypostatic entity that is essentially revelational, not in and for itself, but by its ontological determination from above.

In fact, even in *CD* I/1–2, Barth does not claim that we must "substitute" the notion of God's active presence for biblical reports of events in ordinary history. Van Til misses the meaning of the term "*bloß historisch*" when he describes it as a "past or present or future point in the ordinary historical sense." In the original quote, Barth does not speak of "past or present or future," but of "*bloß historisch*" and "*bloß eschatologisch*"—the bare historical and the bare eschatological.[128]

Barth uses the adjective *bloß* with explicit reference to Kant's

---

127. *Gottes Gnadenwahl*, 15.
128. *KD* I/2, 558.

Religion within the Bounds of Bare Reason.[129] "Bare reason" (*die bloße Vernunft*) refers to naked human reason uncloaked by historical revelation.[130] In dismissing the *"bloß historisch"* and *"bloß eschatologisch,"* Barth has in mind the two major trajectories in neo-Protestantism. One is the neo-Kantian approach to history represented by the Ritschlians, who relied on historical positivism in their attempt to interpret historical facts objectively, apart from the aid of supernatural revelation. The other is the eschatological-metaphysical approach to history represented by Schleiermacher and Ernst Troeltsch (1865–1923), who, also apart from supernatural revelation, saw history as an immanently purposive activity developing towards a consummate end.

What Barth intends to say with the derogative *"bloß historisch"* and *"bloß eschatologisch"* is that apart from revelation, which he identifies with Jesus Christ, we can neither come to an objective interpretation of history (contrary to the neo-Kantians) nor identify a consummate purpose in history (contrary to the idealist metaphysicians):

> The whole doctrine of the Holy Scriptures, and all of church dogmatics and the preaching and sacrament of ecclesiastical proclamation therewith, revolve around this event [of Jesus Christ as revelation]. If we stop revolving around this event in our thinking and speaking, falling into the bare historical or the bare eschatological one way or another—the bare problematic and uncertain of God's Word in the Holy Scriptures—then we certainly do not think and talk in and with the Church, do not think and talk in faith and certainly no longer from the Word of God in the Holy Scriptures, but rather of some surrogate with which we consciously or unconsciously replace this event.[131]

129. *CD* I/2, 785.
130. See my *Immanuel Kant*, 86–87.
131. *KD* I/2, 558. Translation mine.

6. "Barth holds to a 'fallenness view' of Christ's human nature." This misreading has come from both the Barthian and evangelical sides.[132] The fact is that Barth distinguishes between "nature" and "history." The human being (*Sein/Dasein*) is determined from above (*von oben*) by the history of Jesus Christ, and this determination constitutes our nature. Meanwhile, the human being is also determined from below (*von unten*) by the sinful world history of Adam's fallen race. Because human nature is the determination of our being by grace, it is kept intact and undistorted by sin even when the human being is situated in the historical state of fallenness.[133]

God the Son assumed our *history* of fallenness to be attacked by sin from below on our behalf as our covenant partner, but the human *nature* that he assumed cannot be fallen, for fallenness is foreign to nature: sin is an ontological impossibility. Barth is unequivocal about the sinlessness of Christ's human nature in his formulation of the Christ-Adam relation in *CD* IV/1: "This other, too came directly from God, not as a creature only, but as the Son of God and Himself God by nature. He, too, was a sinner and debtor, but as the sinless and guiltless bearer of the sins of others, the sins of all other men."[134] That is, the guilt and sin of Adam's race were imputed to Christ through his union with us. Barth has never stated that Christ assumed fallen human nature. It is in fact a view that he explicitly rejects.[135]

7. "Barth's Christological doctrine of election is an incipient universalism." No, it is not. His mature formulation of double predestination as the "sublation" (i.e., negation) of reprobation

132. For instance, Oliver Crisp, *Divinity and Humanity* (Cambridge: Cambridge University Press, 2007), 90–93, 98; Bruce McCormack, *For Us and Our Salvation* (Princeton: Princeton Theological Seminary, 1993), 21.

133. For more detailed explanations and textual references, see my "Barth on Actualistic Ontology."

134. *CD* IV/1, 512.

135. For a detailed discussion, see my *Barth's Ontology*, 110–12.

in election, along with his emphasis on the election of *all* in Christ, has led many readers to believe that his doctrine inevitably implies some form of universal salvation.[136] The reading of an incipient universalism into Barth was popularized among evangelicals by the English translation of Berkouwer's *Triumph of Grace.* This is still a common misconception among evangelicals. Oliver Crisp, for instance, comments that Barth's openness to the possibility of a final reprobation of those who "choose to reject Christ . . . flatly contradicts other things Barth says about the inexorable nature of our derivative election in Christ."[137]

This misreading is definitively falsified by Barth's perspicuous statements in the 1936 *Gottes Gnadenwahl,* where he sets forth the Christocentric rendition of his doctrine of election for the first time in his career. There he clearly states that his discourse on the election of all leaves "no room for the speculation of an eternal apocatastasis."[138] In *CD* IV/3, he again tells us that his Christological doctrine of election "quite conclusively" proclaims the eschatological condemnation of those who reject the truth of the gospel.[139]

These statements, of course, need to be understood in context, in order to answer those who think that Barth seldom means what he says or that he programmatically contradicts himself. As we saw under the heading of "Particularism" earlier in this chapter, the notion of a *simpliciter* election of *all* is for Barth surely

---

136. Notable examples in recent years include Tom Greggs, "'Jesus Is Victor': Passing the Impasse of Barth on Universalism," *Scottish Journal of Theology* 60 (2007): 196–212; David Congdon, "*Apokatastasis* and Apostolicity: A Response to Oliver Crisp on the Question of Barth's Universalism," *Scottish Journal of Theology* 67 (2014): 464–80.

137. Oliver Crisp, "Karl Barth and Jonathan Edwards on Reprobation (and Hell)," in *Engaging with Barth: Contemporary Evangelical Critiques,* ed. David Gibson and Daniel Strange (Nottingham: Apollos, 2008), 319.

138. *Gottes Gnadenwahl,* 27.

139. *CD* IV/3, 478.

tantamount to an apocatastasis in which the particularity of each elect person is dissolved. The election of *all* (universality) in *Christ* (the particular), by contrast, is a process in which the particularity of Christ as God's elect sublates the universality of the prison of disobedience. In *Gottes Gnadenwahl*, Barth tells us that this forbids us from conjuring up a universal salvation.[140]

But if Christ was reprobated in the stead of all humankind, is not the election of all *in Christ* still, in the final analysis, an election of *all*? In the last resort, does Barth's Christocentric doctrine of election not lead to some doctrine of universal salvation? It is tempting to answer this question in the affirmative, if one neglects the *actualistic* character of his Christocentric particularism.

For Barth, the existential being (*Sein*) of the creature is determined by the history of Christ from above as well as Adam's history of sin from below, but because the history of Christ is not only an eternal history but also a temporal one, it has a past and a future as well. This means that the human essence as God's elect is determined not only vertically from above, but also horizontally by the act of God in both the perfect and future tenses.

In *Gottes Gnadenwahl*, Barth unequivocally affirms the prospect of an eschatological separation of the elect from the reprobate: "There certainly is a predestinedhood of man corresponding to the *praedestinatio* of God. But the separation of men into believers and unbelievers by this concept will become visible—it will become actual—in the last judgment. . . . We are heading towards this actuality."[141] What Barth intends to say with his rejection of the traditional understanding of the absolute decree (*decretum absolutum*) of double predestination is that "we should not make a *present* separation out of this future separation. Rather, we should accept in obedience our situation

---

140. *Gottes Gnadenwahl*, 27.
141. *Gottes Gnadenwahl*, 48.

between Christ's ascension and His return as the situation in which we walk by faith and not by sight."[142]

In *CD* IV/3, Barth revisits this topic in a section titled "The Condemnation [*Verdammnis*] of Man," in §70, "The Falsehood and Condemnation of Man."[143] Here Barth sets forth a twofold two-way determination of the reality of human world history: (1) a vertical determination *from above* by the victory of Christ— or better put, Christ as victor—from and to all eternity, countered by a determination *from below* by the sin of all other human beings; and (2) a horizontal determination by the *perfect tense* of God's reality in Christ accomplished *a priori* (*zum Vornherein*), along with a determination by the *future tense* of God's final condemnation of sinful humankind to which the present actuality of human falsehood points.

In the vertical determination, sin has no power to effect human essence. Because sin has been *a priori* overcome by Christ, it is an ontological impossibility. The horizontal determination, however, is thoroughly God's own act. Barth states that the condemnation of humankind, unlike fallenness and misery, is not the result of sinful human activity or inactivity, but is itself God's act, to which the present actuality of human falsehood points.

In *CD* IV/1–3, Barth defines sin as human pride, sloth, and falsehood. Pride and sloth, respectively, result in the fall and misery of humankind. The consequence of falsehood is divine condemnation. The fall and misery of humankind as consequences of human pride and sloth are only world-historical conditions that will pass away at the end of time because of Christ's *a priori* triumph over what Barth calls "nothingness" (*das Nichtige*—that which is not—manifest in the forms of sin, evil, and spiritual

142. *Gottes Gnadenwahl*, 48 (italics added).
143. See my exposition of this paragraph in "Condemnation and Universal Salvation: Karl Barth's 'Reverent Agnosticism' Revisited," *Scottish Journal of Theology* 71 (2018): 324–38.

death). However, Barth makes it clear that divine condemnation, unlike human fallenness and misery, is God's act, rather than a form of nothingness.

The human being at present is "obviously a human being punished by God [*von Gott gestrafter Mensch*]."[144] Here Barth is employing the verb *strafen* as a dialectical wordplay in the Hegelian grammar of sublation. The German word he uses for "falsehood" is *die Lüge*. While *strafen* on its own means "to punish," the idiom *"Lügen strafen"* means "to belie." In the grammar of sublation, the negation of the negative is always teleological. According to Barth, the present actuality of the punishment that humankind suffers points teleologically to a final condemnation of the human liar who rejects the truth of the gospel.

More concretely, the present punishment is the temporary divine permission for the sinner to exist "in an untrue and falsified situation" as "a bewitched man in a bewitched world."[145] This punishment is not yet "the worst thing"—the sinner is "only moving towards this [worst thing] in this situation and bewitchment."[146] The "worst thing," according to Barth, is "to be sentenced [*verurteilt*], condemned [*verdammt*] and lost" at the end of world history.[147] Sure enough, final divine condemnation has not yet actually happened, "but it is bad enough to be moving towards this," for the present actuality of the punishment of those who reject the gospel is determined by this eschaton.[148]

If there finally comes about a universal pardon at the last judgment, "it can only be a matter of the *unexpected* work of grace and its revelation on which we *cannot count* but for which we *can only hope* as an undeserved and inconceivable overflowing of the

144. CD IV/3, 469; *KD* IV/3, 540. Italics and translation mine.
145. CD IV/3, 469.
146. CD IV/3, 469.
147. CD IV/3, 469.
148. CD IV/3, 469.

significance, operation and outreach of the reality of God and man in Jesus Christ."[149] In other words, the doctrine of election as formulated by Barth theoretically points to a last judgment at which there will be both glorification for the elect and condemnation for the reprobate.

Still, Barth thinks that "there is no good reason why we should forbid ourselves, or be forbidden, openness to the possibility that in the reality of God and man in Jesus Christ there is contained much more than we might expect and therefore the supremely unexpected withdrawal of that final threat."[150] As Barth sees it, with good reason we should be open to the *possibility* of universal salvation.[151] "If for a moment we accept the unfalsified truth of the reality which even now so forcefully limits the perverted human situation, does it not point plainly in the direction of the work of a truly eternal divine patience and deliverance and therefore of an *apokatastasis* or universal reconciliation?"[152]

In a word, Barth's position is that on one hand we must not "count on" the *apokatastasis* "as if we had a claim to it," because the doctrine of election clearly teaches reprobation and final condemnation. On the other hand, however, "we are surely commanded the more definitely to hope and pray for it," though we must "hope and pray cautiously and yet distinctly that, *in spite of* everything which may seem *quite conclusively to proclaim the opposite*, His compassion should not fail."[153]

8. "Barth's theology is dialectical." Yes, it is. But the question is, in what sense is it dialectical? Barth eclectically employs a wide range of dialectics as noetic tools with which to make sense of the particulars of the Christian faith.

---

149. *CD* IV/3, 477 (italics added).
150. *CD* IV/3, 477–78.
151. *CD* IV/3, 478.
152. *CD* IV/3, 478.
153. *CD* IV/3, 478 (italics added).

As far as his mature theology is concerned, the anhypostatic-enhypostatic dialectic of Chalcedonian Christology is the only programmatic one that underlies his entire theological discourse.[154] The formula "God became human without ceasing to be God" consistently undergirds the Christocentric phase of his theology. This formula is sometimes expressed with the dialectical language of Luther's *theologia crucis* (e.g., *Deus absconditus* and *Deus revelatus*), but always with a strong emphasis on the *extra Calvinisticum*.

Besides the two-nature Christology of Chalcedon, no other dialectic occupies such a programmatic role in Barth's mature writings. For instance, we saw that he explicates double predestination with the Hegelian dialectic of sublation. But this dialectic is far from programmatic in Barth's method. He would never apply it to, say, the immanent Trinity, which he explicates in terms of the Trinitarian dialectic of the Niceno-Constantinopolitan Creed.

Evangelicals who follow Van Til's reading of Barth have welcomed the problematic imposition of a "dialectical origin" in the (neo-)Kantian *Realdialektik* on Barth, espoused by leading revisionist Barth scholars of our day. As we have seen, however, this imposition is implausible.

Other evangelical interpreters have associated Barth's theological method with Kierkegaardian dialectics. Sure enough, *Romans* II relies heavily on Kierkegaard.[155] The dialectic that Barth developed in 1924, however, has become distinctively Reformed.[156] Kierkegaardian dialectics remained dominant in Barth only up to 1924.

154. See George Hunsinger, "Karl Barth's Christology: Its Basic Chalcedonian Character," in *The Cambridge Companion to Karl Barth*, ed. John Webster (Cambridge: Cambridge University Press, 2000), 127–42. I have defended this view against its critics in *Barth's Infralapsarian Theology*, 215; *Barth's Ontology*, 115–23.

155. *Pace* Bruce McCormack. See my *Barth's Infralapsarian Theology*, 84–86.

156. Rightly Bruce McCormack, "Revelation and History in Transfoundationalist Perspective: Karl Barth's Theological Epistemology in Conversation with a Schleiermacherian Tradition," *Journal of Religion* 78 (1998): 18–37.

The association of Barth with Kierkegaardian dialectics is further complicated by poor caricatures of Kierkegaard as an irrationalist. John Robbins, an ardent supporter of Gordon Clark, asserts that as a pupil of Kierkegaard, Barth is "guilty" of "a guiding philosophy which holds that the assertion of contrary and even contradictory statements is genuine philosophy and theology."[157] This is a crude imposition of a false reading of Kierkegaard on Barth.[158] Interestingly, Clarkians like Robert Reymond think that Van Til is guilty of the same "irrationalism."[159]

It is true that Barth's strategy in resolving apparently logical contradictions in *Romans* II is strongly Kierkegaardian: God in his freedom is above our understanding of the laws of logic. Kierkegaard employs dramatic irony through Johannes Climacus, the unbelieving pseudonym, to argue that the incarnation, while plausible in paganism, is logically impossible on the Christian presupposition of the infinite qualitative difference between God and humankind.[160] The Christian pseudonym Anti-Climacus, however, contends: "Sometimes the inventiveness of a human imagination suffices to procure possibility, but in the last resort,

157. John Robbins, "Karl Barth," *The Trinity Review* (February 1998): 1. This was originally published as the foreword to Gordon Clark, *Karl Barth's Theological Method* (Philadelphia: Presbyterian and Reformed, 1963).

158. For an explanation of Kierkegaard's notions of paradox and the absurd, see Joel Rasmussen, *Between Irony and Witness* (London: T&T Clark, 2005), 101.

159. Robert Reymond, *The Justification of Knowledge* (Phillipsburg, NJ: Presbyterian and Reformed, 1979), 105.

160. Søren Kierkegaard, *Concluding Unscientific Postscript*, ed. and trans. Alastair Hannay (Cambridge: Cambridge University Press, 2009), 485. Readers like William Barrett have advanced the view of Kierkegaard as an irrationalist on the basis of the Climacus texts. See William Barrett, *Irrational Man* (Garden City, NY: Doubleday, 1962). Such readings exhibit literary insensitivity towards Kierkegaard's use of ironies. Joel Rasmussen explains: "While the more colloquial meaning of 'absurd' as 'foolish' and 'ridiculous' is explicit as regards the perspective of the understanding . . . , the language of the larger interchange suggests that Climacus has orchestrated the entire exchange in such a way as to pun on 'the absurd' as the understanding's unheeding deafness to the paradox" (*Between Irony and Witness*, 93).

that is, when the point is to believe, the only help is this, *that for God all things are possible.*"[161]

The early Barth (wrongly, in my view) takes this to mean that God is free to contradict himself. Resorting to the Kiekegaardian dialectic of the possible and the impossible, Barth sets forth the programmatic expression, "Impossible with man; possible with God!" as the guiding principle underlying *Romans* II.[162] In his *Münster Dogmatics* (1927), he retains the view that "God is a free Lord, not only over the law of non-contradiction, but over his own deity."[163]

In the *Church Dogmatics*, however, Barth revokes this voluntarist view of God's freedom and begins to speak of what God can and cannot do. He now subscribes to the classic distinction between God's *potentia absoluta* and *potentia ordinata*. *Potentia absoluta* refers to, in Richard Muller's words, "the omnipotence of God limited only by the law of noncontradiction. . . . God can effect all possibility, constrained only by his own nature."[164] *Potentia ordinata*, by contrast, is "a limited and bounded power [of God] that guarantees the stability and consistency of the orders of nature and of grace."[165]

Barth is emphatic that even in God's relations to creatures, there are things that God cannot do, because God cannot cease to be God, and because God cannot contradict himself and his own will. For instance, Barth says that once God entered into his

161. Søren Kierkegaard, *Sickness unto Death*, trans. Alastair Hannay (Radford, VA: Wilder, 2008), 30 (italics added).

162. *Romans* II, 75.

163. *Die christliche Dogmatik im Entwurf*, 1. Band: *Die Lehre vom Worte Gottes, Prolegomena zur christlichen Dogmatik* (1927; Zurich: Theologischer Verlag Zürich, 1982), 217, cited by Sebastian Rehman, "Does It Matter If Christian Theology Is Contradictory? Barth on Logic and Theology," in *Engaging with Barth*, 63.

164. Richard Muller, *Dictionary of Latin and Greek Theological Terms Drawn Principally from Protestant Scholastic Theology* (Grand Rapids: Baker Academic, 1985), 231–32.

165. Muller, *Dictionary*, 231–32.

covenant with humankind, he "cannot be God" without being God-for-us.[166] In speaking of what God must or cannot do, says Barth, "we honor the actual will of God visible in the event of His revelation, as the source and inner concept of all necessity. . . . We shall and must acknowledge the necessity of His actual manifest will, His *potentia ordinata*."[167]

We have already discussed Barth's mature view of God's freedom under the rubric of actualism. It suffices here to say that from *CD* I/1 onward, Barth no longer sees God's freedom as a divine license to contradict himself. He denies any element of voluntary caprice (*Willkür*) in God's freedom. When apparent contradictions arise in any theological utterance, the mature Barth would attribute them to the limitations of human reason under the noetic effects of sin. He never claimed that these contradictions are ontic.

9. "Barth rejects the notion of an immanent Trinity back behind the God who is self-revealed in Jesus Christ." Van Til represents Barth's view this way: "To safeguard the Christ-Event . . . , we must . . . remove the idea of a *Logos asarkos* [preincarnate Son]. To maintain the idea of a *Logos asarkos* back of God incarnate in and identical with Jesus is to seek to block the free movement of the grace of God toward man."[168] According to Van Til, Barth's "rejection of the *Logos asarkos*, of the God 'in himself,' . . . spring[s] from his activistic notion of the Christ-Event."[169]

This interpretation can only be the product of extraordinary theological acumen, but it is still wrong. Some of the most authoritative readers of Barth today have also made the assertion that Barth's actualistic ("activistic" is the term Van Til uses) ontology necessitates a rejection of the notion of an immanent

---

166. CD II/2, 7.
167. CD I/2, 41.
168. Van Til, *Christianity and Barthianism*, 104.
169. Van Til, *Christianity and Barthianism*, 107.

Trinity and a preincarnate Logos. According to these revisionist scholars, Barth's actualistic ontology dictates that God's being is indeterminate, apart from his act, and that it is his act of election-in-Christ that determined and constituted his being as the Trinity. For this reason, so they assert, Barth's actualism forbids any theological talk of an immanent Trinity back behind Jesus Christ, who is identical with the electing God (i.e., God's being in the act of election).

No serious revisionist reader of Barth, however, would claim that Barth himself ever reached such a conclusion. Their contention is that Barth's doctrine of the immanent Trinity contradicts his own actualistic ontology. No serious reader of Barth can deny that even as late as *CD* IV/1, Barth continues to speak of the *Logos asarkos* as "the content of a necessary and important concept in trinitarian doctrine when we have to understand the revelation and dealings of God in the light of their free basis in the inner being and essence of God."[170]

The all-important formulation of God's love and freedom in *CD* II/1 in terms of the primary and secondary objectivities of God, as we saw, is clearly based on a distinction between God-in-and-for-himself as immanent Trinity and God-for-us as electing God. Barth does not simply affirm the immanent Trinity. The immanent Trinity occupies a definitive role in his theological ontology. It is the trademark by which he is set apart from, say, Karl Rahner, who abolishes the distinction between the immanent Trinity and the economic.

The consensus even among revisionist scholars is that Barth affirms the immanent Trinity and the *Logos asarkos*. The revisionist contention is not that Barth rejects the *Logos asarkos*, or that the affirmation of the concept is merely lip service. Rather, they see his serious affirmation of the immanent Trinity as "an

---

170. CD IV/1, 52.

inconsistency in Barth's thought," and their proposal is to "register a critical correction" of him on what they deem to be his own actualistic terms.[171]

This assessment of Barth dates back to his own day. Dietrich Bonhoeffer's 1930 *Habilitationsschrift* already suggested that Barth's notion of God's supratemporal essence was at odds with his own actualism in the *Münster Dogmatics*.[172] Later, Emil Brunner asserted that Barth's actualism in the *Church Dogmatics* would lead to the "extraordinary" conclusion that election constitutes the Trinity, though, fortunately in Brunner's view, "Barth does not attempt to deduce" such a conclusion.[173]

It is legitimate to contend that there is an inconsistency in Barth's thought—though I think this reading is wrong—as far as the standards of good academic argument are concerned. It is quite a different thing, however, to draw for Barth conclusions that he never drew, let alone ones that he explicitly and emphatically rejected. In a word, Barth does not reject the notion of the immanent Trinity. He is emphatically unequivocal that God's love and freedom in the immanent Trinity constitute the condition on which God can love us in freedom and be free in loving us in becoming God-for-us without ceasing to be God-in-and-for-himself.

10. "Barth's 'traditional phraseology' is 'new wine in old bottles.'"[174] This assessment is partly true. Barth did break with classical Reformed theology and the broader Western tradition at important junctures. The consequence was that he had to

171. Bruce McCormack, "Grace and Being: The Role of God's Gracious Election in Karl Barth's Theological Ontology," in *The Cambridge Companion to Karl Barth*, ed. John Webster (Cambridge: Cambridge University Press, 2000), 193.

172. Dietrich Bonhoeffer, *Act and Being*, ed. Hans-Richard Reuter and Wayne Whitson Floyd, trans. H. Martin Rumscheidt (Minneapolis: Fortress, 1996), 83–87.

173. Emil Brunner, *Dogmatics*, vol. 1, *The Christian Doctrine of God*, trans. Olive Wyon (Philadelphia: Westminster, 1950), 315.

174. Van Til, *Christianity and Barthianism*, 2.

add new content to terms like "revelation," "election," "creation," "reconciliation," "justification," and "union with Christ." What complicates the matter is that he does not simply replace the old content with the new, and that the extent to which he revised different types of theological vocabulary varied.

The term "election," for example, is a high-level word in the hierarchy of dogmatic vocabularies, in that it is the name of a doctrine, and not just a theological notion such as *"potentia ordinata."* On this level, the redefinition of traditional terms involves doctrinal reformulations.

Aside from doctrinal reformulations, however, Barth usually retains the traditional definitions of historic terms and phrases, and his revisions thereof are usually by addition rather than subtraction or alteration. Take the term "human nature" for example. He never replaced the traditional definition of "nature" with a modern, historicist one. He retains the traditional definition of "nature" as the formal-causal aspect of different kinds of substances. Even as late as *CD* IV/2, he continued to hold that "'human nature' means quite simply that which makes a man a man as distinct from God, angel or animal . . . , his *humanitas.*"[175]

Of course, with the Christocentric reformulation of the doctrine of creation, Barth had to add something to this historic definition of "human nature." He added that human nature is a determination from above by the covenantal history of God and humankind in Jesus Christ. With this revision, Barth gives to the historic notion of human nature a modern, historicist twist. Therewith he further contends that sin is an ontological impossibility for God's creatures. This contention carries profound implications, some of which may be unacceptable to mainline evangelicals (see chapter 3).

In any case, while the "new wine in old bottles" description

---

175. CD IV/2, 25.

may be true to an extent, it should only be taken as an objective description that is somewhat inadequate, rather than a judgmental accusation. Where Barth disagreed with the tradition, he was always clear about it, and we should not assume that there is any deceptive intent in his use of "traditional phraseology."

True enough, Barth's thought may be difficult in its sophistication, his bombardment of the reader with erudite philosophical terms befuddling, his sentences fraught with subordinate clauses, "like a dog that jumps into the Atlantic Ocean, swims all the way across to the other side, and climbs out at the end with a verb in his mouth"—a quip by Mark Twain on German sentences, as paraphrased by Professor Hunsinger.[176] (*Voilà*, a one-sentence paragraph.)

Yet, the difficulty of Barth's writing does not mean that it is "unclear" because of "insincerity . . . which motivates" him "to disguise his true intention and meaning by using words in equivocal and subversive ways."[177] If one were allowed to judge Barth's intent this way, then every American could pass the same verdict on the seventeenth-century Puritans (e.g., "I cannot ascribe the superlative degree to anything of which I deny the positive"— guess who penned it!), and every Scot is entitled to accuse the Teutons of perpetual deception by the very nature of their language. But has the Lord not taught us not to judge?

Barth's use of traditional phraseology is not intended for deception, and his texts are, though difficult, perspicuous. Even though there is a cocktail of old and new liquors in his bottle that is eclectically old and new, the connoisseur can discern the intricacies therein. Evangelical critiques of Barth become fruitful only when we truly understand and appreciate—however critically—what is in his bottle and what his bottle is made of.

176. Hunsinger, *How to Read Karl Barth*, 27.
177. Robbins, "Karl Barth," 2.

Conclusion

In the foregoing discussions, I have tried, in a subtle way, to address a certain evangelical complaint about "the sheer vastness and complexity of the *Church Dogmatics*, which militated against a unified and coherent account of his [Barth's] thought, something that should surely be basic to any positive interaction."[178] The fact that "there sometimes seem as many Barths as there are Barthians" has discouraged many evangelicals from seriously engaging with his writings.[179] Though I have not been able to introduce the less influential paradigms (e.g., the historicized Barth advanced by Robert Jenson, the postmodern Barth espoused by William Stacey Johnson, and the postcolonial Barth of Asian theology), my presentation of the traditionalist and revisionist paradigms has underscored the possibility of an objective interpretation that honors both text and context.

My hope is that by offering a sketch of Barth's intellectual biography and outlining the basic motifs governing his theological development, we can come to a rereading of Barth that, to the best of our abilities, allows his text to speak for itself from its proper context. The fact that there is no unified and coherent account of, say, Augustine, has not discouraged evangelicals from trying to interpret him objectively. It is the case with almost every great thinker that his thought is subjected to a wide variety of interpretations. Evangelicals can, of course, opt out of such academic debates, but such an option comes at a great cost, for separatism almost inevitably leads to post-truth anti-intellectualism. Thankfully, as demonstrated towards the end of chapter 1, evangelicals in the last two decades have produced fruitful scholarship on Barth. I hope that the guidelines offered in this chapter will

178. Carl Trueman, "Foreword," in *Engaging with Barth*, 14.
179. Trueman, "Foreword," 14.

contribute to further evangelical interactions with Barth that are at once critically charitable and charitably critical, for the sake of the ongoing edification of evangelical theology in general and confessional Reformed theology in particular. It is with this intention that we now turn to the next chapter.

3

ENGAGING WITH BARTH: AN EVANGELICAL REFORMED PERSPECTIVE

Having offered a summary of Barth's thought, we now return to the question raised at the end of chapter 1: what can evangelicals gain from reading Barth? I will outline four points below and discuss how we can turn to classical Reformed theology and neo-Calvinism on these points for the edification of evangelical theology today. This list is by no means exhaustive, but it seeks to address issues in evangelical theology that I take to be urgent.

Mediated Knowledge of God in Historic Reformed Theology

Barth, as we saw, is emphatic on the immediate nature of revelation. What he means, primarily at least, is that, as creatures, we cannot possibly have immediate epistemic access to God's essence *ad intra*. Knowledge of God's essence can be mediated to us only through his *ad extra* act of self-revelation in creaturely and historical forms, because human cognition is restricted to the realm of experience.

Barth's mature view of the necessarily indirect nature of creaturely knowledge of God—if it is not misconstrued in the problematic interpretational framework of a post-Kantian *Realdialektik* or allegedly Kierkegaardian dialectics—is actually well in line with Protestant orthodoxy and mainline Western theology. The mature Barth appropriates Kant's insights only eclectically, and there is one particular Kantian doctrine that both Barth and Herman Bavinck have deemed correct by the standards of orthodox Christianity: "Kant is perfectly correct when he says that our knowledge does not extend farther than our experience. If God has not revealed himself, then neither is there any knowledge of him."[1]

⌐ Bavinck also stresses the necessarily indirect nature of God's self-revelation in the realm of human experience: "In a strict sense there is no immediate revelation either in nature or in grace. God always uses a means—whether taken from among creatures or chosen freely—by which he reveals himself to human beings."[2] Bavinck is emphatic that "in this dispensation all revelation is mediate."[3] As far as the present age is concerned, "no creature can see or understand God as he is and as he speaks in himself. Revelation is therefore always an act of grace; in it God condescends to meet his creature, a creature made in his image. All revelation is anthropomorphic, a kind of humanization of God."[4]⌐

We can see here that Bavinck's view of the indirect and analogical nature of revelation goes hand in hand with the Reformed understanding of divine condescension or accommodation. The

1. Herman Bavinck, *Reformed Dogmatics*, ed. John Bolt, trans. John Vriend, 4 vols. (Grand Rapids: Baker, 2003–8), 2:50.
2. Bavinck, *Reformed Dogmatics*, 1:309.
3. Bavinck, *Reformed Dogmatics*, 1:310.
4. Bavinck, *Reformed Dogmatics*, 1:310.

accommodatio has been confessionally defined and carries normative authority among those who subscribe to the Westminster Standards:

> The distance between God and the creature is so great, that although reasonable creatures do owe obedience unto him as their Creator, yet they could never have any fruition of him as their blessedness and reward, but by some voluntary condescension on God's part, which he hath been pleased to express by way of covenant. (Westminster Confession, 7.1)

The Confession teaches a twofold necessity for divine condescension, the first occasioned by the ontological distance between the Creator and creatures, and the second occasioned by the gulf of sin. God's covenantal condescension is effected in the realm of experience and in the form of history.

God reveals himself progressively in and through redemptive history as well as world history, such that at no point of his covenantal condescension does he reveal himself as mechanical parts. Rather, the living God always reveals himself as an organic whole through his covenantal activity. This is akin to how the essence of a plant is given as a whole living entity in every stage of its development, albeit in different forms. This organicism implies that propositions such as "God is immutable" must not be understood in terms of an abstract notion of immutability. Rather, believers come to understand the concrete immutability of God's being through his covenantal activities, culminating in and centering on his becoming human without ceasing to be God. For Bavinck, the organicist nature of revelation as such necessitates mediacy: to say that "revelation always occurs organically" is to say that it always occurs "mediately."[5]

---

5. Bavinck, *Reformed Dogmatics*, 1:309.

Regrettably, one dominant evangelical view of revelation, most famously represented by Carl Henry's *God, Revelation and Authority* (1976), has explicitly departed from the norm stated in the Westminster Confession and taught in the broader Western tradition. Professor Michael Horton has helpfully suggested that the Barthian and postliberal understanding of the indirectness of revelation is, in one important aspect, more faithful to the classical Protestant tradition than Henry's mechanistic view of propositional revelation.[6]

Henry's contention is that the verbal inspiration of biblical propositions makes God's essence immediately knowable to finite creatures. Quantitatively, human knowledge is of course finite and God's knowledge infinite, and so in this sense human beings cannot know God comprehensively as God knows himself. The inspiration of Scripture as propositional revelation, however, enables a kind of human knowledge of God that is qualitatively the same ("univocal") as God's self-knowledge, according to Henry.

This view is propagated in our day by Robert L. Reymond.[7] He rejects Calvin's doctrine of divine accommodation—the notion that, in Reymond's words, "because of our finitude God could not give to us a univocal verbal depiction of himself as he is in himself. What we possess is at best only a finite representation of God, and thus ours is an understanding of him 'as he seems to us' and not as he is in himself."[8] Reymond suggests that

> we should not follow Calvin here since we can know on the
> basis of God's verbal self-revelation many things about him

6. Michael Horton, "A Stony Jar: The Legacy of Karl Barth for Evangelical Theology," in *Engaging with Barth: Contemporary Evangelical Critiques*, ed. David Gibson and Daniel Strange (Nottingham: Apollos, 2008), 377.

7. See Robert Reymond, "Calvin's Doctrine of Holy Scripture (1.6–10)," in *A Theological Guide to Calvin's Institutes*, ed. Peter Lillback and David Hall (Phillipsburg, NJ: P&R, 2008), 44–64.

8. Reymond, "Calvin's Doctrine of Holy Scripture," 57.

in the same sense that he knows them. That is why God gave us the Bible in the first place—that we might know him. Of course, we will not know God exhaustively, but we can know him truly as he is in himself.[9]

Professor Horton points out that such a view is "unsatisfying at least to those of us who hold the traditional Protestant distinction between archetypal and ectypal knowledge and refuse to reduce the concept of truth to propositional statements without remainder."[10] Historic Protestantism and the broader Western tradition understand the difference between God's self-knowledge and our knowledge of God to be *both* quantitative and qualitative. Incomprehensibility, traditionally understood, means both that our knowledge of God cannot quantitatively match God's self-knowledge, and that even his own verbal expressions of his essence in creaturely language—and consequently our knowledge of God's inward essence—cannot be univocal with his own inward wisdom.

The qualitative aspect of the traditional doctrine of incomprehensibility is expressed by the formula of God's unknowability *per essentiam.* This formulation of the essential unknowability of God is closely related to the traditional doctrine of transcendence defined in terms of the Creator-creature distinction, which gives rise to the fundamental theorem "*finitum non capax infiniti* (the finite cannot contain the infinite)." It does not require a mathematician to know that the difference between the finite and the infinite is not only quantitative, but also qualitative. The doctrine of God's essential unknowability, defined as his qualitative incomprehensibility, is emphatically affirmed by Thomas, Luther, Calvin, Reformed orthodoxy, and neo-Calvinism. If there

9. Reymond, "Calvin's Doctrine of Holy Scripture," 57.
10. Horton, "A Stony Jar," 377.

is to be any true knowledge of God's essence, the knowledge can only be analogical (though the nature of the analogy has been among the most debated topics in the Western tradition).

Bavinck reports that for "Thomas Aquinas . . . , there is no knowledge of God's essence, his 'whatness,' in terms of its uniqueness; we only know his disposition toward his creation. There is no name that fully expresses his essence."[11] God's essential unknowability and ineffability eventually came to be "ecclesiastically defined" in Catholicism, and "the theology of the Reformation did not modify this view."[12] Instead, the Reformed orthodox followed through with it more tenaciously than theologians of any other tradition. "Their profound aversion to all forms of idol worship made them everywhere distinguish sharply between that which is of God and that which is creaturely. More than any other theology they took seriously the proposition that 'the finite cannot contain the infinite.'"[13]

The historic formula of God's essential unknowability has often been misunderstood by evangelical theologians today.[14] It is misleadingly described as the doctrine that "only God knows himself completely, comprehensively, while human beings know God derivatively and in accord with their limitations as finite creatures."[15] This description rightly summarizes the doctrine of God's incomprehensibility, but the formula of God's essential unknowability is a very specific aspect of the doctrine of incomprehensibility.

The argument advanced by theologians wishing to abandon the formula of essential unknowability further demonstrates

11. Bavinck, *Reformed Dogmatics*, 2:39.
12. Bavinck, *Reformed Dogmatics*, 2:40.
13. Bavinck, *Reformed Dogmatics*, 2:40.
14. E.g., Vern Poythress, *The Mystery of the Trinity* (Phillipsburg, NJ: P&R, 2020), 624–25.
15. Poythress, *Mystery of the Trinity*, 624.

their serious misunderstanding of the historic position. It is argued: (1) if we do not know God's essence, while (2) God *is* his essence, then (3) we do not know God.[16]

What is missing in this line of argument is the awareness that in the historic Latin formulation of divine unknowability *per essentiam*, God's *essentia* is not a general designation of what God *is* in an Aristotelian sense, but rather a specific reference to God's triune being in his *opera ad intra*. The doctrine of essential unknowability teaches that God's triune essence *ad intra* is unknowable to human reason, fallen or not, and that human beings can only come to know this essence indirectly through God's *opera ad extra*, manifested in the creaturely realm. Even those who affirm that reason can attain to some knowledge of God's essence in a general sense would deny that God's triune essence *ad intra* is accessible to human cognition apart from mediatory revelation.

Furthermore, we must not overlook the Nicene Fathers' drastic redefinitions of Aristotelian substance terminology.[17] While they generally rejected Peripatetic doctrine (not least because of its rejection of the immortality of the soul), the rules regulating Greek philosophical vocabularies in the Patristic period were largely delimited by Aristotelianism, which makes no distinction between *hypostasis* (ὑπόστασις) and *ousia* (οὐσία). However, the Nicene Fathers required vocabulary adequate to convey the biblical doctrine that God is an immutable and simple being eternally existing in the dynamic relations of the eternal acts of Father, Son, and Holy Spirit. They adopted *ousia* to designate God's immutable and simple being and referred to the coequal and coeternal agents of God's inward activity as *hypostases*. This drastic redefinition of Aristotelian terminology already signaled a rejection of classical Greek substantialism.

16. Poythress, *Mystery of the Trinity*, 626–67.
17. See Bavinck, *Reformed Dogmatics*, 2:297.

When Augustine (baptized 387) expounded the Trinitarian doctrine established at Nicaea (325) and solidified at Constantinople (381), he rendered *ousia* interchangeably as *essentia* and *substantia*, but clearly preferred *essentia*.[18] Bradley Green points out that this translation is an "un-Aristotelian move" on Augustine's part.[19] Green quotes Augustine's *De Trinitate*: "God is a substance (*substantia*), or perhaps a better word would be being (*essentia*); at any rate what the Greeks call *ousia*. . . . We have the word 'being' (*essentia*) from 'be' (*esse*)."[20]

Augustine preferred *essentia* as a rendering of *ousia* because he understood God's immutable and simple substance as a being in perpetual *opera ad intra*. It is insufficient to understand God only as "Being Itself" (*ipsum esse*), as Exodus 3:14 reveals to us. The aseity of God has to be understood in light of 1 John 4:16: "God *is* love." Augustine explains that "love is of some one that loves, and with love something is loved. Behold, then, there are three things: he that loves, and that which is loved, and love."[21] God does not need an *ad extra* object to *become* love. God *is* love *a se* as the triune subject, object, and act of love, expressed in the *opera ad intra* of eternal generation and procession.

Although later Latin theology made *substantia* the standard translation of *ousia* in order to emphasize the immutability and simplicity of the Godhead, which, according to Augustine, is "simple and manifold," the Trinitarian connotation of *essentia* is preserved.[22] Thomas Aquinas may use *essentia* in an Aristotelian sense in the *praeambula fidei*, but when it comes to the doctrine

18. See Ronald Teske, "Augustine's Use of '*Substantia*' in Speaking about God," *Modern Schoolmen* 62 (1985): 149.

19. Bradley Green, *Colin Gunton and the Failure of Augustine* (Eugene, OR: Pickwick, 2011), 163–64.

20. Green, *Colin Gunton*, 148.

21. Augustine, *On the Holy Trinity*, ed. Philip Schaff, trans. Arthur Haddan (Edinburgh: T&T Clark, 1887), 124.

22. Augustine, *On the Holy Trinity*, 101.

of faith, he clearly denies the immediate knowability of God's triune essence *ad intra*.

The doctrine of essential unknowability, affirmed by the Reformed more tenaciously than any other Western tradition (with Lutheranism as an arguable—though, in my view, inconsistent—exception), does not deny that we can come to true and even systematic knowledge of God's essence *indirectly and analogically* (neither univocally nor equivocally). We may reflect on God's *ad extra* works of creation, providence, and redemption, which are all revelatory of God's inward being.

Reflections on the empirical cognition of creaturely realities, moreover, must find their starting point in faith in God's triune essence, revealed supremely in the person and work of Christ.[23] Faith plays a crucial role in the establishment of our mediated knowledge of God's essence, because it is by faith that we know the crucified one as the firstfruits of the resurrected, the man Jesus as the Christ, and the Son of God promised to the Jews as God the Son.

It is the Holy Spirit, the giver of faith, who teaches us these things and reminds us of what our Lord said to us (John 14:26): "I and the Father are one" (John 10:30). Christ, the very *I AM*, not by himself, but eternally of the Father and with the Father, invites his people to faith in his oneness with the Father: "Believe me when I say that I am in the Father and the Father is in me" (John 14:11).

This faith is not blind, for it is through the works Christ performed on earth that we reasonably come to believe in his own proclamation: "It is the Father, living in me, who is doing his work" (John 14:10). By contemplating the works of Christ, we

---

23. *Pace* Barth's misreading of the *vestigium Trinitatis*, this Christ-centered *credo ut intelligam* program is precisely Augustine's teaching in the very beginning of *De Trinitate*, book 9, which must be read in light of book 4. See Augustine, *On the Holy Trinity*, 125.

come to believe, under the illumination of the Holy Spirit, that he is of the Father (*ex essentia Patri*), and that in him the fullness of God's essence is revealed to us through the hiddenness of his flesh. Thereby we know the hidden (*absconditus*) and revealed (*revelatus*) God as one. And because all God's works prior to the incarnation pointed to the person and work of Christ, the saints of the Old Testament were also enabled to come to know God through the mediation of Christ, apart from whom there can be no true or saving knowledge of God.

The central role of Scripture is such that it documents the history of redemption centered on Christ the Mediator. The inspiration of the Holy Spirit was "to commit . . . wholly unto writing" God's self-revelation "at sundry times, and in divers manners" (Westminster Confession, 1.1—the reference to Hebrews 1:1 here implies a Christ-centered understanding of the history of redemption). Scripture does not give us any immediate revelation of God *per essentiam* through abstract propositions. Confessional Reformed theology requires us to understand revelation as mediatory, rather than immediate.

When theologians of old decided on the formula of God's essential unknowability, then, they not only honored the Creator-creature distinction, but also the person and work of Christ as revealed to us in Scripture and confessed in the historic creeds of the church. Apart from Christ's work, our faith in his person has no reasonable ground. Apart from his person, our faith in the triune God has no reasonable ground. And apart from God's works in the history of redemption, culminating in the person and work of Christ, all theological talk of God's essence would be idolatrous, because God's essence *a se* is unknowable to creatures.

To deny the classic *formula* of essential unknowability because of misunderstandings of key theological terms is tolerable by the standards of creedal orthodoxy. The proposal made by Henry and Reymond, however, is to do away with the *substantive* teaching of essential unknowability and *accommodatio*. This is not only an explicit rejection of the Reformed standard stated in Westminster Confession 1:1 and 7:1. It amounts to a violation of the very axiomatic doctrine of the Creator-creature distinction and a denial of any genuinely Christ-centered and redemptive-historical understanding of biblical revelation.

On this point, evangelicals, without adopting a Barthian paradigm wholesale, can be positively reminded by Barth's relational-analogical view of revelation in terms of God's covenantal history with creatures in Jesus Christ. According to Barth, the ectypal history of God and humankind in Jesus Christ is relationally analogous to the archetypal *opera ad intra* of God's triune essence (see chapter 2). Scripture does not give us immediate knowledge of God's essence, but rather mediates the knowledge of God's essence to us through the history of God's covenant with us in Christ. Because the self-revealed God is the living God who has made our history his own, we do not know God in abstractly propositional terms. Barth insists, as we saw, that subject-predicate relations in propositions like "God is love" and "God is being" must never be reversed. God is always the subject who acts, and only through his historical activity in Christ, to which Scripture attests, do predicates such as "love" and "being" become concretely knowable to us.

Mediatory and Propositional Revelation: A Reformed-Covenantal Approach to General and Special Revelation

There are many things in Barth's discourse on revelation that can be agreeable to evangelicals who, dissatisfied with Henry's view, wish to abide with traditional doctrine. Sebastian Rehnman helpfully summarizes the doctrine in his fine work on John Owen's theological methodology: "In the Christian tradition revelation is such an epistemological concept that generally involves making the unknown known (or knowable), unveiling the veiled, dispelling ignorance, or exposing the obscure."[24] Against those who directly identify revelation with Scripture without distinction, Rehnman reminds us that in traditional Christianity,

> revelation and Holy Scripture are logically distinct but not separable. God has made himself known in nature and history, and thus has placed man in a religious relationship to himself. But following the fall into sin God revealed himself in a special and redemptive way which culminated in Christ. This way is known through Holy Scripture. . . . Through these writings humanity is connected to the redemptive acts of God.[25]

Although Barth's formulation of the three forms of the Word of God is problematic from a normative evangelical perspective—not least because of his denial of the verbal inspiration and infallibility of Scripture—the distinction *per se* is in fact derived from historic Reformed orthodoxy. Owen, responding to the fallacious argument that "Christ is the Word of God, thus Scripture is not the Word of God," makes the distinction: "Christ is the essential Word of God [*verbum Dei essentiale*], God the Word [*verbum Deus*] . . . ; Scripture the Word of God written [*verbum Dei scriptum*]."[26]

Here Owen follows the Reformed orthodox convention in positing a "triplex" Logos as "hypostatic, implanted, and

---

24. Sebastian Rehnman, *Divine Discourse: The Theological Methodology of John Owen* (Grand Rapids: Baker Academic, 2002), 73.

25. Rehnman, *Divine Discourse*, 73.

26. John Owen, *Pro sacris scripturis*, in *The Works of John Owen*, ed. Thomas Russell, 21 vols. (London: Richard Baynes, 1826), 4:553. Translation mine here and henceforth.

prophesied."[27] The terminology may vary from one theologian to another, but, as Rehnman shows, this threefold distinction of the Word of God was indeed conventional among Reformed orthodox writers.[28]

Barth departs from Reformed orthodoxy in his rejection of the *Logos endiathetos*, the Word of God naturally implanted in human reason. His formal distinction (leaving aside the substantive revisions he made) between the Word of God revealed and the Word of God written, however, points us back to the distinction between the essential (hypostatic) Logos and the written Logos in the Reformed tradition. We are reminded, against Henry, that Scripture as a verbal account of the redemptive history that centers on the person and work of Christ is an *ad extra* act of God. Scripture does not make God's essence immediately accessible to our knowledge. Scripture is *originally* divine as God's very own speech in creaturely language, but this divinity is not *essential* in a *hypostatic* sense (i.e., it does not pertain to God's inward being); it is *original* only in the sense that it is an accomplished *act* of God *ad extra*.

The inseparability between these two forms of the Word of God means that in our exegetical practice, we are not permitted to interpret *in abstracto* theological or ethical propositions in Scripture apart from the redemptive history that centers on Christ—something that evangelicals in the footsteps of Henry are often prone to do. Of course, this is not to say that evangelicals should adopt a Barthian or postliberal view of Scripture by relinquishing the commitment to propositional revelation and the verbal inspiration of Scripture.

The Barthian dichotomy between Christocentric revelation and propositional revelation is really quite foreign to historic

---

27. Owen, *Pro sacris scripturis*, 4:546.
28. Rehnman, *Divine Discourse*, 85.

Reformed theology, but, as far as I can see, Barth's own doctrine of Scripture does not necessitate such a dichotomy. My suggestion to the Barthian and perhaps the postliberal reader is to reconsider the possibility of incorporating the notion of propositional revelation into their narrative approaches.

My suggestion to evangelical readers is to adopt the other evangelical mainstream, of which J. I. Packer is among the early representatives. In his celebrated *Knowing God*, Dr. Packer writes: "Right from the start of the Bible story, through the wisdom of divine inspiration, the narrative is told in such a way as to impress upon us the twin truths that the God to whom we are being introduced is both personal and majestic."[29] The God who is at once personal as Immanuel (God-with-and-for-us) and majestic as Yahweh (God-in-and-for-himself) is the God who is self-revealed in Jesus Christ, God the Son in whom is the fullness of the Godhead, who became human without ceasing to be fully and truly God. The love of God that is *a se*, according to Packer, is revealed to us in the person and work of Christ alone. Scripture serves to document the redemptive history that centers on Christ. Scripture as such is primarily narrative, and biblical propositions serve to guide us in understanding "the Bible story."

My suggestion for evangelicals to follow this line of evangelicalism resonates with Professor George Hunsinger's advice for evangelicals in an article titled "What Can Evangelicals and Postliberals Learn from Each Other?" which has been warmly accepted by none other than Professor Michael Horton.[30] Professor Hunsinger relies on Professor Richard Gaffin in presenting "the view taken by [Abraham] Kuyper and Bavinck when

29. J. I. Packer, *Knowing God* (Downers Grove, IL: InterVarsity Press, 1993), 83–84.

30. See George Hunsinger, *Disruptive Grace* (Grand Rapids: Eerdmans, 2000), 338–60, cited by Horton, "A Stony Jar," 376–79.

they come to the question of Scripture's factuality."[31] Citing Professor Gaffin, Professor Hunsinger stresses that for both Kuyper and Bavinck, "'pushing infallibility into the limelight is intellectualism' of the kind 'that began with the rationalists,'" and that "infallibility for Kuyper and Bavinck . . . is not the kind of intellectualistic doctrine that it is for someone like Henry. It does not function as the linchpin of objectivity, certainty, and truth."[32]

It may be added here that Kuyper and Bavinck, following Reformed orthodoxy, do not defend biblical infallibility apologetically the way Henry and certain modern inerrantists do. (As a note of explanation, I, following the tradition, make no distinction between infallibility and inerrancy). Professor Gaffin observes that "Kuyper's views" expressed "in the *Dictaten* . . . (1.66)," stand in

> basic continuity with classical Reformed orthodoxy. . . . We do not begin . . . , Kuyper says, with the question: Is Scripture infallible? For "If Satan has brought us to the point where we are arguing about the infallibility of Scripture, then we are already out from under the authority of Scripture. . . . The older Reformed theology . . . dealt not with the Bible's infallibility, but with its authority and necessity (in which infallibility was accepted without hesitation, as [implied])."[33]

In other words, whereas neo-Calvinism and Reformed orthodoxy treat biblical infallibility as a starting point in the faith-seeking-understanding program, modern inerrantists like Henry tend to make inerrancy a rationalistic *praeambula fidei*. Biblical inerrancy as such is, supposedly, rationally and evidentially deducible apart from faith in the God who is self-revealed

31. Hunsinger, *Disruptive Grace*, 356.

32. Hunsinger, *Disruptive Grace*, 357, citing Richard Gaffin, "Old Amsterdam and Inerrancy?," *Westminster Theological Journal* 44 (1982): 272.

33. Gaffin, "Old Amsterdam and Inerrancy?," 271–72.

in the redemptive history set down in the *verbum Dei scriptum*. The authority of Scripture is then subjected to the scrutiny of the modern sciences, especially the natural and historical sciences. When one claims that the Bible is scientifically and historically inerrant, what is often implied is that the modern sciences carry the authority to judge whether biblical accounts are true and factual. This is precisely the rationalistic intellectualism of which Professor Gaffin speaks.

Neo-Calvinism and Reformed orthodoxy, in contrast to this school of inerrantism, normatively understand infallibility to be a function of the doctrine of faith (in contrast to a preamble of faith). Revealed doctrine teaches us who God is and what he has done for us. Only on this basis can we proceed to make sense of Scripture as the authoritative Word of God.

Objectively, Scripture "doth abundantly evidence itself to be the Word of God"; subjectively, "our full persuasion and assurance of the infallible truth and divine authority thereof, is from the inward work of the Holy Spirit bearing witness by and with the Word in our hearts" (Westminster Confession, 1.5). It is in this way that "the authority of the Holy Scripture . . . dependeth not upon the testimony of any man, or Church; but wholly upon God (who is truth itself) the author thereof: and therefore it is to be received, because it is the Word of God" (Westminster Confession, 1.4).

John Flavel (1628–91), following the Westminster tradition, writes: "It may be fairly inferred from this proposition, that the scriptures are the word of God . . . , the perfection of the scriptures, which being the only rule given by God, must therefore be perfect."[34] That the Reformers understood inerrancy to be implied by the revealed doctrine of God is evident in the teaching

---

34. John Flavel, *The Works of John Flavel*, vol. 6 (Edinburgh: Banner of Truth, 1968), 144.

of Heinrich Bullinger (1504–1575): "God is by His nature truthful, just, good, pure, immortal, and eternal. Correspondingly, God's Word, which comes out of His mouth, is also truthful, just, without deceit or guile, free of error and wicked motives, holy, good, immortal, and eternal. For the Lord says in the Gospel, 'Thy Word is truth' (John 17:17)."[35]

Our affirmation of the entire trustworthiness of Scripture, in other words, springs forth from our knowledge of the God who is self-revealed in the Christ of Scripture. Thus Packer:

> In face of these [biblical] claims [of Jesus that as God the Son he never ceased to be fully and truly God in becoming human], only two courses are open. Either we accept them and ascribe full divine authority to all that Jesus taught, including his declarations of the inspiration and authority of the Old Testament, or else we reject them and call into question the divine authority of his teaching at every point.[36]

For Dr. Packer, the verbal inspiration and thus the authority and inerrancy of Scripture are a function of who Jesus is and what he has done for us. It is Christ who teaches us to submit to the authority of the verbally inspired Word of God. Without knowing Christ, any argument for the verbal inspiration of Scripture would be little more than intellectualistic hubris.

Professor Hunsinger cites Professor Gaffin's quotation of Bavinck: "'It is not even [Scripture's] purpose to provide us with an historical account according to the standard of reliability which is demanded in other areas of knowledge.'"[37] The "histori-

---

35. Walter Hollweg, *Heinrich Bullingers Hausbuch: Eine Untersuchung über die Anfänge der reformierten Predigtliteratur* (Gießen: Münchowsche Universitätsdruckerei, 1956), 364–65. Translation mine.

36. Packer, *Knowing God*, 61.

37. Hunsinger, *Disruptive Grace*, 356, citing Herman Bavinck, *Gereformeerde*

cal narratives of Scripture . . . do not intend to convey 'historical, chronological, geographical data . . . in themselves'; rather, what they intend to attest is 'the truth, poured out on us in Christ.'"[38] Of course, compared to "postliberal theologians like Frei and Lindbeck," who "see a greater discrepancy between biblical narrative and historical fact than their predecessors," Kuyper and Bavinck retain a more traditional understanding of "scriptural unity, factuality, and truth" as conditions for our knowledge of God's self-revelation through redemptive history.[39]

Furthermore, unlike Henry, Bavinck makes no dichotomy between the historical and the propositional in his doctrine of revelation:

> From this [redemptive] history we discover that revelation is not exclusively addressed to the human intellect. In Christ, God himself comes to us in saving power. At the same time we must not make the opposite error and deny that revelation communicates truth and doctrine. Revelatory word and deed belong together in God's plan and acts of salvation.[40]

On this point, I suggest to both evangelical and Barthian readers that we consider, in addition to Kuyper and Bavinck, the Christocentric and organic view of propositional revelation espoused by Geerhardus Vos. Vos appeals to Jesus' own exegesis to show that treating Scripture as propositional revelation need not be "stigmatized as literalistic and mechanical," as long as we

---

dogmatiek, 4 vols. (Kampen: J. H. Kok, 1976), 1:356, as translated by Richard Gaffin, "Old Amsterdam and Inerrancy?," *Westminster Theological Journal* 45 (1983): 229.

38. Hunsinger, *Disruptive Grace*, 356, citing Bavinck, *Gereformeerde dogmatiek*, 564–65, as translated in Gaffin, "Old Amsterdam and Inerrancy?," 259, taken from Jack Rogers and Donald McKim, *The Authority and Interpretation of the Bible* (San Francisco: Harper & Row, 1979), 389.

39. Hunsinger, *Disruptive Grace*, 357.

40. Bavinck, *Reformed Dogmatics*, 1:324.

take the propositions to be "an organic expression of the truth and will of God."[41]

As I demonstrate in the Hegel volume in the present series, Vos's organicism interacts closely with German idealism. In this respect, Vos and Barth share many similar concerns. They both want to ensure that the *historical* nature of revelation be upheld in their respective theologies. They share a similar view of history as God's purposive activity *ad extra*, unfolded in the arena of creation as its outward basis. For both, history is inherently *covenantal*, in that it consists in God's dealings with humankind. Both understand covenantal history to be Christocentric, in that it revolves around what Vos calls the believer's "organic mystical union" with Christ.[42]

Vos and Barth part ways in their specific understandings of the covenantal nature of history. For Barth, there is only one covenant—God's eternal decision to be *pro nobis* in the act of election in Christ. The whole of creation is ontologically determined by this covenant, accordingly. This Christocentric ontology leaves no room for a covenant of works prior to the covenant in Christ, and thus no general revelation prior to and distinct from special revelation.

Barth's view incurs a number of losses. For example, can theology be "scientific" in the same way that all other systems of knowledge are said to be "scientific"? This is a question that we will address soon. Another example: the natural law tradition in the field of jurisprudence, partly developed in the seventeenth century by the likes of Samuel Rutherford (ca. 1600–61) and John Locke (1632–1704) on the basis of the historic Reformed notion of the *tabula rasa* in the doctrine of natural revelation, as well as the notion of *imago Dei* in the broader Western tradition,

41. Geerhardus Vos, *Biblical Theology: Old and New Testaments* (Eugene, OR: Wipf and Stock, 2003), 359.
42. Vos, *Biblical Theology*, 385.

would call for a radically new foundation within a Barthian paradigm, and whether a Barthian reconstruction of natural law could contribute to public discourse remains to be seen. After all, can a Barthian affirm, as a neo-Calvinist would, that the cherished statement, "All men are created equal and endowed by their Creator with certain unalieanable rights," is capable of making *general* (as distinct from salvific) sense to a nation that comprises both Christians and non-Christians? If a positive answer is to be given, then the Barthian view of covenantal-historical and Christocentric revelation would at least need to be significantly reworked and further developed.

By contrast, historic Reformed theology has a ready framework within which to explicate this matter. Vos subscribes to the confessionally Reformed distinction between the covenant of works in Adam and the covenant of grace in Christ in his creation-fall-redemption construct of redemptive history. On this basis, Vos affirms a natural knowledge of God given through creation.

The ostensible problem here is: if there was indeed a period in the history of God's covenant(s) with humankind in which Christ was not our federal head, does this not imply that creaturely history is not entirely determined *in Christo*? Then what happens to Vos's Christocentrism? Does his position not invite Barth's charge that Reformed orthodoxy is guilty of natural theology, and is this not precisely the reason why Barth felt the need to do away with the *Logos endiathetos* (implanted Word) in his reformulation of the *triplex verbum Dei*?

Vos's genius is partly reflected by his demonstration of the relevance of historic doctrine to modern theology. He is able to retain the traditional Reformed doctrine of humanity's natural knowledge of God, given through creation, without compromising the thoroughly Christocentric nature of revelation, because he recognizes the importance of the historic doctrine of the "pact of salvation" (*pactum salutis*), also known as the "covenant of redemption" or the "council of peace."

Mark Jones offers a succinct explanation of the *pactum salutis* as the notion of "the eternal transactions between the Father and the Son" in which "the Son promised to act as a surety for the elect and so 'satisfy his Father for all the Wrong . . . done to him.'"[43] This is sometimes accompanied by the addition that the totally depraved sinner will come to faith in the Son on the terms of the covenantal agreement of the Father and the Son with the Holy Spirit. Many biblical passages point to this notion of an eternal *pactum* between the persons of the Godhead, one of the most obvious being Jesus' prayer prior to his arrest: "I have revealed you to those whom you gave me out of the world. They were yours; you gave them to me and they have obeyed your word" (John 17:6).

Vos aptly observes:

> If man already stood in a covenant relation to God before the fall, then it is to be expected that the covenant idea will also dominate in the work of redemption. God cannot simply let go of the ordinance which He once instituted, but much rather displays His glory in that He carries it through despite man's sin and apostasy. It was merely the other side of the doctrine of the covenant of works that was seen when the task of the Mediator was also placed in this light. A *Pactum Salutis*, a Counsel of Peace, a Covenant of Redemption, could then be spoken of. There are two alternatives: one must either deny the covenant arrangement as a general rule for obtaining eternal life, or, granting the latter, he must also regard the gaining of eternal life by the Mediator as a covenant arrangement and place the establishing of a covenant in back of it. Thus it also

43. See Mark Jones, *Why Heaven Kissed Earth: The Christology of the Puritan Reformed Orthodox Theologian, Thomas Goodwin (1600–1680)* (Göttingen: Vandenhoeck & Ruprecht, 2010), 128 (quoting Goodwin).

becomes clear how a denial of the covenant of works sometimes goes hand in hand with a lack of appreciation for the
counsel of peace.[44]

Bavinck takes a similar stance on the import of the *pactum
salutis*. He is wary that the doctrine of a covenant of works in
Adam, taken on its own, could lead to the kind of natural theology
to which both he and Barth are averse. Bavinck is emphatic in his
dogmatic prolegomena that "the covenant of works (*foedus ope-
rum*) is not a covenant of nature (*foedus naturae*) in the sense that
it arises from a natural human proclivity but is a fruit of supernatural revelation."[45] But the question remains: is the covenant of
works a supernatural act of God apart from Christ?

The answer is found in Bavinck's discussion of Christ the
Redeemer. He observes that Scripture identifies only two covenants that God made with humankind, namely, "the covenant of
works and the covenant of grace."[46] Sure enough, the covenant of
works was "made with humankind in Adam" for "the unfallen,"
and not with "humankind in Christ."[47]

Both of these covenants made with humankind, however,
were established under the provisions of the intra-Trinitarian
covenant of redemption made before the foundation of the
world. "In the pact of salvation Christ can never even for a second be conceived apart from his own."[48] In the intra-Trinitarian
pactum salutis, just as in the covenant of grace made with humankind, "the mystical Christ . . . acts as the negotiating party."[49]

44. Geerhardus Vos, "The Doctrine of the Covenant in Reformed Theology," in
Redemptive History and Biblical Interpretation: The Shorter Writings of Geerhardus Vos,
ed. Richard B. Gaffin, Jr. (Phillipsburg, NJ: P&R, 1980), 245.
45. Bavinck, *Reformed Dogmatics*, 1:308.
46. Bavinck, *Reformed Dogmatics*, 3:228.
47. Bavinck, *Reformed Dogmatics*, 3:228.
48. Bavinck, *Reformed Dogmatics*, 3:228.
49. Bavinck, *Reformed Dogmatics*, 3:228.

And since (as is evident from 1 Cor. 15:45ff.) Adam was a
type of Christ even before the fall, so the covenant of grace
was prepared, not first by Noah and Abraham nor first by the
covenant of grace with Adam, but already in and by the covenant of works. God, who knows and determines all things and
included also the breach of the covenant of works in his counsel when creating Adam and instituting the covenant of works,
already counted on the Christ and his covenant of grace.[50]

Although the Reformed orthodox debate certain details
of the *pactum salutis,* most would agree with Patrick Gillespie:
"This transaction having been from eternity, it was a concluded
bargain before the creatures had a being."[51] Yet, because this pact,
as an *ad extra* act of God in eternity, actually comes into effect in
redemptive history, it indirectly reveals to us the glory of God's
triune essence through tangible means.

Granted that God's triune essence is not immediately accessible to human knowledge, John Owen suggests that Christ's incarnation, oblation, and intercession give us a glimpse into the eternal
pact between Father, Son, and Holy Spirit, a covenant made *ad
extra* that corresponds to God's loving faithfulness *ad intra.* "Now,
this emptying of the Deity, this humbling of himself, this dwelling
amongst us, was the sole act of the second person, or the divine
nature in the second person, the Father and the Spirit having no
concurrence in it but by liking, approbation, and eternal counsel."[52]

Professor John Fesko offers an incisive analysis of the crucial role of the *pactum salutis* in the Christocentric character of
the Reformed doctrine of revelation: "Since the *pactum* entails
the incarnation, this requires divine revelation to prepare for the

---

50. Bavinck, *Reformed Dogmatics,* 3:228.

51. Patrick Gillespie, *The Ark of the Covenant Opened* (London: Parkhurst, 1677), 59.

52. John Owen, "The Death of Death in the Death of Christ," in *The Works of
John Owen,* ed. William Goold, 23 vols. (Edinburgh: Banner of Truth, 1967), 10:175.

advent, incarnation, and subsequent explanation of the significance of the Son's work."[53] Professor Fesko points to Charles Hodge as a prime example of a modern theologian appealing to the classic *pactum* for the construal of a Christocentric view of revelation:

> Hodge locates the pinnacle of God's self-disclosure in the incarnation of Christ, which means not only that God designs humanity with the capacity to receive revelation, but also that this design is irrefragably connected to the incarnation of Christ. The connections between anthropology, Christology, revelation, and epistemology find their genesis in the *pactum*.[54]

In fact, well before Barth and Schleiermacher, and Vos and Hodge, the Reformed orthodox were already sharply aware that any theological speculation apart from Christ would be futile and destructive to true knowledge of God. Thus Owen:

> The person of Christ is the foundation of all the counsels of God, as unto his own eternal glory in the vocation, sanctification, and salvation of the church. . . . Thus it is said of him, with respect unto his future incarnation and work of mediation, that the Lord possessed him in the beginning of his way, before his world of old; that he was set up from everlasting, from the beginning, or ever the earth was.[55]

Owen is aware that non-Christological speculations about God's eternal decrees inevitably lead some to portray God as a capricious tyrant. It is precisely God's flesh-*becoming* that reveals

---

53. John Fesko, *The Covenant of Redemption: Origins, Development, and Reception* (Göttingen: Vandenhoeck & Ruprecht, 2016), 232.

54. Fesko, *Covenant of Redemption*, 158.

55. John Owen, "A Declaration of the Glorious Mystery of the Person of Christ," in *Works of John Owen*, ed. Goold, 1:54.

the immutability of his *being* and the constancy of his will, manifest through the covenant of redemption. So, although the "first spring or original [of God's eternal decrees] was in the divine will and wisdom alone," such that "no reason can be given, no cause assigned, of these counsels, but the will of God alone," Owen insists that "the design of their accomplishment was laid in the person of the Son alone. As he was the essential wisdom of God, all things were at first created by him. But upon a prospect of the ruin of all by sin, God would in and by him—as he was fore-ordained to be incarnate—restore all things."[56] It is through this Christocentric way of understanding God's eternal will and temporal works that classical Reformed theology comes to inquire about God and everything that is not God.

The historic Reformed insistence on Christocentric, redemptive-historical revelation goes hand in hand with the doctrine of divine incomprehensibility as God's unknowability *per essentiam*. Indeed, in classical Reformed theology, the unity-in-distinction of *verbum Dei essentiale* and *verbum Dei scriptum* precludes an abstractly propositional view of biblical revelation void of Christocentric and redemptive-historical content. This distinction is in fact reflective of the more quintessentially Reformed distinctions between the different forms of *gloria Dei*.

More than any other tradition, the Reformed tradition consistently holds to the invisibility of God's *essential glory*. Even in Eden, according to Reformed orthodoxy, Adam could only behold the face of God in an earthly form. Thus Bavinck: "There was supernatural revelation also in Paradise (Gen. 1:28f.; 2:16f.). Revelation was therefore not first made necessary by sin. Even in the state of integrity, there was a revelation of grace."[57]

God's *manifest glory* through creation is not the light of light,

56. Owen, "Person of Christ," 62.
57. Bavinck, *Reformed Dogmatics*, 1:359.

nor is it even a refraction of the true light. It is only the created light of God's handiwork *ad extra*. This glory is analogous to God's essential glory in an archetype-ectype relation.

The Reformed, following Nicene-Chalcedonian orthodoxy, also speak of the *personal* or *hypostatic glory* of God. Christ is "light of light, very God of very God, begotten, not made, consubstantial with the Father; by whom all things were made; who for us men and for our salvation came down from heaven and was incarnate by the Holy Spirit of the Virgin Mary, and was made man" (Nicaea-Constantinople, 381).

Whereas even the Lutherans would speak of a *genus maiestaticum* in which the essential glory of God is shared between Christ's two natures through the *communicatio idiomatum*, the Reformed have consistently insisted, in the pattern of the *extra Calvinisticum*, that the *gloria* and *maiestas Dei* remain peculiar to Christ's deity. Bavinck stresses that Christ in his human nature "was not a comprehensive knower, that he walked by faith and hope, not by sight, that he did not yet share the 'beatific knowledge' (*scientia beata*) here on earth."[58]

It should be noted that the Reformed rendition of the beatific vision is such that even in the new heaven and the new earth, we behold not the essential glory of God, but still the personal glory in the Lamb that was slain (Rev. 5:12). Thus Owen on our "beatifical" sight of God: "*All communications* from the Divine Being and infinite fulness in heaven unto glorified saints, are in and through Christ Jesus, who shall for ever be the medium of communication between God and the church, even in glory."[59] In other words, according to Reformed orthodoxy, knowledge of God's essence will always be mediated to us in and through Christ, even in the beatific state.

---

58. Bavinck, *Reformed Dogmatics*, 3:312.

59. Owen, "Meditations and Discourses on the Glory of Christ," in *Works of John Owen*, ed. Goold, 1:414–15 (italics original).

True enough, Reformed theologians often speak of some form of "contemplation (*visio*)" and "understanding (*comprehensio*)" of God given to the redeemed "directly, immediately, unambiguously, and purely" upon the renewal of creation.[60] Such statements, however, must be accompanied by the qualification that glorified saints "will all know of [God], each in the measure of his mental capacity, with a knowledge that has its image and likeness in God's knowledge."[61] That is, our knowledge of God remains analogical—never univocal—even in the new creation.

The immediacy of the beatific vision is not a denial of Christ's mediatorship there and then. Christ's "mediatorship of reconciliation" ends at the new creation, but "what remains is the mediatorship of union. Christ remains Prophet, Priest, and King as this triple office is automatically given with his human nature, included in the image of God, and realized supremely and most magnificently in Christ as the Image of God."[62] The blessed "will together be filled with all the fullness of God (Eph. 3:19; Col. 2:2, 10), inasmuch as Christ, himself filled with the fullness of God (Col. 1:19), will in turn fill the believing community with himself and make it his fullness . . . (Eph. 1:12; 4:10)."[63] The beatific vision is not a sight and comprehension of God apart from Christ, but rather a vision and understanding mediated through Christ. In a word, the Reformed view of revelation so normative to evangelicalism teaches that we will never have immediate epistemic access to God's inward essence. God always reveals himself to us by way of self-condescension in the form of covenant in Christ.

The foregoing analysis shows that there is no reason for evangelicals who respect the Reformed tradition to be appalled

60. Bavinck, *Reformed Dogmatics*, 4:722.
61. Bavinck, *Reformed Dogmatics*, 4:722.
62. Bavinck, *Reformed Dogmatics*, 2:482.
63. Bavinck, *Reformed Dogmatics*, 4:723.

by the Barthian contention that revelation is indirect, so long as this contention is not interpreted within the problematic framework of (neo-)Kantian or allegedly Kierkegaardian dialectics so often imposed on Barth. My suggestion, of course, is not that we should adopt Barth's Christocentric ontology as an alternative to Henry's view of revelation—this should be clear from the foregoing discussion.

My proposal is that evangelicals like myself, who hold to propositional revelation and the verbal inspiration of Scripture, should be critically reminded by Barth that our living <u>God reveals himself not through abstract propositions, but rather through propositions concretely determined by the covenantal-redemptive history of his dealings with us in Christ.</u> Barth's insistence on the indirectness of revelation reminds us, against Henry, that by virtue of being creatures and not God, we cannot gain unmediated knowledge of God *per essentiam* through propositional revelation. Our knowledge of God's essence is mediated by covenantal-redemptive history, centered on the person and work of Christ. This knowledge is only an ectype of God's archetypal self-knowledge, and the two can never be univocal. With a positive reminder from Barth, I suggest that we heed the shared advice of Professor Horton and Professor Hunsinger, and follow the examples of Kuyper and Bavinck—and Vos— and turn to classical Reformed theology for resources within our own tradition for the edification of evangelical theology.

Saga versus Proposition: Historical Objectivity of the Resurrection

Barth's placement of the biblical narratives in the genre of saga has been a significant point of contention between evangelicals and Barthians. This classification means that while, say, Christ's resurrection really happened in history, the biblical reports surrounding this event inevitably involve what one might identify with Robert Alter as "historicized fiction" or "fictionalized history." On a Barthian view, these reports are like the story of Barth citing the lyrics to "Jesus Loves Me": there are different accounts of how and where it happened, and we are never fully certain if it really happened—though it probably did—but it is a revelatory story about Barth anyway.

Now if biblical narratives fall under the category of saga in such a way, and if these stories are written in and for the church, then the most reasonable hermeneutic would seem to be the "testimony and trial" model proposed by Walter Brueggemann. Some of Brueggemann's more general descriptions of the Old Testament in fact apply to the New Testament as well, when it is read as what Barth categorizes as saga. For instance, Brueggemann describes the Old Testament as a "polyphonic" text, bearing different and often contradictory testimonies about God, with many "dialectical" theological claims expressed with a kind of rhetoric that is "characteristically ambiguous and open."[64] This would also apply to the New Testament narratives when they are understood as saga in a Barthian sense.

The task of the theologian, then, would naturally be the "work of fashioning a larger, coherent portrayal" of God based on testimonies that do not "fit together" well.[65] The method of this portrayal is described with the metaphor of "testimony and trial": the task of the ecclesial interpretive community is to examine the utterances of various witnesses to arrive at a construal of divine reality.[66] It is in this sense that "testimony becomes revelation," and that biblical witnesses are said to be "reliable."[67] The

64. Walter Brueggemann, *Theology of the Old Testament* (Minneapolis: Fortress, 1997), 106, 112.

65. Brueggemann, *Theology of the Old Testament*, 267.

66. Brueggemann, *Theology of the Old Testament*, 121.

67. Brueggemann, *Theology of the Old Testament*, 121.

authority of Scripture consists in "human testimony" deemed "truthful" in the ecclesial courtroom, rather than in the "scholastic categories of inspiration and revelation."[68]

Of course, Barth would never go so far as to agree with Brueggemann's appeal to Lyotard and Derrida in "the deconstruction of that in which Christian faith is embodied."[69] Deconstructionism in general does not follow from Barth's view of Scripture, much less the specific deconstruction of the Christian faith.

What seems naturally deducible from Barth's categorization of the biblical narratives as saga, however, is Brueggemann's "testimony and trial" hermeneutic. Because there are so many witnesses who differ in their reports of events and theological viewpoints, we need the church as an interpretive community to gather from them a theology that is more or less coherent. In practice, this ascribes to the church the authority of a jury judging the biblical witnesses. In the saga model, then, the regulating authority of Scripture over ecclesial dogmas becomes fairly thin in comparison to models that acknowledge propositional revelation and verbal inspiration. The church, and consequently individual theologians like Barth himself, would be permitted by the category of saga to take more liberty with the text of Scripture than any verbal inspiration model would allow. After all, the saga model does not require *ad litteram* interpretations of the biblical text.

One example is Barth's own treatment of the New Testament term "all" (*panta*) in his construction of the doctrine of election. Professor Hunsinger comments that "Barth's doctrine of universal objective participation breaks with almost the entire Latin theological tradition. . . . One has to go all the way back to early

---

68. Brueggemann, *Theology of the Old Testament*, 121.
69. Brueggemann, *Theology of the Old Testament*, 332.

Greek fathers such as Athanasius to find relatively comparable associations of the phrase *in Christ* with the word *all*."[70] In reading the "all" into the "in Christ," the extent of the liberty that Barth takes with the New Testament text is comparable to the spiritual (allegorical) interpretation of the Greek fathers.

??? Arrogant?.

Because the New Testament is understood as saga, Barth is not bound to any literal interpretation of the word "all." This stands in sharp contrast to Owen's comprehensive study of the New Testament uses of the word "all" in his rebuttal against the doctrine of hypothetical universalism advanced by the School of Saumur.[71] Owen's view of biblical revelation requires him to come to an understanding of how the word "all" is literally used in New Testament texts before he can come to any doctrinal conclusion.

The question then arises: if propositional revelation is completely replaced by Barth's narrative approach to Scripture as saga, then to what extent is the believer's faith regulated by the dogmas of the church, and to what extent are the dogmas of the church regulated by the narratives of Scripture? The answer seems quite indefinite, for one who adopts the Barthian view can be as traditional and confessional as Professor Hunsinger, but Barth's view of Scripture as saga can also allow for the highly revisionary approach to Scripture and ecclesial dogmas that we find in, say, Stanley Hauerwas.

Still, there are strengths to Barth's identification of biblical narratives as saga worthy of consideration on the part of evangelicals. I have in mind specifically his refusal to test the historical veracity of biblical narratives against the criteria of modern historical criticism. This becomes especially valuable in his treatment of the resurrection of Christ and the empty tomb.

70. George Hunsinger, "A Tale of Two Simultaneities: Justification and Sanctification in Calvin and Barth," in *Conversing with Barth*, ed. John McDowell and Mike Higton (Aldershot, UK: Ashgate, 2004), 77 (italics original).

71. Owen, "Death of Death," 303–9.

Recall Barth's insistence that modern historiography, with all the naturalistic and positivistic assumptions underlying its methodology, is incapable of verifying or falsifying the historicity of the resurrection. This insistence serves to remind us of the limitations of historical-critical inquiries.

Take the example of Matthew the evangelist. Matthew tells us that in his day and age, the empty tomb was an accepted historical fact. Both followers and opponents of Jesus knew that the tomb became empty on the third day, and both parties were eager to interpret this neutral fact within their respective presuppositional frameworks.

The "story" that "circulated among the Jews" up to Matthew's "very day" was that Jesus' "disciples came during the night and stole him away" while the guards were asleep (Matt. 28:11–15). The guards were the propagators of the false report, and they knew it was false, but they, in the spirit of Thomas Kuhn's natural scientist, adopted this interpretation of the neutral fact of the empty tomb for the sake of profit (v. 15).

Matthew gives us convincing historical evidence of the absurdity of this explanation of the empty tomb: the tomb was "made . . . secure by putting a seal on the stone and posting the guard" (27:66). In fact, under Pilate's command, the tomb was made "as secure as" the priests and Pharisees "[knew] how" (27:25). The priests and Pharisees knew very well that the tomb became empty when it was still sealed watertight, and yet they still chose to adopt the story that later circulated among the Jews, because this was the post-truth explanation that fitted well with the presuppositional framework of their theology.

What is interesting here is that this Pharisaic theory about the empty tomb is a feasible thesis on the naturalistic assumptions of modern historical criticism, while the evangelical thesis is not. The modern scientific mind might give in to the evidences that Matthew provides, and conclude that the Pharisaic thesis is highly improbable. Still, there must be a natural cause and thus a naturalistic explanation of the empty tomb, insists the modern historian. The proclamation that Christ is risen is simply not a feasible thesis on naturalistic assumptions.

Modern historians study history by the method of analogous events within Kantian limitations.[72] They presuppose that what happens today and what happened a thousand years ago are causally linked, and there is always an analogy between every cause-effect event of the same nature. The most obvious causal continuity between the past and the present is that the sun rises every morning. Although we observe only the *correlation* between morning and sunrise, Kant has authorized historians to speak of *causal* relations between the two. Causal regularities like this lend modern historians after the post-Kantian turn to history the basis on which to understand things that happened thousands of years ago. Historians study events that belong to the natural order of things in which every phenomenon occurs by natural causes.

The resurrection, however, is not an event of this sort. Its cause is supernatural: "God raised him from the dead" (Acts 3:15; 4:10; 13:30–34; 17:31; Rom. 10:9; Col. 2:12; 1 Peter 1:21)—"incorruptible" (1 Cor. 15:20, 42)! The resurrection, then, was not causally linked to any past event in history; it was only negatively conditioned by the crucifixion, but not efficiently caused thereby. Moreover, there has never been any past event remotely analogous to Christ's resurrection—not even the resurrection of Lazarus, who was raised with a corruptible body. There are no regular patterns of historical events that give the modern historian a basis on which to investigate Christ's resurrection. The resurrection as a historical event was unique and singular. Its historicity cannot be subjected to modern historical criticism.

72. See Karl Ameriks, *Kant and the Historical Turn* (Oxford: Oxford University Press, 2006).

Furthermore, the Lord was evidently raised to be above the conditions of space and time. Though he did not become omni-present, he was able to appear and disappear instantaneously. The modern study of history, however, is conditioned by spatio-temporality: it was the Kantian view of spatio-temporality as the precondition of empirical knowledge of reality that gave rise to what is known as modern historical consciousness in the post-Kantian generation. More simply put, the modern science of history is the study of events conditioned by space and time, and historians have no right to verify or falsify the reality of the reports of a person who was lifted above the condition of spatio-temporality.

Upon the assumptions of modern historical criticism, then, reported sights of Jesus after the crucifixion might possibly be explained by the thesis that he never really died, but reports of his sudden appearances and disappearances can only be discredited as unfalsifiable witness. The modern historian, by virtue of being "modern," cannot possibly explain the neutral fact of the empty tomb by presupposing who Christ is *kata pneuma* (Rom. 1:4).

The only thing that the modern historian can do in favor of the resurrection thesis is to show by an argument *reductio ad absurdum* that all other possible theories fail to be probable. The modern historian is then capable of showing that the only way to reasonably make sense of the evidences at hand is to accept by faith that Christ is risen, recognizing that the tenets of faith, though unfalsifiable, are the only rational presuppositions with which to explain empirical evidences.

The lesson here is that there is no such thing as what Van Til calls a "neutral historian"—his presuppositionalist rejection of scholarly neutrality is in fact in agreement with Barth's criticisms of modern historiography.[73] For Barth, the neutral facts

73. Van Til, *Christianity and Barthianism*, 14.

of history are always interpreted within definite presuppositional frameworks that are ultimately theological. Objective interpretation of these facts, Barth reminds us, cannot possibly come from the theological framework to which modern historiography is committed. On this point, Van Til may very well agree with Barth. Both Van Til and Barth would tell us that the only objective interpretation of the empty tomb is the proclamation, "Christ is risen."

The objectivity of this interpretation becomes fairly weak, in my view, if we follow Barth in taking the Easter narratives as sagas, because the category of saga allows for too much liberty with the text. If the truthfulness of every report of an event is open to question, then the truthfulness of all the witnesses and the factuality of the event become questionable. But once we accept that Christ is risen, then all the evangelical reports about the risen Lord can be taken as revelatory stories that may or may not be true. When the truthfulness of biblical witnesses and propositions are relativized in this way, as I argued earlier, their regulative authority over ecclesial dogmas and personal theologizing is significantly weakened. The meaning of the resurrection can be understood as truly salvific in a traditional Protestant sense, but it can also be interpreted as an event aimed at political liberation.

On the other hand, if we suppose with Henry that the Bible makes God's essence immediately knowable to us through verbal propositions, then we really do not need to care about the historicity of the resurrection anymore, as far as revelation is concerned. We would still need the risen Lord to accomplish our redemption, and we would still need the Bible to tell us that this redemption has been completed, but we do not need the historicity of the event as a means by which to reflect upon God's essence, because it can be given to us univocally through verbal revelation anyway. Salvation is then severed from revelation. Biblical revelation of God's essence as special revelation, thus seen apart from redemptive history, is no longer understood as salvific, that is, necessitated by the noetic effects of sin. Yet the soteriological emphasis on the inward illumination of the Holy Spirit goes hand in hand with the historic Reformed view of biblical revelation as primarily a narration of redemptive history. If biblical propositions on God's essence were as unequivocal—univocal—as Henry claims, then his subscription to the historic doctrine of inward illumination would lose its ground. Gone with the axiom *finitum non capax infiniti*, then, is the other axiom, *homo peccator non capax verbum Dei*. But when salvation no longer depends on the historicity of revelation, we no longer need to care about the factuality of biblical narratives. We might well say that the Bible is theologically inerrant in that the propositions it makes about God are entirely true, but we would no longer need to affirm the historical truthfulness of the Bible, except for the sake of an abstract notion of inerrancy.

When we understand "for the Bible tells me so" in terms of verbally inspired propositions concretely determined by God's *ad extra* activity in redemptive history, however, we are, in my view, more likely to establish a strong objectivity in our knowledge of the risen Lord and all the historical details surrounding his resurrection that the New Testament authors deemed relevant to the faith. We can trust that, say, the narrations of the woman or women at the empty tomb and of the disciples' reactions (Matt. 28:1–10; Mark 16:1–8; Luke 24:1–12; John 20:1–18) are of a different nature than the varying accounts of Barth citing "Jesus loves me." They are not fictionalized pieces of history, much less historicized fictions, providing inspiring materials for theological construction despite their alleged discrepancies. They are truthful reports of God's concrete dealings with particular human beings at particular times and particular places, in the particular person of Jesus Christ. Sound theology cannot be separated from firm and certain knowledge of what God actually did for us in Jesus Christ, and for this very reason, evangelical theology normatively affirms that historical revelation and verbal inspiration go hand in hand.

Theology as Science: The Possibility
of a Christian Worldview

Both Bavinck and Barth sought to secure the "scientific" status of theology in the modern sense of the term. As suggested in chapter 2, Barth succeeded in ensuring that theology truly consists of human knowledge of God—what Kant would call "theoretical knowledge" (i.e., not just "we ought to affirm that God is," but simply, "God is"), no less.

What might be added here in Barth's favor is that he is not as averse to humanity's *natural* knowledge of God as he has been portrayed in some circles. T. F. Torrance has argued that Barth "rejects" the "status" of

> natural theology . . . as a *praeambula fidei*, that is, as a preamble of faith, or an independent conceptual system antecedent to actual knowledge of God, which is then used as an epistemological framework within which to interpret and formulate actual empirical knowledge of God, thereby subordinating it to distorting forms of thought. . . . However, instead of rejecting natural theology *tout court*, Barth has transposed it into the material content of theology where in a changed form it constitutes the epistemological structure of our knowledge of God.[74]

When Torrance presented this argument to Barth himself, Torrance says, "Barth expressed full agreement." Torrance's interpretation of Barth here is worked out from the "Anselmian method" stated in the 1931 booklet and the "epistemological

---

74. T. F. Torrance, *Space, Time and Resurrection* (Edinburgh: T&T Clark, 1976), x.

structure" that Barth "deployed and developed" in *CD* I/1 and II/1 on the basis of *Anselm*.[75] With an Anselmian method of reflective after-thinking (*Nachdenken*), Barth successfully established the rational nature of theology as the theoretical study of God.

Here we may observe yet another point of similarity between Barth and Bavinck. Bavinck aligns himself with "the Reformation," which "indeed adopted" the "natural theology" of medieval scholasticism "along with its proofs but, instead of treating it prior to the doctrine of faith, incorporated it in the doctrine of faith."[76] Unlike Barth, however, Bavinck acknowledges that in a certain sense, "natural theology used to be correctly denominated a 'preamble of faith,' a divine preparation and education for Christianity."[77]

The key difference between Barth and Bavinck is that, for Bavinck, "general revelation is the foundation on which special revelation builds itself up," such that with a starting point in faith, the believer may seek to understand general revelation regressively (to borrow a Kantian term, if I may) through the spectacles of special revelation.[78] Barth, by contrast, denies the distinction between general and special revelation, and concomitantly dismisses any attempt at *systematic* knowledge of God and creation as essentially Hegelian.

Barth's position, it seems to me, would imply that the sense in which he describes theology as a "science" must be different from the way all other academic disciplines are said to be "scientific." To be sure, Torrance has pointed out similarities between the mode of scientific inquiry in Barth's theology and that in modern physics.[79] This resemblance, however, does not diminish the fact that modern physicists are still in search of a grand

75. Torrance, *Space, Time and Resurrection*, x.
76. Bavinck, *Reformed Dogmatics*, 2:78.
77. Bavinck, *Reformed Dogmatics*, 1:322.
78. Bavinck, *Reformed Dogmatics*, 1:322.
79. Torrance, *Space, Time and Resurrection*, x.

unifying theory that systematically bridges the gap between quantum mechanics and general relativity. Such systematic knowledge, according to Barth, can never be established in theology: only God knows himself systematically and immediately. Any attempt at a theological worldview similar to string theory in physics, according to Barth, would lead us right back into the errors committed by post-Kantian idealism.

One further problem arises when we consider Barth's rejection of the distinction between general and special revelation as a corollary to his Christocentric refusal to acknowledge the possibility of a Christian worldview. For him, all revelation is in Christ, in whom nature and world history are entirely determined ontologically. Paradoxically, this easily leads to the conclusion that there is no distinction between theology as the science of God and all other sciences.

This is, of course, not a conclusion that Barth himself ever drew, just as he never explicitly stated the difference between theological "science" and all other "sciences." In actual practice, Barth was attentive to the findings of the diverse sciences in his own theological inquiries. He practically treated theology as a science distinct from and yet analogous to other sciences, such that there can be positive interactions between theology and other academic disciplines. Yet, as far as I know, how this practice squares with Barth's own rejection of a Christian worldview and of the distinction between general and special revelation is a problem that remains to be solved in Barthian theology. (The trajectory taken by Sigurd Baark, mentioned in chapter 2, seems to promise a convincing solution.)

On this point, evangelicals can cherish the tradition handed down from the Reformation through the likes of Bavinck, and Barthians may also find Bavinck helpful. Bavinck envisions general and special revelation not as two separate spheres, but rather as two concentric circles centered on Jesus Christ. They are distinct yet inseparable. "All revelation [singular!]—general and special—finally finds its fulfillment and meaning in Christ. . . . God is one and the same loving God in creation and redemption; grace restores nature."[80]

The inseparable unity and abiding distinction between general and special revelation in Bavinck's reception of traditional Reformed doctrine can be understood by borrowing Barth's phraseology: general revelation is the outward basis of special revelation, and special revelation is the inward basis of general revelation. "Special revelation should never be separated from its organic connection to history, the world, and humanity."[81]

> General revelation is the foundation on which special revelation builds itself up. . . . The rich significance of general revelation comes out in the fact that it keeps nature and grace, creation and re-creation, the world of reality and the world of values, inseparably connected. Without general revelation, special revelation loses its connectednesss with the whole cosmic existence and life. . . . It is one and the same God who in general revelation does not leave himself without a witness to anyone and who in special revelation makes himself known as a God of grace. Hence general and special revelation interact with each other.[82]

The Trinitarian doctrine of the *pactum salutis*, as we saw, ensures the Christ-centeredness of general revelation. This serves to ascertain that Christian scholars can study everything that is not God with a Trinitarian and Christ-centered worldview, while preserving the distinction between the theological science and all other sciences.

80. Bavinck, *Reformed Dogmatics*, 1:302.
81. Bavinck, *Reformed Dogmatics*, 1:353.
82. Bavinck, *Reformed Dogmatics*, 1:322.

Furthermore, Bavinck's critical treatment of Kant and Hegel from the starting point of a confessionally Reformed theology succeeds, in my view, in securing the status of theology as a systematic science that regulates our thinking in all other sciences. Bavinck, like Barth, resorts to a method of reflective *Nachdenken* to arrive at the knowledge of God's triune essence. Unlike Barth, who insists on a particularistic approach to the knowledge of everything through Christ, Bavinck resorts to the Trinity as the concrete universal through which the unity in diversity and diversity in unity within creation and world history can be understood.

Barth's rejection of *Weltanschauung*, as we saw in chapter 2, is a result of his refusal to arrive at universal statements about God from the starting point of intuiting individual phenomena in the world. Hegelian and Schleiermacherian *Weltanschauungen* can only result in essentially anthropological theologies. Bavinck is well aware of this danger, and he, too, appeals to Ludwig Feuerbach and David Strauss to disclose the idolatries of Hegelian and Schleiermacherian worldviews.[83]

Bavinck's proposal of a Christian worldview is carefully designed to avoid the idolatries disclosed by Feuerbach and Strauss. Instead of trying to arrive at universal predications about God from particular intuitions of this-worldly phenomena, Bavinck's notion of the Christian worldview is such that we must explicate our empirical intuitions in light of the triune God as the concrete universal.

God's triune essence, of course, is not immediately knowable to us. It is revealed to us only through the mediation of Christ. Yet, the very mediatory nature of our knowledge of the triune essence means that our reflective after-thinking of this essence can serve to govern our studies of God's handiwork, because it ensures to us a correspondence between God's essence *ad intra*

---

83. Bavinck, *Reformed Dogmatics*, 1:166.

and his acts and works *ad extra,* and thus an analogy between God's self-knowledge as the archetype and our knowledge of him as the ectype. The archetype-ectype distinction-in-relation and relation-in-distinction between the triune God's omniscience and our knowledge of God in relation to everything that is not God allow for a systematic study of God that governs the diverse studies of his creation.[84]

Bavinck's dogmatic system calls for a Christian worldview in which we can embrace Peter Bulkeley's famous words from the seventeenth century: "If God be over us we must yield him universal obedience in all things. He must not be over us in one thing, and under us in another, but he must be over us in every thing."[85] The personal sanctification and obedience that this worldview demands, both intellectually and ethically, as we shall see in this chapter's conclusion, is almost absent in the actualistic and particularistic Christocentrism of Barth's theology.

Conclusion: Christocentrism, the Quest for Godliness, and Doxological Theology

My concluding appraisal of Barth from an evangelical perspective is more substantive than methodological. It is about the most prominent feature of Barth's theology, namely, its thoroughly Christocentric character. We have discussed the Christocentric shape of historic Reformed theology above. What Barth did with this Christocentrism was to develop it into an ontology. It is, to be sure, not an ontology of theology proper,

---

84. This was the salient point in my volumes on Kant and Hegel in the present series. Readers interested in an in-depth exploration of Bavinck's development of theology as a science are advised to turn to the outstanding monograph on this topic by Nathaniel Gray Sutanto titled *God and Knowledge: Herman Bavinck's Theological Epistemology* (London: T&T Clark, 2020).

85. Cited by Leland Ryken, *Worldly Saints* (Grand Rapids: Zondervan, 1986), 208.

in which even God's inward essence is said to be determined by the incarnation. However, Barth has so reformulated the traditional ontology of creation handed down from Augustine, that the whole of creation is now described as an entity without an essence of its own, apart from Christ.

Calvin, in his soteriology, famously ascribes to our "mystical union" with Christ "the highest degree of importance."[86] Barth expands on Calvin's doctrine and makes *unio Christi* an ontological reality that determines the whole of creaturely existence. Barth even renders this ontological union determinative of God's being as God-for-us (but never of God-in-and-for-himself, of course). Ingolf Dalferth explains Barth's view well: "Our world of common experience is an *enhypostatic reality* which exists only in so far as it is incorporated into the concrete reality of God's saving self-revelation in Christ. Taken by itself natural reality is an anhypostatic abstraction, unable to exist on its own and systematically at once removed from the texture of concrete reality."[87]

It is hardly imaginable, as far as I can see, that evangelicalism would adopt this Christocentric ontology wholesale, or even accept its infrastructure as a paradigm, as that would require relinquishing some of the most basic convictions that underlie normative evangelical theology. What evangelicals can learn from Barth, however, is the idea that natural world history would be void of meaning and rationality apart from the covenantal history of redemption centered on the person and work of Christ. Barth's famous formulation of the covenant as the inward basis of creation and creation as the outward basis of the covenant can

86. John Calvin, *Institutes of the Christian Religion*, ed. John T. McNeill, trans. Ford Lewis Battles, 2 vols. (Philadelphia: Westminster, 1960), 3.11.10, at 1:737.

87. Ingolf Dalferth, "Karl Barth's Eschatological Realism," in *Karl Barth: Centenary Essays*, ed. Stephen Sykes (Cambridge: Cambridge University Press, 1989), 28–29, cited by John Bolt, "Exploring Barth's Eschatology: A Salutary Exercise for Evangelicals," in *Karl Barth and Evangelical Theology: Convergences and Divergences*, ed. Sung Wook Chung (Grand Rapids: Baker Academic, 2006), 216–17 (italics original).

easily be transformed into a neo-Calvinist formulation: redemptive history is the inward basis of natural world history, while natural world history is the outward basis of redemptive history.

The problem with Barth's Christocentric ontology is not that it leads to an incipient universalism—we have seen that it does not. The chief problem has to do with his radical redefinition of sin. Whereas the Western tradition—Catholic and Protestant alike—follows Augustine in defining sin as a *corruptio* and *privatio* of the good nature with which God created us, Barth says that sin is a second determination "from below" (*von unten*) of our existential being (*Sein/Dasein*) by the history of our sinful acts and decisions. Sin as such is totally foreign to our nature, for "nature" denotes the ontological determination of our essential being (*Wesen*) "from above" (*von oben*) by the history of God's covenant with us in Jesus Christ. The two determinations stand in a *totus-totus* relation in the grammar of the Protestant *simul*.

Whereas the magisterial Reformers and the Reformed and Lutheran orthodoxies thereafter describe justification as an *existential* reality effected by faith as its instrumental cause, Barth's Christocentric ontology dictates that justification constitutes the essential determination of human nature. Justification becomes the *ontological* reality of humankind, and sin becomes an ontological impossibility.

As Professor Hunsinger points out, Barth's elevation of the Reformation *simul* from an existential level to an ontological one basically excludes "Calvin's emphasis on the gradual," and this "incur[s] certain losses."[88] Both Luther and Calvin "retained a definite place for the gradual in a way that Barth simply did not."[89] The personal sanctification and obedience that the Christian tradition as a whole demands on biblical grounds then

88. Hunsinger, "Two Simultaneities," 86.
89. Hunsinger, "Two Simultaneities," 86.

becomes a striking lacuna in Barth's theology under the terms of his Christocentric ontology. It is, in Professor Hunsinger's words, "a large logical space" in Barth's theology "that remains to be more adequately filled."[90]

Professor Christiane Tietz's splendid construal of Barth's biography as a "life in conflict" is all too demonstrative of how this theological weakness manifested itself in his own life.[91] The ontological *simul* was used as a justification for the ethical contradictions in his personal life, notwithstanding his political witness in the public arena during the Second World War.[92] Of course, by no means am I bringing up this point as an *ad hominem* attack to discredit Barth's theology. I have always insisted that unless an evangelical is willing to give up the theological convictions endorsed by George Ladd because of the unrepentance of his later life, he or she should never attempt to invalidate Barth's theology by referring to his moral shortcomings.

What I am suggesting here is merely that Barth's Christocentric ontology does not seem to have offered him sufficient motivation for the mortification of sin. His ontological *simul* can easily leave room for excuses to remain in sin, and any good Barthian should recognize this flaw in Barth's theology and try to amend it in further theological construction. His Christocentric ontology, as it stands before further amendment, offers little *credo ut intelligam* help in making sense of the biblical command, "Be holy, for I am holy" (1 Peter 1:16; Lev. 11:45).

This is not to say, of course, that Barthian theology encourages complacency with sin or that it contradicts this

90. Hunsinger, "Two Simultaneities," 86.

91. Christiane Tietz, *Karl Barth: Ein Leben im Widerspruch* (Munich: C. H. Beck, 2019). English translation: Christiane Tietz, *Karl Barth: A Life in Conflict*, trans. Victoria Barnett (Oxford: Oxford University Press, 2021).

92. See especially Christiane Tietz, "Karl Barth and Charlotte von Kirschbaum," *Theology Today* 74 (2017): 110.

command—it does not. Yet it does not adequately encourage the quest for godliness and mortification of sin, either. As Professor Hunsinger puts it, "Barth does not eliminate entirely" the "possibility of growth and progress in the Christian life," and yet it is still an aspect of Barthian theology that needs to be more adequately developed.[93]

On this point, evangelicalism has a clear advantage over Barthianism. Of course, given its denominational diversity, evangelical theology can be legalistic in some instances and antinomian in others. However, the definitive evangelical doctrine of penal substitutionary atonement, which the late J. I. Packer famously described as "the heart of the gospel," along with the pneumatological doctrine of the application of redemption, serves as the central motivation for evangelical piety.

The salvific work of the Holy Spirit is such that he unites us to Christ through the gift of faith, not only for our justification, but also for our sanctification. Sanctification consists in spiritual renewal through repentance, and repentance hinges "upon the apprehension of God's mercy in Christ to such as are penitent," such that the sinner "so grieves for and hates his sins, as that he turns from them all to God, purposing and endeavoring constantly to walk with him in all the ways of new obedience" (Westminster Larger Catechism, 76). In his practical instructions on the mortification of sin, Owen writes: "Let faith look on Christ in the gospel as he is set forth dying and crucified for us. Look on him under the weight of our sins, praying, bleeding, dying; bring him in that condition into thy heart by faith; apply his blood so shed to thy corruptions: do this daily."[94]

Barth insists that there can be no true knowledge of sin apart from our knowledge of Christ, and Owen would agree, except

93. Hunsinger, "Two Simultaneities," 86.
94. John Owen, "Of the Mortification of Sin in Believers," in *Works*, ed. Goold, 6:85.

that Owen understands Christ's atoning work as the satisfaction of God's vindicatory justice. Towards the end of his treatise on the necessity of penal substitutionary atonement, Owen stresses that sin is revealed truly only in light of the wrath that Christ suffered on the cross. At Golgotha, it is revealed that sin, "by its most pernicious power of metamorphosing, hath transformed angels into devils, light into darkness, life into death, paradise into a desert, a pleasant, fruitful, blessed world into a vain, dark, accursed prison, and the Lord of all into a servant of servants."[95] The propitiation that Christ accomplished forbids any Mozartean attitude towards sin. Rather, it demands the most serious mortification of sin in the daily life of the believer.

Yet, it is also at Golgotha that the love of God is revealed. In his celebrated *Knowing God*, the late Dr. Packer, my beloved teacher, offers a pithy discussion of God's free love and loving freedom revealed to us through Christ's work of propitiation. He also addresses the problem of the apparent "incoherence and paradox" in the biblical author's use of words. These are themes that dominate Barth's theology as a whole, and Dr. Packer's presentation gives us a definitively evangelical view on this core subject of Christian theology. It would be befitting, then, to conclude the present volume, dedicated to Dr. Packer, with his take on the atoning love of Christ that compels us not only to mortify our sin, but also to partake of God's glory in doxology—the final purpose of evangelical theology:

> Paul prays that the readers of his Ephesian letter "may have power, together with all the saints, to grasp how wide and long and high and deep is the love of Christ, and to know this love that surpasses knowledge" (Eph. 3:18–19). The touch of incoherence and paradox in his language reflects Paul's

---

95. John Owen, "A Dissertation on Divine Justice," in *Works*, ed. Goold, 10:620.

sense that the reality of divine love is inexpressibly great; nevertheless, he believes that some comprehension of it can be reached. How?

The answer of Ephesians is, by considering propitiation in its context—that is, by reviewing the whole plan of grace set forth in the first two chapters of the letter (election, redemption, regeneration, preservation, glorification), of which plan the atoning sacrifice of Christ is the centerpiece. . . .

Christ's love was free, not elicited by any goodness in us (2:1–5); it was eternal, being one with the choice of sinners to save which the Father made "before the creation of the world" (1:4); it was unreserved, for it led him down to the depths of humiliation and, indeed, of hell itself on Calvary; and it was sovereign, for it has achieved its object—the final glory of the redeemed, their perfect holiness and happiness in the fruition of his love (5:26–27), is now guaranteed and assured (1:14; 2:7–10; 4:11–16; 4:30). Dwell on these things, Paul urges, if you would catch a sight, however dim, of the greatness and the glory of divine love. It is these things that make up "his glorious grace" (1:6); only those who know them can praise the name of the triune Jehovah as they should.[96]

---

96. Packer, *Knowing God*, 197.

GLOSSARY

absolute. Originally Hegelian term designating being "in-and-for-itself" (*an-und-für-sich*). Barth contends against Hegel that the triune God is unsublatably (see *sublation*) absolute. Appealing to the Augustinian notion of the subjectivity, objectivity, and activity of love within the immanent Trinity, Barth insists that God is absolute *a se*. He coins the terms "primary absoluteness" and "primary objectivity" (see *objectivity, primary/secondary*) to describe the freedom of God as the aseity of his eternal being in the act of love.

abstract. Technical term critically borrowed from Hegel to describe empty and meaningless subjects and predicates. Barth rejects Hegel's definition of concretion as the epitome of a universal predicate in a particular object. For Barth, God is already concrete in and for himself as the triune God. Human thinking of God becomes concrete when it corresponds to God's self-revelation in Jesus Christ. Also see *concrete*.

actualism. The philosophical program that understands "being" in terms of "activity." At the heart of Barth's mature actualism is the notion of "being-in-act" (*Sein-in-der-Tat*). His actualism is not a general program from which he proceeds to talk concretely about God. Theological speech, according to Barth, must begin concretely with God's self-revelation in Jesus Christ, and so his actualism is a function of revealed doctrine, rather than the other way around. In Jesus Christ, the electing God and elected man (see *Christ as electing God and elected man*), God reveals himself to be the God self-determined through the act of election to *become* God-for-us. This indirectly reveals to us the immanent Trinity, who is unsublatably in-and-for-himself in the *opera ad intra* of love. The Godhead is not a static substance. "There is no Godhead in itself" (*CD* II/2, 115). By this statement, Barth is not denying the immutable *essence* of the immanent Trinity. What he means is that God's immutable essence is not statically and inactively "in itself," but rather is active and relational, both in itself and for itself: "Godhead is always the Godhead of the Father, the Son and the Holy Spirit" (*CD* II/2, 115). God's essence, in other words, must be understood in light of the *opera ad intra*, which grounds and makes possible his *ad extra* act of electing to be God-for-us. Human beings made in the *image of God* are also beings determined by activities. From above, the human essence is ontologically determined by the divine act of election; from below, the human *being* (*Sein/Dasein*) is determined by particular acts, decisions, and histories of pride, sloth, and falsehood.

actual (*aktuell/wirklich*). That which is actualized, that is, made real by decisions and acts. Though "actuality" (*Wirklichkeit*) can be synonymous with "reality" (*Realität*), Barth makes "actuality" a more technical term that carries actualistic connotations. Thus, he sometimes uses *wirklich* interchangeably with *aktuell* (active, current, ongoing), a German word with its etymological origin in the Latin *actus* (act). Barth resorts to Niceno-Constantinopolitan and Augustinian Trinitarianism to contend that the immanent Trinity is fully actual in and for himself. God does not need contingent beings other than himself to actualize himself as God. He is fully actual by his immutable *opera ad intra* in his eternal being-in-act, which we come to know reflectively by thinking-after (*nachdenken*) his self-revelation in Jesus Christ. In this sense, Barth speaks of the immanent Trinity as *actus purus* (pure act). What sets him apart from Thomist philosophy is that he does not proceed from general, philosophical understandings of potentiality and actuality to deduce God's pure actuality. Rather, he begins concretely with God's self-revelation in Jesus Christ in order to think-after the truth of God's pure activity as immanent Trinity.

Adam. A universal (as opposed to particular) notion designating fallen humankind. In Barth's mature theology, the Christ-Adam dialectic is formulated in terms of election and the covenant. Adam has no independent existence apart from Christ. From the beginning (*zum Vornherein*: also meaning "*a priori*"), Adamic history has been assumed by the Son of God as his own history, the history of God-for-us and God-with-us, and so Adamic history had been (Barth intentionally uses the pluperfect) overcome by the history of God's covenant with his creatures in Jesus Christ.

after-thinking (*Nachdenken*). A crucial step in the method of speculation in the Augustinian-Anselmian tradition. This method is characterized by the faith-seeking-understanding program. Programmatically, it states that genuine knowledge begins with faith in *a priori* truth(s) that is/are self-evident. The quest for understanding proceeds by thinking-after, that is, interpreting, empirical matters of fact on the basis of faith. Then truths that are not immediately cognizable to us will be reflectively mediated to us (as in reflection from a mirror). Barth uses the terms "speculation" and "speculative" derogatively, because it had become a trademark of Cartesian-Hegelian rationalism in his intellectual-historical context. Cartesian and Hegelian speculation begins with faith in the rational human *ego* to reflectively deduce the existence of God by thinking-after phenomenal realities. Despite his rejection of this brand of speculative philosophy, Barth adopts the Augustinian-Anselmian mode of speculation that begins with faith in Jesus Christ as God incarnate, and programmatically employs the term *Nachdenken* in his writings. In his mature theology, knowledge of God begins with our faith in Christ as electing God and elected man. On this basis, we can proceed to think-after matters of fact such as the new life of the believer, the community of the elect (i.e., the reality of the church on earth), the *missio Dei* on earth, etc. Reflective after-thinking of God's acts and works *pro nobis* mediates to us knowledge of God's triune *essence* in-and-for-himself.

analogy of faith (*analogia fidei*). The *correspondence* or conformation of the understanding of the believer to the dogmatic proclamation of the church, of the proclamation of the church to Scripture, and of Scripture to Jesus Christ, the Word of God revealed. Barth's actualistic formulation of the *analogia fidei* is deeply rooted in the Anselmian program of *fides quaerens intellectum*. See *after-thinking* and *Word of God, three forms of.*

analogy of relations (*analogia relationis*). The ontological analogy between the *ad intra* relations of active love within the triune Godhead and the God-human relationship in Jesus Christ. The archetype-ectype analogy is "not . . . an *analogia entis* [analogy of being]," that is, similarity and correspondence between two nonactive and nonrelational substances, but rather an "*analogia relationis*" that "consists in the fact that the freedom in which God posits" himself as the triune God "is the same freedom as that in which he is the Creator of man, in which man may be his creature, and in which the Creator-creature relationship is established by the Creator" (*CD* III/2, 220). "In this [covenantal] relationship *ad extra*, God repeats a relationship proper to himself in his inner divine essence" (*CD* III/2, 218, rev.). The human essence is determined by this relationship in Jesus Christ, who is the very *image of God*.

a priori (*zum Vornherein*). What is true and real apart from our experiences and cognitions. Barth's use of "*zum Vornherein*" carries historicist connotations handed down from post-Kantian idealism, and so in the Torrance-Bromiley translation of the *Church Dogmatics*, it is variously rendered as "from the beginning" or "from the very first," that is, prior to the historical actualization of anything sensible and cognizable to us. Because Jesus Christ is the beginning of all God's ways and works *pro nobis* (distinct but inseparable from God-in-and-for-himself), *nothingness* is described as having been defeated *zum Vornherein* in the *history* of Jesus Christ. Grammatically, Barth insists that God's triumph over nothingness as our covenant partner in Christ—accomplished *zum Vornherein* by the sublation of reprobation in the act of election—can only be described properly in the "pluperfect tense" (*CD* IV/1, 502).

being (*Sein/Dasein*). What something *actually* is. German idealism envisions "being" as a function of "becoming": "being" is determined (see *determination*) by "becoming." Barth, in his mature theology, rejects the idealist form of *actualism*, which speaks of what a thing is in terms of its being-*as*-act. When he speaks of God's being (i.e., what God actually is), he sets forth the programmatic notion of being-*in*-act.

He retains the traditional understanding of God's triune being as an essence complete in and for itself. Meanwhile, he stresses that the triune essence is a being in the eternally active relations between the persons of the Godhead in the *opera ad intra*. God's being in-and-for-himself in his intra-Trinitarian acts is the ground upon which he can *become* (i.e., determine himself as) being-for-us without ceasing to *be* God-in-and-for-himself. The human being is also determined by activities. Essentially, the human being is essentially determined by God's act of *election* in Jesus Christ. Yet, paradoxically, the human being is also a being in the act of sin, in that it is determined from below by the sinful activities and histories of his own life and the history of his Adamic race.

bondage of the will (*servum arbitrium*). The fallen human being's actual inability not to sin, which Barth expresses by the present active indicative: *non potest non peccare*. Barth thinks (rightly or wrongly) that Augustine's notion of the bondage of the will is based on a basically Platonic meontology (the philosophical view of evil as nonbeing), which teaches that evil consists of imperfect representations of the forms that define various kinds of beings. Barth departs from Augustine when Barth claims that our good human essence, determined from above by God's covenant with us in Christ, remains totally intact and undistorted in the *status corruptionis*, and that our actual inability to sin is determined from below by the *history of Adam*. That is, the bondage is not fatalistically predetermined by the corruption of human nature, but rather is created by the ongoing actuality of sin. Also see *sin* and *nothingness*.

caprice (*Willkür*). The will's unbound and lawless power of choice. In post-Kantian philosophy, *Willkür*, which Kant defined neutrally as "choice," gradually came to designate an independent power of the will unbound by any law, be it the laws of nature or of morality. The earlier Barth holds to a voluntaristic view of God's freedom, asserting that God is above the law of noncontradiction, and that God is free even to contradict himself. The Barth of the *Church Dogmatics*, however, is emphatic that God cannot contradict himself. Resorting to the classic Reformed notions of *potentia absoluta* and *potentia ordinata*, Barth states that (1) God cannot contradict his own nature, and that (2) God cannot contradict his own will. He would say, for instance, that "God cannot be God" without being God-for-us, once God has decided to enter into covenant with his creatures in Jesus Christ (*CD* II/2, 7). Barth stresses that "there is no caprice about the freedom of God" (*CD* II/1, 358). Election is not based on God's groundless choice: it is not "the caprice of a tyrant" (*CD* II/2, 45). Rather, the relationship between the electing God and elected human in Jesus Christ is grounded in, and made possible by, the loving relations within God's triune essence, which is eternal and immutable. Also see *freedom* and *bondage of the will*.

Christocentrism. The guiding ontological (see *ontology*) principle of Barth's mature theology, which states that Jesus Christ is the beginning of all God's ways and works from and to all eternity; with the epistemological corollary that no creatures can attain to any genuine knowledge of God or of anything that is not God, apart from his self-revelation in Jesus Christ. Barth's theological ontology underwent a thoroughly Christocentric reorientation in 1936, when he identified election with the incarnation in *Gottes Gnadenwahl*. This enabled him to claim knowledge of God's immutable essence as Trinity, a knowledge mediated to us in and through Jesus Christ. The Trinitarian aspect of Barth's Christocentric ontology finds a full-blown expression in

CD II/1 under the rubric of "The Being of God as the One
Who Loves in Freedom" (§28). The all-important formula
of *Christ as electing God and elected man* in *CD* II/2 serves
to facilitate the application of the Christocentric principle
to other aspects of Barth's subsequent theology, including the doctrines of creation and reconciliation. Barth's
Christocentrism differs from that of traditional Reformed
theology: traditional Reformed Christocentrism is redemptive-historical, while Barth's Christocentrism is ontological. In Barth, all beings and nonbeings are ontologically
determined or undetermined (see *determination*) by God's
willing and nonwilling in Jesus Christ. Even God's own
being is self-determined in Christ to become God-for-us,
albeit without ceasing to be God-in-and-for-himself. Barth's
Christocentrism makes Christ's relationship to God ontologically determinative of the essence and nature of all
human beings. Also see *Christ, union with.*

Christ as electing God and elected man. A formula set forth in
CD II/2 (1942) to express the Christocentric doctrine of
election developed in *Gottes Gnadenwahl* (1936). The precise function of this formula in Barth's theological *ontology*
is among the most debated topics in contemporary Barth
studies. Although the precise wording of this formula was
set forth in *CD* II/2, the notion was already in place in
Gottes Gnadenwahl, where Barth writes: "The eternal God
and thus also the eternal Son of God is the electing God,
and the electing God is none other than the eternal God
and thus the eternal Son Himself in the communion with
the Father and the Holy Spirit, who assumed human nature
in His birth from the Virgin Mary" (p. 46). There Barth
makes it clear that the "identity" between the electing God
and Jesus Christ is not *simpliciter* valid, but rather an indirect
and mediate identity "made recognizable to us" in creaturely

form (p. 45). Barth not only maintains this position, but also makes it even clearer and more emphatic in 1942: "As the Son of the Father He has no need of any special election" (*CD* II/2, 103). When Barth says that God the Son *is* the elected human, the word "is" refers to God's being-in-becoming. God the Son is *simpliciter* God with the Father and the Holy Spirit, and *secundum quid* the elected man as electing God. By the same token, Jesus Christ is *secundum quid* the electing God by virtue of the identity of God's eternal counsel with our time. Election does not determine what God is in-and-for-himself. Rather, God's essence as Father, Son, and Holy Spirit grounds and makes possible his act of electing to become God-for-us. Also see *Christocentrism*.

Christ, threefold office of. Christ's office as priest, king, and prophet, which he exercises in the accomplishment of the work of reconciliation. Barth adopts the classic Reformed formula of Christ's threefold office as the framework in which he develops the doctrine of reconciliation. *CD* IV/1 focuses on Christ's priestly office, which Barth unfolds under the rubric of "Jesus Christ, the Lord as Servant" (chapter 14, §§59–63); *CD* IV/2 expounds Christ's royal office in a chapter titled "Jesus Christ, the Servant as Lord" (chapter 15, §§64–68); *CD* IV/3 treats Christ's prophetic office under the title "Jesus Christ, the True Witness" (chapter 16, §§69–73). The highly pneumatological nature of Barth's doctrine of reconciliation reflects his Reformed heritage and his application of the *extra Calvinisticum*: Christ's earthly ministry was not an exercise of his *genus maiestaticum* as Son, but rather the power of the *Holy Spirit* poured out upon him.

Christ, union with. The essential reality of all creation, established by God's gracious election, an eternal act of God *in Christo* that ontologically determines the covenantal relationship of God to all creatures and all creatures to God. The person and work of Jesus Christ, according to Barth, comprises at once a person in whom two natures are inseparably united with abiding distinction (as traditionally understood), as well as a history of active relationship between the electing God and elected man. This ectypal relationship corresponds perfectly to the archetypal relations of love within the immanent Trinity (see *analogy of relations*). Jesus Christ is the very image of God in this relational sense, and all human beings are created in this image to partake of Christ's essential relationship to God. This makes our union with Christ an ontological reality accomplished from all eternity, and the existential aspect of this reality is actualized in the here-and-now by the Holy Spirit's reenactments of Christ's perfectly accomplished work. In the Christological dimension, all creatures are ontologically united to Christ by God's eternal election, and thus justified from all eternity. In the pneumatological dimension, we are existentially united to Christ by faith alone, and thus justified by faith alone. The Christological dimension of *unio Christi* does not render the pneumatological redundant or unnecessary. Barth is unequivocal in both *Gottes Gnadenwahl* and *CD* IV/2 that one's present lack of faith, which consists in the actual refusal to live one's life in accordance with one's ontological union with Christ, actualistically corresponds to a final condemnation on Judgment Day, where there will be a separation of the elect from the reprobate. Also see *Christocentrism*.

Church. The form of the one community of the elect summoned to faith in Jesus Christ to represent God's mercy. Under the rubric of "The Election of the Community" (*CD* II/2, §34), Barth sets forth the definitive elements of his ecclesiology. The eternal election of the man Jesus Christ and of all God's elect *in Christo* is historically actualized by the Holy Spirit's work of faith *in nobis* to accomplish the election of the community. The "election of the many" is "included" in the election of the one Jesus Christ (*CD* II/2, 195), and as such these are not two separate elections. The election of the community is the historical reenactment of the eternal election of Jesus Christ: these are two distinct yet inseparable aspects of one and the same act of divine election. The historical election of the community is represented in two forms at two different stages. Israel is the form that serves to represent God's judgment; the church, God's mercy. These are not two separate communities, but rather two temporal forms of the same community, testifying to the world the *sublation* of God's judgment by his mercy in the eternal election of Jesus Christ. The primary duty and mission of the church is to proclaim Christ's work of reconciliation that fulfills God's eternal covenant with us (*CD* IV/3, §§71–72). Because the church is a special community of the elect, summoned by the Holy Spirit, her proclamation of and witness to Jesus Christ is a form of the Word of God endowed with regulative authority over individual Christian proclamations, theologizing, and biblical interpretations (see *Word of God, three forms of*).

conceptual necessity (*Denknotwendigkeit*). (Neo-)Kantian term referring to the logical consequences drawn necessarily from the application of analytic judgments to nonempirical concepts or ideas. Analytic judgments, according to Kant, are propositions in which the predicate is already included in the subject (e.g., "All boys are male"). An analytic judgment serves to clarify the concept or idea that it analyzes, but does not demonstrate the existence of the object or type of objects corresponding to the concept or idea. Hegel's absolute idealism is partly aimed at arguing that the existence of God is a conceptual necessity. Barth consistently refuses to reduce dogmatics to a system of conceptual necessities. Meanwhile, he also insists against neo-Kantianism that theology constructed on the basis of empirical objectivity (see *empirical object*) can never consist of genuine knowledge of God, because God transcends the sensible world. Theology, as the science of God, insists Barth, consists of reflective *after-thinking* (*Nachdenken*) of the self-revelation of the transcendent God in the immanent world. From 1936 onward, Barth's *credo ut intelligam* reflections consistently started with Jesus Christ, the electing God and elected man (see *Christ as electing God and elected man*). God's eternal election to be God-for-us is neither a "conceptual necessity" nor an "empirical object," but rather the "truth of revelation [*Offenbarungswahrheit*]. . . . More concretely: it is biblical truth. With complete concreteness: it is truth in Jesus Christ" (*Gottes Gnadenwahl*, 11–13).

concrete. Technical term critically borrowed from Hegel to describe the particularity of God's being and activity. Hegel contrasts the concrete to the abstract. The term "abstract" describes an indeterminate (see *determination*) object in our conception. Hegel uses "concrete" to describe the consummate unity between particulars and the universal, and envisions God as the concrete universal. God, according to Hegel, becomes concrete through the historical process of self-determination. Barth insists against Hegel that God is concrete and determinate in and for himself as the triune God, prior to and apart from any *ad extra* activity of self-determination. This particular God, who is self-revealed in Jesus Christ as Father, Son, and Holy Spirit, is not the universal concept of divinity that philosophy and religion seek to explicate. Human understanding of this particular God becomes concrete only when it finds its *credo* *ut intelligam* starting point in faith in Jesus Christ, the God self-determined to become God-for-us without ceasing to be God-in-and-for-himself.

correspondence (*Entsprechung*). Actualistic analogy, that is, archetype-ectype analogy in the form of acts, relations, decisions, and histories. God's act of electing to be God-for-us in Jesus Christ is an act that corresponds perfectly to God's *opera ad intra*. The relationship between the electing God and elected man in Jesus Christ corresponds perfectly to the loving relationship immanent in the triune Godhead (see *analogy of relations*). God's patience in the time that he has for us in Jesus Christ corresponds perfectly to the eternal time that God has in and for himself. The Holy Spirit's activation of faith and obedience *in nobis* corresponds to the already accomplished work of Christ *extra nos*. Believers are called to live their *actual* lives in correspondence to their essential being *in Christo*.

constitutive principle. Technical term critically borrowed from (neo-)Kantianism to refer to a postulate that we can ascertain by reason, so long as this postulate provides a certain determinate condition that is absolutely necessary for what we know to be true and real. A constitutive principle is contrasted to a *regulative principle*. In Kant, God, as the ideal of pure reason, remains a regulative principle in the theoretical use of reason (the inquiry of reason into "what is") and becomes immanent and constitutive only in the practical use of reason (the inquiry of reason into "what ought to be"). Barth appropriates these two (neo-) Kantian terms and places them within an Anselmian program of *fides quaerens intellectum*. In this epistemological program, the regulative principle is the *regula fidei* that serves as the starting point of any genuine knowledge of God in relation or nonrelation to everything that is not God. "The doctrine of predestination," for instance, "is not a constitutive principle, but rather a regulative one" (*Gottes Gnadenwahl*, 35). The subjection of our knowledge and knowing to the *regula fidei* gives rise to what Kant would call theoretical knowledge of God, that is, knowledge of the *God is*. Barth's identification of the articles of faith as regulative rather than constitutive principles serves to underscore his rejection of absolute idealism, which avers that human reason can know God with absolute logical certainty.

covenant. The pact that God made with humankind to be *pro nobis* by his gracious Yes in Jesus Christ, who is himself the covenant maker as the electing God and covenant receiver as elected man. The covenant is anchored in the eternal election of Jesus Christ and enacted in the Adamic world in the form of a *history*. The covenantal history of God and humankind in Jesus Christ determines the very *essence* of all God's creatures made in his image (see *image of God*). In *CD* III/2, §45, Barth spells out the notion that humankind is ontologically determined to be God's covenant partner. As the Lord of this covenant, God confronts on our behalf the *nothingness* that threatens to dissolve our ontological relationship to God. God carries out the history of the covenant in this world by his providential works of preservation, accompaniment, and government (*CD* III/3, §§49–50). Barth's entire discourse on creation and providence is based on the paradigmatic formulation of "creation as the external basis of the covenant" and "the covenant as the internal basis of creation" (*CD* III/1, §41). This formula conveys the actualistic understanding that creation is the stage on which the eternal covenant made in Jesus Christ is historically enacted, and that the history of the covenant is the very rationality, the rational *telos*, of world history. This paradigmatic formula can be applied to all aspects of Creator-creature relationships in Barth's actualistic ontology. Golgotha, for instance, can be understood as the external basis of election, and election the internal basis of the crucifixion.

creation. The outward basis on which the *covenant* is actualized. Creation is a work of God *ad extra*, and as such it is not an emanation of God's essence and possesses no divine nature. However, the work corresponds (see *correspondence*) perfectly to God's eternal election to be our covenant Lord in Jesus Christ, and this eternal act of God *ad extra* corresponds perfectly to his *ad intra* essence as the triune God. Creation is thus ontologically determined to be preserved, accompanied, and governed by the Creator on the terms of the covenant made in Jesus Christ. Barth insists that the doctrine of creation "is a doctrine of faith" (*CD* III/1, 4). It is the church's confession of God "as the Creator of heaven and earth," and the truth of *creatio ex nihilo* that it entails is an article of the *regula fidei* that "cannot be known by the light of nature" (*CD* III/1, 4). The truth of *creatio ex nihilo* is of course not immediately clear from the biblical texts. Rather, it stems from the Christian confession that God alone is transcendent as the Creator, that everything other than God is a creature, and that there is not a third kind of beings that is neither God nor creature. The traditional Augustinian understanding of *creatio ex nihilo* is necessary to exclude its "antithesis—the mythological acceptance of a primeval reality independent of God," even though Barth rejects the differentiation between form and matter in the tradition (*CD* III/1, 103). The most definitive element in Barth's doctrine of creation is the formulation of "creation as the external basis of the covenant" and "the covenant as the internal basis of creation" (*CD* III/1, §41). See *covenant*. For the creation of humankind, see *image of God*.

creation, shadow side of. An aspect of the good order of God's creation, alongside the brighter side. The shadow side (*Schattenseite*) of creation pertains to the good order of God's handiwork and is not to be confused with the chaotic darkness that Genesis 1:2 sets forth. In *CD* III/1, Barth speaks of the frontier between light and darkness, life and death, and the brighter and darker sides of human existence, as the good ordinance of God's creation. In *CD* IV/2, §65, "The Sloth and Misery of Man," Barth explains that nothingness arises from the shadow side of creation when the sinner refuses to stand with Christ as victors at the frontier. Natural death as the "approaching shadow of the frontier" is not itself a form of nothingness (*CD* IV/2, 469). Nothingness in the form of death refers to the natural death that actually becomes a threat to our covenant relationship in Jesus Christ when we refuse to embrace this death with Christ on the cross. It is in this sense that God says No to the shadow that has and presently continues to become a form of nothingness through the sinful acts and decisions of humankind.

decretum absolutum. Jesus Christ as the absolute decree of God in the act of election, in which reprobation is posited and sublated (see *sublation*). In historic Reformed theology, *decretum absolutum* refers to God's double decree of election and reprobation. Barth reinterprets double predestination using the Hegelian grammar of sublation. Reprobation is the negation of sin and nothingness—of humankind's No to God's ways and works. God's No to nothingness serves the purpose of his Yes to his creatures. God's eternal decree is thus the sublation of reprobation in the election of Jesus Christ. Barth trades on the Hegelian connotations of the term "*absolute,*" defined as being in-and-for-oneself. God is absolute as immanent Trinity, and the *decretum ad extra* that he made in Jesus Christ to become God-for-us is grounded in and made possible by his being in-and-for-himself. Because Jesus Christ is himself the electing God, and the electing God-for-us and the triune God-in-and-for-himself is one and the same God, Jesus Christ is, *secundum quid*, the absolute decree of God.

determination (*Bestimmung*). Technical term critically borrowed from Hegel to refer to the act and process of establishing or receiving the defining characteristics of a thing (i.e., its essential nature) by entering into relationship with otherness. The Leibnizian-Wolffian tradition before Hegel tended to speak of determination in the nominal infinitive, *das Bestimmen*, and Kant also adopted this usage. Hegel transformed the architectonic notion of *Bestimmen* into an organic notion of *Bestimmung* to convey the view that truth and reality are not characterized by being and nonbeing (*is* and *is not*), but rather by the dialectical process of establishing or receiving essential natures through active relationships with otherness. Barth rejects Hegel's view that God needs the world as an other in order to determine himself as God, but he critically adopts the Hegelian grammar of "determination" as an overarching notion supporting the construct of his actualistic ontology. A determination, according to Barth, qualifies but does not constitute an entity's nature or essence. In the case of God, Barth stresses against Hegel that the triune essence is determinate in and for itself, apart from and prior to any *ad extra* activity or process. In the case of humankind, Barth says that the human essence (*Wesen*) is determined from above (*von oben*) by the history of God's covenant with his creatures, grounded in the election of Jesus Christ. There is, however, a second and nonessential determination of the human being (*Sein/Dasein*), namely, a determination from below (*von unten*) by the history of Adamic sin.

dialectics. The manner of intellectual inquiry that seeks to
uncover the truth by considering mutually opposing voices.
Barth's theology is dialectical in a wide variety of ways.
The Hegelian dialectic of *sublation*, for instance, features
prominently in Barth's Christocentric reformulation of the
historic Reformed doctrine of double predestination in
Gottes Gnadenwahl and *CD* II/2. In *CD* III/3, he adopts
the Kierkegaardian dialectic of possibility and impossibility
to speak of sin as an absurd "impossible possibility," a term
that he stopped using after *Romans* II, in which God's activities in this world are described as "impossible possibilities."
If there is one overarching dialectic everywhere applicable
in Barth's mature theology, it is the Chalcedonian dialectic
of inseparable union and abiding distinction, which can be
expressed by the classic formula "God became human without ceasing to be God."

divine accompaniment (*concursus Dei*). See *providence*.

divine preservation (*preservatio Dei*). See *providence*.

divine ruling (*gubernatio Dei*). See *providence*.

double predestination. See *decretum absolutum*.

election. God's eternal self-determination to be God-for-us in,
by, and through the incarnation. Barth's Christocentric
doctrine of election, developed in 1936, lies at the heart
of his actualistic ontology (see *ontology*). Having identified election as God's eternal (see *eternity*) decision to
become incarnate, Barth comes to insist that the truth of
election must be reflected point by point by thinking-after
(see *after-thinking*) the history of Jesus Christ as what the
Reformers called *speculum electionis* (mirror of election).
Christ took on sinful flesh to be forsaken by God at the
cross, and the negation of sin at Golgotha led to Christ's
resurrection as a declaration of our justification before God.
The path Christ traversed in our history reveals an eternal

sequentiality in the divine act of predestination: reprobation is the negation of sin, and election is the *sublation* of
reprobation. Also see *actualism, Christocentrism, Christ as
electing God and elected human,* and *decretum absolutum.*

empirical object (*Erfahrungsgegenstand*). Technical term critically borrowed from (neo-)Kantianism to refer to humanly
cognizable objects in the sensible world conditioned by
spatio-temporality. Barth stresses that God's eternal essence
and activity transcend the sensible world, and so they cannot be objects of experience. We can only come to indirect
and mediated knowledge of God's eternal *essence* and activity by thinking-after (see *after-thinking*) his works in the
sensible and mutable world. In Jesus Christ, God became
an immanent object of experience without ceasing to be the
immutable God who transcends the humanly cognizable
world. Also see *conceptual necessity* (*Denknotwendigkeit*).

essence (*Wesen*). What a thing is prior to external acts, decisions,
and histories. "Essence" is distinguished from both *"nature"*
(*Natur*) and *"being"* (*Sein/Dasein*). Barth notes that in Latin
theology, "the essence [*das Wesen*] of God is the being [*Sein*]
of God as divine being" (*CD* I/1, 349). The word *"essentia"*
primarily signifies something concrete and actual. Only in a
derivative sense does *"essentia"* refer to *"nature"* (*natura*) as
the formal cause of a certain kind of things. Barth follows the
Latin convention and uses *Wesen* as the German rendering
of *"essentia."* However, he adds to this notion an actualistic
dimension. God's triune essence is complete in and for itself,
prior to *ad extra* activities, in that within this essence is an
endless encounter of persons in the act of love. The human
essence is not complete in and for itself, and yet it is still
complete apart from and prior to the human being's activities in history, for it is determined *a priori* by the history and
activity of Jesus Christ, who is the very *image of God.*

eternity. The uncreated time of God-in-and-for-himself and the time he self-determined to have for us in Jesus Christ prior to the creation of our time. On the one hand, Barth agrees with the historic Western definition of eternity as timelessness and successionlessness, in the sense that eternity transcends fleeting temporality. On the other hand, Barth stresses that in another sense, eternity "is not in any way timeless" (*CD* III/1, 67). He speaks of eternity as "God's time": "as the source of [creaturely] time," eternity "is supreme and absolute time" (*CD* III/1, 67). In speaking of "absolute" time, Barth has in mind the Trinitarian notion of God-in-and-for-himself (see *absolute*). Within the triune essence there is endless and immutable activity or interaction, namely, the *opera ad intra* of the Trinity. Activity involves time and process, and, in this sense, we can speak of an eternal and immutable time within the triune Godhead. There is also some sense of succession or sequence—of past, future, and present—within the "supreme and absolute time," though this unfathomable time ought to consist of "the immediate unity of present, past and future; of now, once and then; of the center, beginning and end; of movement, origin and goal" (*CD* III/1, 67). This temporal tri-unity is "the essence of God" (*CD* III/1, 67). In this sense, "God is Himself eternity" (*CD* III/1, 67). Barth describes this Trinitarian understanding of eternity in the Boethian grammar of *simultaneity*: as "the Eternal," God is "simultaneously before time, above time, and after time" (*CD* III/1, 67). Eternity as God's time is the "prototype" of creaturely time (*CD* III/1, 67). In contradistinction to eternity, creaturely time, as the "form of the existence of the creature," consists of "the one-way sequence and therefore the succession and division of past, present, and future" (*CD* III/1, 67–68).

faith. See *justification by faith*.

fall of humanity. The beginning of world history as a result of Adamic pride. Following the Augustinian tradition, Barth states that "the fall of man … comes in and with the pride of man": "he falls in exalting himself where he ought not to try to exalt himself, where, according to the grace of God, he might in humility be freely and truly man" (*CD* IV/1, 478). Humankind fell into a state of corruption (*status corruptionis*). This is not a corruption of the good essence created by God, as Augustinian meontology would have it. The good essence of the human creature, according to Barth, remains intact and undistorted in the state of fallenness. This good *essence* (*Wesen*) is determined (see *determination*) from above by God's covenant with us in Jesus Christ, and sin is totally foreign to our essence—it is an ontological impossibility. The *status corruptionis* is a second determination of the existential human being (*Sein/Dasein*) by the actual sins of Adam's race in world history. The human being is simultaneously determined from above and from below, by the history of the covenant and the history of corruption. Both determinations are total with regard to the existential human being at present, but only the determination from above is ontological and essential. The determination from below has no ontological status—it is mere *nothingness* (*das Nichtige*: that which is not). Nothingness, however, is actual. It has the power to determine the existential state of the human being at present, leading to actual sins in the forms of sloth and falsehood. The falsehood of the sinner, moreover, corresponds to a present state determined not by the history of fallenness from below, but by the prospect of God's condemnation from the future. It is thus untrue that Barth's Christocentric ontology renders the doctrine of the fall redundant and meaningless, as if fallenness would have no eschatological bearing on any of God's creatures.

fides quaerens intellectum. See *after-thinking, analogy of faith,* and *regulative principle.*

freedom. In the primary sense, to be what one truly is; in the secondary sense, the correspondence of *ad extra* decisions and acts to *ad intra* essence. God is free in the primary sense of being *a se*: as the triune God, he is love in-and-for-himself prior to his loving relationship with us. He is free in the secondary sense that his love *pro nobis* corresponds perfectly to his love *a se*. The human creature is free when his will and actions conform to his ontological essence determined *in Christo*, which is an essence to be for God as God is for us. Following the Augustinian-Kantian tradition, Barth differentiates between freedom and *caprice*.

God. All that God is in Jesus Christ, which is one and the same as, albeit abidingly distinct from, all that God is in and for himself as Father, Son, and Holy Spirit. Failure to appreciate the basically Chalcedonian character of Barth's mature theology has led some of his supporters, as well as some of his critics, to think that he rejects divine attributes such as immutability, impassibility, and pure actuality, as in the classic doctrine of God. Barth is unequivocal in the Christocentric revision of his theological ontology in 1936, that "the immutability of God cannot be questioned whatsoever" (*Gottes Gnadenwahl*, 47). However, human cognition and knowledge are conditioned by spatio-temporality. In our "human mutability," we can only perceive God's "act" in historical actuality: "we have to gaze upon God's immutability in human mutability" (*Gottes Gnadenwahl*, 48). Yet, we do know by faith that Jesus Christ *is* God, and so by faith and "only by faith can we speak about God's immutability and faithfulness and identity," the identity between the *Deus absconditus* and *Deus revelatus* (*Gottes Gnadenwahl*, 48).

historiography (*Historie*). The scientific, critical study of *history*

(*Geschichte*) that arose in the post-Kantian era. Barth is severely critical of the hubris of the modern historian who thinks that historical criticism, with all its positivistic and naturalistic assumptions, is capable of objectively interpreting historical events in ways that the ancient authors of Scripture could not. For Barth, there can be no objective interpretation of history apart from revelation, and God alone possesses an ultimately objective view of history.

history (*Geschichte*). Events that happened in time, be it the supreme and absolute time of God (see *eternity*), the time of God's creatures (see *time of humankind*), or God's time for us in Jesus Christ that is a union of the two times (see *time of Jesus Christ*). Barth differentiates between *Historie* and *Geschichte*, but makes no systematic dichotomy between them. *Historie* refers to human interpretation of the history of this world, and Barth usually uses the term to refer to modern historiography. World history (*Weltgeschichte*) is the transient history of the world fallen *in Adamis*, and the historian—ancient or modern—is incapable of any genuinely objective interpretation of world history, for world history is ontologically determined (see *determination*) by the history of God's covenant with us in Jesus Christ. The *Geschichte* of Jesus Christ as God's time for us is the *assumptio* of Adamic history by God the Son from the eternal *Geschichte* of God's loving *opera ad intra*. Only the believer, who is essentially a theologian, regardless of his trade, who after-thinks (see *after-thinking*) historical phenomena with a starting point of faith in Jesus Christ, can participate, in a creaturely form by the work of the Holy Spirit, in God's objective knowledge of world history.

Holy Spirit. Agent of the triune Godhead, whose primary work is to reenact here and now, in secondary and dependent forms, the work Christ accomplished perfectly there and then. The volumes prior to *CD* IV everywhere presuppose the work of the Holy Spirit, though in these volumes Barth does not bring the Holy Spirit to the foreground nearly as often as he does Jesus Christ. In *CD* IV, however, the role of the Holy Spirit in the work of reconciliation dominates nearly half of the text. According to Barth's mature theology, the actualization of our covenant relationship with God, determined *a priori* (*zum Vornherein*) by the election of Jesus Christ and fulfilled by the *work* of *reconciliation*, hinges *completely* upon the reenactment of Christ's grace *extra nos* by the renewing work of the Holy Spirit *in nobis*. More simply, what Christ accomplished in his finished and perfect work of salvation there and then, the Holy Spirit actualizes in us here and now in a secondary and dependent form. The Holy Spirit's work is especially prominent in Barth's discourse on the *missio Dei* in *CD* IV/3, even before the pneumatological paragraphs (§§71–73).

image of God (*imago Dei*). Jesus Christ as the relational ectype of God's triune essence, which determines the similarity and correspondence between God's relational essence and ours. Barth defines essence in terms of acts and relations, and so the *imago Dei* cannot be the analogy between two non-active and non-relational substances. Rather, Jesus Christ is the very *imago Dei*. "The term 'image'" refers to "a correspondence and similarity between the two relationships," namely, "the relationship within the being of God on the one side" and "between the being of God and that of man on the other" (*CD* III/2, 220). The human essence is determined from above by the God-human relationship in Jesus Christ, who is the image of God. Christ the electing God is for himself as the elected man, and he as the elected man is for himself as electing God. Human beings created in his image as such are ontologically determined to be for

God, as God is *pro nobis* in Jesus Christ. Also see *analogy of relations.*

immediacy [*Unmittelbarkeit*]. Without mediation. Barth uses this term in the context of post-Kantian idealism and romanticism. Barth insists that human knowledge of God is necessarily indirect and mediated, and from the Christocentric reorientation of his doctrine of election in 1936 onward, he would consistently maintain that knowledge of God's eternal being and act is mediated to us in and by none other than Jesus Christ.

incarnation. The Son's becoming human without ceasing to be God; the actualization of God's self-determination to be God-for-us and God-with-us, grounded in and made possible by God's being in-and-for-himself; the process in and by which the electing God becomes one with the elected man in Jesus Christ. The mature Barth adopts a basically Chalcedonian understanding of the incarnation as the anhypostatic-enhypostatic union of two natures in one person. He adds to Chalcedonian Christology actualistic, historicist, and relational dimensions that are characteristically modern. For instance, he speaks of the *time of Jesus Christ* as the *assumptio* of our time by the time of God. Also see *Christ as electing God and elected man* and *Christocentrism.*

justification by faith. The imputation of righteousness and nonimputation of sin by our ontological union with Christ. Whereas historic Reformed theology speaks of our mystical union with Christ, the formal cause of our justification, as an existential reality established by faith as the instrumental cause of justification wrought by the Holy Spirit *in nobis,* Barth envisions union with Christ (see *Christ, union with*) and thus our justification in him as an ontological reality. While Barth retains the key terms in the Protestant doctrine of justification, he does not use the scholastic language of causality. He replaces this metaphysical vocabulary with personalist terms (see *personalism*): "the crucified and risen Jesus Christ ... lives as the author and recipient and revealer of the justification of all men" (*CD* IV/1, 629). With the Reformed tradition, Barth stresses that Christ alone justifies, and that faith is merely an "empty vessel" (*CD* IV/1, 628) and a "vacuum" (*CD* IV/1, 630). Faith is not merely noetic. Faith is a "real apprehension of [our] real being in Christ" (*CD* IV/1, 636). Therefore, "even in its emptiness and passivity, justifying faith has this character of supreme fullness and activity" (*CD* IV/1, 636). The character of fullness and activity is "proper to [faith]," only "because Jesus Christ is ... its author and finisher, and therefore the One who forms it" (*CD* IV/1, 615). Faith was originally wrought in Christ by the *Holy Spirit*, and the same Spirit repeats (see *repetition*) *in nobis* the work that faith accomplished perfectly *in Christo*. What Christ accomplished in his finished and perfect work of justification there and then, the Holy Spirit actualizes in us here and now in a secondary and dependent form. The event of our justification, though *a priori* (*zum Vornherein*) accomplished *in Christo* from the beginning of all God's ways and works, does not *become* a fully actualized reality until we actually believe in Christ by the work of the Holy Spirit *in nobis*.

love. The dynamic triune essence that God freely is in-and-for-himself, and the creaturely essence that God repeated (see *repetition*) *ad extra* in Jesus Christ. Following the Augustinian tradition, Barth states that love consists of the lover, the beloved, and the act of love. God's love *pro nobis* in Jesus Christ mediates to us the knowledge of God's love as the triune God *a se*. The freedom of God must be understood in terms of God's love in-and-for-himself and his love for us. Creaturely love is made in the *image of God*, and Jesus

Christ is this very image. The theme of God's love and freedom undergirds Barth's doctrine of election and governs all
aspects of his mature theology. Also see *actualism, freedom,
Trinity (immanent)*, and *objectivity (primary and secondary)*.

nature (*natura*). The formal-causal attributes of God and various
kinds of things that are not God, determined by concrete
activities. Barth retains the traditional Latin definition of
natura as formal-causal attributes. He never completely historicized or actualized the category of nature to eliminate
its substantialistic and essentialistic dimension. Even as late
as *CD* IV/2, he would continue to speak of "human nature"
as "quite simply that which makes a man a man as distinct
from God, angel or animal . . . his *humanitas*" (*CD* IV/2,
25). However, he adds to this substantialistic dimension
an actualistic one. God's faithfulness, for instance, is not an
abstract attribute, but an attribute of the concrete relations
and acts of love within the triune essence. Similarly, human
nature is determined actualistically by the history of God's
covenant with us in Jesus Christ.

natural theology. The metaphysical study of God with a starting
point in *a posteriori* cognitions and concepts. Barth's use of
the term "natural theology" is heavily informed by Kant,
who distinguishes between transcendental and natural theologies. Whereas transcendental theology appeals to pure
reason alone, natural theology resorts to experience. Natural
theology as such, according to Kant, cannot be truly theological on its own, for apart from transcendental concepts,
it ultimately reduces God to nature. Barth adopts this Kantian view of natural theology, and thinks that German idealism after Kant, as Feuerbach has disclosed, is guilty of the
idolatry of natural theology. Instead of jettisoning the entire
enterprise of natural theology, however, Barth salvages it by
denying its status as *praeambula fidei* and bringing it under

the *regulative principle* of the articles of faith in a basically Anselmian program of *fides quaerens intellectum.*

nothingness (*das Nichtige*). That which is not, actual in the forms of sin, evil, and death. The English translation is admittedly misleading (*CD* III/3, 289: see editor's note). It is not meant to convey the quality of nonexistence: it is not *die Nichtigkeit* or *das Nichts* (*CD* III/3, 349). He chooses the unusual term "*das Nichtige,*" and gives it the "definitions and delimitations, of 'that which is not'" (*CD* III/3, 289n2). It is not God; it is not God's creature. Everything that *is*, however, is either God or God's creature; there is not a third type of being. Thus, nothingness cannot be identified. It negates both the Creator and the creature, and has been negated by God. The term "nothingness," then, is not even a meontological one, but a thoroughly apophatic one. Barth follows through with his Christocentric principle (see *Christocentrism*) and proposes to explicate the reality of nothingness in light of Golgotha. Sin is that form of nothingness whereby the creature resists God's gracious Yes. Nothingness consists of *actual* negations of our covenantal essence determined in Jesus Christ, and thus of the good ordinance of God's creation. Nothingness in the form of death, in particular, arises when we refuse to stand with Christ at the frontier facing the shadow side of creation and embrace natural death as God's gracious ordinance in Jesus Christ (see *creation, shadow side of*).

objectivism. Theological motif undergirding Barth's theology, namely, the conviction that the event of Jesus Christ is an objective one that occurred *extra nos*—outside the subjective sphere of our knowledge and experience. See chapter 2 for more details.

objectivity (*Gegeständlichkeit*), *primary and secondary.* The presence of an object of love within the triune Godhead (primary objectivity) and the presence of an object of God's love *ad extra* in Jesus Christ (secondary objectivity). See *actualism, freedom, love,* and *Trinity, immanent.*

ontology. The study of, or any discourse on, the notion of being. George Hunsinger issues the caveat that we must distinguish between two senses in which the term is used. In a more general sense, ontology refers to any discourse on the notion of being, and in this sense we can speak of Barth's theological ontology as "actualistic," "Christocentric," and what not. However, ontology can also refer to a mode of metaphysical inquiry that begins with a universal and programmatic definition of "being," to which the concept of God is tailored. In this sense, Barth's theology is antiontological and antimetaphysical. Also see *metaphysics.*

overflow (*Überfluß*). Originally Platonist term that Barth adopted through the Augustinian tradition to describe the actualistic *correspondence* between the love that God essentially is in the primary objectivity of the triune Godhead and the love of God *pro nobis* in Jesus Christ. The overflow is not a substantial emanation. Rather, the love that overflows from God's inward essence is an *ad extra* act corresponding perfectly to God's *opera ad intra.* In CD II/2, Barth describes the election of Jesus Christ as the overflow of God's love, defined in terms of God's primary and secondary objectivities set forth in CD II/1 (see *freedom, love,* and *objectivity, primary and secondary*). In CD III/2, Barth describes the overflow as an *analogy of relations* (*analogia relationis*): the loving relationship between God and humankind in Jesus Christ is an ectype of the archetypal love within God's triune essence.

participatio Christi. See *Christ, union with.*

particularism. Barth's "concerted attempt always to move from the particular to the general rather than from the general to the particular" (George Hunsinger, *How to Read Barth*, 32). After the Christocentric reorientation of his doctrine of election in 1936, it was guided by "an almost ruthless particularity, a concentration of the imagination on one point and one point only: the name of Jesus, his absolute specific as 'this one,' the first and the last and the most simple thing" (John Webster, *Karl Barth*, 62). See chapter 2 for more details.

personalism. The relationalist dimension of Barth's ontology that emphasizes interpersonal encounters. See *justification by faith* for an example. See chapter 2 for more details.

providence. God's covenantal work of preserving, accompanying, and ruling over creation. Barth retrieved the originally Lutheran construct of *preservatio, concursus,* and *gubernatio* from the orthodox Continental Reformed tradition. Under the threat of deism and pantheism in early modern Continental philosophy, Reformed theologians in the seventeenth century made *concursus* the underlying principle of both *preservatio* and *gubernatio.* Simply put, *concursus Dei* refers to how every event in this world is totally the result of natural causation and totally the work of God's own hand. Barth sees the two major strains of liberal theology—neo-Kantianism and metaphysical idealism—as intellectual descendants of early modern deism and pantheism, and so he finds in the classic Reformed formulation of providence powerful answers to theological liberalism. He incorporates the *totus-totus* grammar of the *concursus* into his Christocentric ontology: all events in world history are totally determined from above by the history of God's covenant in Jesus Christ and from below by the history of Adam's sin. God preserves and rules over creation by accompanying creation in the *time of Jesus Christ* as the union of two times.

regulative principle. Technical term critically borrowed from (neo-)Kantianism to refer to a logical and ontological starting point that, among other possible starting points, directs the understanding to the highest degree of unity and coherence. Barth rejects the (neo-)Kantian position that we can never ascertain—not even by a *reductio ad absurdum*—the validity or actuality of a regulative principle. He redefines "regulative principle" as the *regula fidei* in the Anselmian program of *fides quaerens intellectum*. This allows him to claim what Kant would call "theoretical" knowledge of God (i.e., knowledge of the *God is*), which Kant distinguishes from the practical (i.e., knowledge that God ought to be). Also see *constitutive principle*.

reconciliation. The fulfillment of God's covenant with humankind in Jesus Christ, God-with-us. Reconciliation is the work of God as God-with-us, and it presupposes the covenant that God made with us in Jesus Christ. "The fellowship which originally existed between God and man, which was then disturbed and jeopardized, the purpose of which is now fulfilled in Jesus Christ in the work of reconciliation, we describe as the covenant" (*CD* IV/1, 22). Christ accomplished the work of reconciliation in his threefold office as priest (*CD* IV/1, chapter 14, §§59–63), king (*CD* IV/2, chapter 15, §§64–68), and prophet (*CD* IV/3, chapter 16, §§69–73) (see *Christ, threefold office of*). Through the dynamic work of the Holy Spirit, who repeats the otherwise unrepeatable work of Christ accomplished *once and for all*, the reconciliation between God and sinners perfectly established in Jesus Christ takes place in our lives *again and again, more and more*, until he comes.

repetition (*Wiederholung*). Actualistic term referring to ecytypal acts and works of God corresponding (see *correspondence*) to respective archetypes. The God-human relationship that God created in Jesus Christ, for instance, is an *ad extra* repetition of the essential relationship within the triune Godhead. The election of the community is a present repetition of the eternal election of Jesus Christ. The crucifixion is a repetition of reprobation, while the resurrection is a repetition of election. What Christ perfectly accomplished there and then, the Holy Spirit repeats here and now in a secondary and dependent form.

reprobation. God's No to sin and nothingness, sublated (see *sublation*) in God's gracious election of Jesus Christ. Reprobation is actualized in the person of Christ upon the cross, where he became the one reprobate man in the stead of all others. See *Christ as electing God and elected man, condemnation, decretum absolutum,* and *election.*

resurrection of Christ. The work of the Holy Spirit in raising Jesus to life from the dead, "bodily, visibly, audibly, perceptibly, in the same concrete sense in which He died" (*CD* IV/1, 351–52). The resurrection has to be an *articulus fidei.* It is not a *praeambula fidei* that the allegedly neutral historian is capable of verifying or falsifying. Faith in the resurrection is a starting point in our attempt to understand world history as a history taken up by God himself in the *history of Jesus Christ.* The resurrection is crucial to Barth's doctrine of *reconciliation.* Christ's bodily resurrection was a sensible manifestation and actualization of our eternal justification and sanctification. That he is *Christus Victor* as our covenant partner is revealed supremely by his resurrection from the dead. This historical event is the in-breaking of eternity into world history and the anticipation of the consummation of our history *in Christo.* The resurrection inaugurates a new era, a time between the times of his ascension and second coming, in which his work of reconciliation continues on earth in the form of the promise of the Holy Spirit.

revelation. God's act of disclosing to us his otherwise hidden ways and works, which are indirectly reflective of his essence, in the history of Jesus Christ. For Barth, revelation is necessarily indirect, because of the axioms *finitum non capax infiniti* and *homo peccator non capax verbum Dei.* Strictly speaking, only Jesus Christ, very God and very man, *is* revelation. As electing God and elected man (see *Christ as electing God and elected man*), he revealed to us by his life on earth the eternal covenantal love that overflowed (see *overflow*) from the inward essence of the triune God. Scripture *is* and *becomes* the Word of God as human witness to revelation. Ecclesial proclamation *becomes* the Word of God in conforming to the *regula fidei* of Scripture to point the world to Jesus Christ. Barth rejects the distinction between special revelation and general revelation. All creation is ontologically determined *in Christo*, and so ultimately speaking there can be no genuinely profane speech in the world. All creaturely speech, however secular it may seem, is ultimately a form of the Word of God testifying to Jesus Christ. Yet even the most devout speech about God, if not understood in light of Jesus Christ, can be nothing to the hearer but a profane word.

saga. The literary genre adopted by the biblical authors to narrate the history of Jesus Christ. In identifying the biblical narratives, especially those of creation and the resurrection, as saga, Barth's intention is to repudiate historical-critical approaches to the Bible. He is especially opposed to the Bultmannian bias "that an event alleged to have happened in time can be accepted as historical only if it can be proved to be a 'historical fact'" on the assumptions of "modern historical scholarship" (*CD* III/2, 446). In biblical saga, "intuition and imagination are used but in order to give prophetic witness to what has taken place by virtue of the Word of God in the (historical or prehistorical) sphere where there can be no historical proof" (*CD* IV/1, 508).

sanctification. The ontological determination of our essence as saints by the life of the man Jesus as the Holy One, and the activation of this essence in our actual lives by the work of the Holy Spirit *in nobis*. See *reconciliation*.

simul iustus et peccator. The *totus-totus* realities of our essential being (*Wesen*) as justified saints in Jesus Christ and of the determination of our existential being (*Sein/Dasein*) by *sin*. Whereas the magisterial Reformers and the Reformed and Lutheran orthodoxies thereafter describe justification as an *existential* reality effected by faith as its instrumental cause, Barth's Christocentric ontology dictates that justification constitutes the essential determination of human nature. Justification becomes the *ontological* reality of humankind, and sin becomes an ontological impossibility that is nevertheless actual and totally determinative of our lives, decisions, activities, societies, and other aspects of existence. Also see *justification by faith*.

sin. The form of *nothingness* that arises from and becomes actual through human activity and inactivity. As a form of nothingness, it negates God and all his ways and works. More concretely, it consists of all the active and passive human refusals and failures to live in actual conformity with our essential being *in Christo*. Sin is actual in the forms of pride (*CD* IV/1, §60), sloth (*CD* IV/2, §65), and falsehood (*CD* IV/3, §70). Pride and sloth result in the fall and misery of humankind, respectively. Sin in the form of falsehood leads to the condemnation of the human liar who rejects God's truth in Jesus Christ. Fallenness and misery are part and parcel of sin as a form of nothingness. Condemnation, however, is not a form of nothingness, but rather an eschatological act of God that has yet to be actualized. In *CD* IV/3, Barth sets forth the actualistic construct of twofold, two-way determinations of the human being (*Sein/Dasein*). From above, the human being is ontologically determined *in Christo*. From below, the human being is determined by the history of Adamic sin. By God's gracious activity completed in Christ, the human being is ontologically justified from the very beginning of God's ways and works. The present punishment of the sinner who rejects the truth of Jesus Christ, however, points us to the prospect of final condemnation, by which the present state of the sinner is determined. Barth is unequivocal in his mature writings that there will be an eschatological separation of the reprobate from the elect, though he also states that the patience of God revealed in the work already accomplished in and by Jesus Christ warrants us to hope and pray for the final salvation of all.

sin, ontological impossibility of. The total foreignness of the actuality of sin to the ontological *essence* (*Wesen*) of the creature. The essence of God's creatures is ontologically determined in Jesus Christ to be justified and sanctified, and so it is ontologically impossible for us to acquire some sinful nature through the fall. Sin is not a second nature, but rather a second *determination* of human existence, which is foreign and contradictory to our nature. In this way, Barth rejects the Western scholastic distinction—one adopted by historic Reformed theology—between original goodness as our essential nature and fallenness as our accidental nature. Also see *actualism*, *sin*, and *nothingness*.

sublation (*Aufhebung*). Technical term critically borrowed from Hegel to denote the teleological process of the negation of the negative for the uncovering and accomplishment of the consummate rationality of the entire process. Barth adopts the Hegelian language of sublation to describe a number of God's acts and works *ad extra*, most notably election as the sublation of reprobation (see *Christ as electing God and elected man* and *decretum absolutum*). This Hegelian dialectic is by no means programmatic in any phase of Barth's theological development. It must be noted that he never applies the dialectic of sublation to God's essence. Sigurd Baark has made an important contribution to contemporary Barth studies by stressing that the basically Anselmian mode of speculation in Barth's mature theology subscribes to the "unsublatable subjectivity" of the triune God in the act and process of revelation.

theology. The science of God regulated by the church, with a starting point in faith in the Christ of Scripture, established by the program of *fides quarens intellectum*. See *after-thinking* and *Word of God (three forms of)*.

time of God. See *eternity*.

time of humankind. The "form of the existence of the creature," which consists of "the one-way sequence and therefore the succession and division of past, present, and future," created in the image of eternity as God's supreme and absolute time (*CD* III/1, 67–68). See *eternity*.

time of Jesus Christ. The time that God self-determined to have for us; the ectypal image of God's supreme and absolute time, the image in which the *time of humankind* is created. The time of Jesus Christ is the union of two times, namely, the eternal time of God and the fleeting time of the creature. God in his eternity has time in-and-for-himself, and eternity as God's own time grounds and makes possible God's time for us. That God has time for us is the concrete meaning of God's patience. Because God has self-determined to have time for us, "there was no time when God was not the Covenant-partner of man" (*CD* III/2, 218). This is not to be taken as a denial of God's absolute time in-and-for-himself. Rather, it is meant to convey the basically Nicene-Chalcedonian understanding that the time of Jesus Christ *is* the time of God. Barth stresses that the time of Jesus Christ reveals to us that "there is freedom in God, but no caprice [see *caprice*]" (*CD* III/2, 218–19). The time of Jesus Christ is grounded in and made possible by God's time in-and-for-himself. These are not two different and separate times. They are one and the same time, albeit in two distinct modes: the one *ensarkos*, and the other *asarkos*. Also see *eternity*.

Trinity, immanent. God's essential being-in-act *ad intra* that grounds and makes possible all God's ways and works *ad extra*. Barth describes the immanent Trinity in the Hegelian language of the *absolute*, defined as God's being in-and-for-himself. Contrary to Hegel's notion of a logical trinity that *becomes* absolute by and through a process of self-determination (see *determination*), Barth resorts to a basically Nicene and Augustinian understanding of objectivity (see *objectivity, primary and secondary*) and activity within the Godhead to contend for the unsublatable (see *sublation*) subjectivity of the immanent Trinity. Also see *actualism* and *Christocentrism*.

unio Christi (*union with Christ*). See *Christ, union with*.

witness. Proclamation of the ways and works of God, grounded in the prophetic office of Christ and reenacted by the Holy Spirit *in nobis* in between the times of his ascension and second coming. Jesus Christ as electing God and elected human is the true Witness who reveals to us the *love* that overflowed (see *overflow*) from God's triune essence (*CD* IV/3, 382). The election of the community of faith in this world (see *Church*), which corresponds to the eternal election of Jesus Christ, establishes a community of witnesses *in Christo*. Israel and the church are prophetic, insofar as they are the community gathered by the Holy Spirit to proclaim

God's ways and works in Jesus Christ. Scripture is the Word of God, insofar as it testifies with Christ, the true Witness, to the God of the man Jesus.

Word of God, three forms (or *threefold form*) **of.** The Word of God revealed, written, and proclaimed. Scripture is not itself revelation: it is and becomes the Word of God by essentially being (*Wesen*) and actually becoming (*Sein-im-Werden*) a human *witness* chosen by God and formed by his providence to testify to Jesus Christ. Christ alone as true Witness *is* essentially God's revelation as *verbum Dei essentiale*. Whereas Scripture essentially *is* a human witness to revelation, the proclamation of the community of the elect only *becomes* witness to revelation by the free act of the Holy Spirit in the here-and-now. Scripture is the supreme *regula fidei* in the community of faith, but individual interpretations of Scripture must conform to the church's dogmatic proclamation in the pattern of an *analogia fidei*.

world history (*Weltgeschichte*). See *history* (*Geschichte*).

worldview (*Weltanschauung*). Immediate intellectual cognition of the world within a philosophical framework of interpretation; better translated as "world-intuition." For Barth, the idealist attempt to attain to immediate cognition—intellectual or otherwise—of reality within an established philosophical system is symptomatic of sinful human pride.

BIBLIOGRAPHY

Primary Sources by Karl Barth (German)

Anselm: Fides quaerens intellectum. Zurich: Theologischer Verlag Zürich, 1931.

Die christliche Dogmatik im Entwurf. 1. Band, *Die Lehre vom Worte Gottes, Prolegomena zur christlichen Dogmatik,* 1927. In *Gesamtausgabe* II.14. Zurich: Theologischer Verlag Zürich, 1982.

Gottes Gnadenwahl. Munich: Chr. Kaiser, 1936.

Die kirchliche Dogmatik. 4 vols. in 12 parts (I/1–IV/4). Zollikon-Zurich: Evangelischer Verlag, 1932–67.

Offene Briefe 1945–1968. In *Gesamtausgabe* V.15. Zurich: Theologischer Verlag Zürich, 1984.

Die protestantische Theologie im 19. Jahrhundert: Ihre Geschichte und ihre Vorgeschichte. Zurich: Theologischer Verlag Zürich, 1994.

Rechtfertigung und Recht, Christengemeinde und Bürgergemeinde, and *Evangelium und Gesetz.* Zurich: Theologischer Verlag Zürich, 1998.

Der Römerbrief. 1922; Zurich: Theologischer Verlag Zürich, 1999.

Die Theologie Calvins, 1922. In *Gesamtausgabe* II.23. Zurich: Theologischer Verlag Zürich, 1993.

Die Theologie der reformierten Bekenntnisschriften, 1923. In *Gesamtausgabe* II.32. Zurich: Theologischer Verlag Zürich, 1998.

Unterricht in der christlichen Religion 1924–1926. 3 vols. In *Gesamtausgabe* II.17, 20, 38. Zurich: Theologischer Verlag Zürich, 1985, 1990, 2003.

Primary Sources by Karl Barth
(English and English Translation)

Anselm: Fides Quaerens Intellectum. Translated by Ian Robertson. London: SCM, 1960.

Church Dogmatics. 4 vols. in 12 parts (I/1–IV/4). Edited by Geoffrey W. Bromiley and Thomas F. Torrance. Translated by Geoffrey W. Bromiley. Edinburgh: T & T Clark, 1956–1975.

Community, State, and Church: Three Essays. Translated by A. M. Hall and G. Ronald Howe. Garden City, NY: Doubleday, 1960.

The Epistle to the Romans. Translated by Edwyn Hoskyns. Oxford: Oxford University Press, 1933.

The Göttingen Dogmatics. Vol. 1, *Instruction in the Christian Religion.* Edited by Hannelotte Reiffen. Translated by Geoffrey Bromiley. Grand Rapids: Eerdmans, 1991.

Protestant Theology in the Nineteenth Century. Translated by Brian Cozens and John Bowden. London: SCM, 2001.

Primary Sources by Confessional
Reformed Theologians

Bavinck, Herman. *Philosophy of Revelation.* Edited by Cory Brock and Nathaniel Gray Sutanto. Peabody, MA: Hendrickson, 2019.

————. *Reformed Dogmatics*. Edited by John Bolt. Translated by John Vriend. 4 vols. Grand Rapids: Baker, 2003–8.

Baynes, Paul. *A Commentary upon the First Chapter of the Epistle to the Ephesians*. London, 1618.

Berkhof, Louis. *Systematic Theology*. Edinburgh: Banner of Truth, 1958.

Beza, Theodore. *The Christian Faith*. Translated by James Clark. Lewes: Focus Christian Ministries, 1992.

Calvin, John. *Institutes of the Christian Religion*. Edited by John T. McNeill. Translated by Ford Lewis Battles. 2 vols. Philadelphia: Westminster, 1960.

Charnock, Stephen. *The Existence and Attributes of God*. Vol. 1. Grand Rapids: Baker, 1996.

Edwards, John. *Veritas Redux*. Andover, MA: Gale, 2010.

Flavel, John. *The Works of John Flavel*. 6 vols. Edinburgh: Banner of Truth, 1968.

Gillespie, Patrick. *The Ark of the Covenant Opened*. London: Parkhurst, 1677.

Goodwin, Thomas. *The Works of Thomas Goodwin*. 12 vols. Grand Rapids: Reformation Heritage Books, 2006.

Hodge, Charles. *Systematic Theology*. 3 vols. Grand Rapids: Eerdmans, 1989.

Kuyper, Abraham. *Encyclopedia of Sacred Theology: Its Principles*. New York: Scribner's, 1898.

————. *Lectures on Calvinism*. Grand Rapids: Eerdmans, 1931.

Maccovius, Johannes. *De aeterna Dei electione*. Franeker, 1618.

Owen, John. *The Works of John Owen*. Edited by William Goold. 23 vols. Edinburgh: Banner of Truth, 1967.

————. *The Works of John Owen*. Edited by Thomas Russell. 21 vols. London: Richard Baynes, 1826.

Perkins, William. *A Christian and Plaine Treatise of the Manner and Order of Predestination, and of the Largeness of Gods Grace*. London, 1606.

Sibbes, Richard. "To the Reader." In Paul Baynes, *A Commentary upon the First Chapter of the Epistle to the Ephesians*. London, 1618.

Turretin, Francis. *Institutes of Elenctic Theology*. Edited by James Dennison. Translated by George Giger. 3 vols. Phillipsburg, NJ: P&R, 1992–97.

———. *Institutio Theologicae Elencticae*. 3 vols. Geneva, 1679.

Vos, Geerhardus. *Biblical Theology: Old and New Testaments*. Eugene, OR: Wipf and Stock, 2003.

———. *Redemptive History and Biblical Interpretation: The Shorter Writings of Geerhardus Vos*. Edited by Richard B. Gaffin, Jr. Phillipsburg, NJ: P&R, 1980.

Other Primary Sources

Anselm of Canterbury. *Cur Deus Homo*. Translated by Sidney Deane. Chicago: Open Court, 1903.

Augustine. *On the Holy Trinity*. Edited by Philip Schaff. Translated by Arthur Haddan. Edinburgh: T&T Clark, 1887.

Bonhoeffer, Dietrich. *Act and Being*. Edited by Hans-Richard Reuter and Wayne Whitson Floyd. Translated by H. Martin Rumscheidt. Minneapolis: Fortress Press, 1996.

Brueggemann, Walter. *Theology of the Old Testament*. Minneapolis: Fortress, 1997.

Brunner, Emil. *Dogmatics*. Vol. 1, *The Christian Doctrine of God*. Translated by Olive Wyon. Philadelphia: Westminster, 1950.

Buber, Martin. *I and Thou*. Translated by Walter Kaufmann. New York: Charles Scribner's Sons, 1970.

Cyril of Alexandria. *On the Unity of Christ*. Yonkers, NY: St. Vladimir's Seminary Press, 1997.

Feuerbach, Ludwig. *The Essence of Christianity*. Translated by George Eliot. New York: Prometheus, 1989.

Gunkel, Hermann. *Genesis*. Translated by Mark Biddle. Macon, GA: Mercer University Press, 1997.

Hauerwas, Stanley. *After Christendom?* Nashville: Abingdon, 1991.

Heppe, Heinrich. *Die Dogmatik der evangelisch-reformierten Kirche.* Whitefish, MT: Kessinger, 2010.

———. *Reformed Dogmatics.* Edited by Ernst Bizer. Translated by G. Thomson. London: Wakeman, 2010.

Kant, Immanuel. *Kritik der reinen Vernunft.* Wiesbaden: Fourier, 2003.

———. *Religion within the Bounds of Bare Reason.* Translated by Werner Pluhar. Indianapolis: Hackett, 2009.

Kierkegaard, Søren. *Concluding Unscientific Postscript to the Philosophical Crumbs.* Edited and translated by Alastair Hannay. Cambridge: Cambridge University Press, 2009.

———. *Sickness unto Death.* Translated by Alastair Hannay. Radford, VA: Wilder, 2008.

Lindbeck, George. *The Nature of Doctrine: Religion and Theology in a Postliberal Age.* Louisville: Westminster John Knox, 1984.

Luther, Martin. *The Bondage of the Will: A New Translation of De Servo Arbitrio (1525), Martin Luther's Reply to Erasmus of Rotterdam.* Translated by J. I. Packer and O. R. Johnston. Old Tappan, NJ: Fleming H. Revell, 1957.

Maury, Pierre. "Erwählung und Glaube." In *Theologische Studien* 8. Zurich: Evangelischer Verlag Zürich, 1940.

Moltmann, Jürgen. "The Election of Grace: Barth on the Doctrine of Predestination." In *Reading the Gospels with Barth*, edited by Daniel Migliore. Grand Rapids: Eerdmans, 2017.

———. *Der lebendige Gott und die Fülle des Lebens: Auch ein Beitrag zur gegenwärtigen Atheismusdebatte.* Gütersloh: Gütersloher Verlagshaus, 2014.

———. *The Trinity and the Kingdom.* Minneapolis: Fortress, 1993.

———. *The Way of Jesus Christ.* Minneapolis: Fortress, 1993.

Pannenberg, Wolfhart. *Problemgeschichte der neueren evangelischen Theologie in Deutschland: Von Schleiermacher bis zu Barth und Tillich.* Göttingen: Vandenhoeck & Ruprecht, 1997.

————, ed. *Revelation as History*. London: Macmillan, 1969.

————. *Systematic Theology*. Translated by Geoffrey Bromiley. 3 vols. Grand Rapids: Eerdmans, 2009.

Schaff, Philip, ed. "The Canons and Decrees of the Council of Trent." In *The Creeds of Christendom*, vol. 2. Grand Rapids: Baker, 1983.

Schleiermacher, Friedrich. *The Christian Faith: A New Translation and Critical Edition*. Translated by Terrence Tice, Catherine Kelsey, and Edwina Lawler. Louisville: Westminster John Knox, 2016.

————. *On Religion: Speeches to Its Cultured Despisers*. Edited and translated by Richard Crouter. Cambridge: Cambridge University Press, 1996.

Schweizer, Alexander. *Die Glaubenslehre der evangelisch-reformieten Kirche, dargestellt und aus den Quellen belegt*. 2 vols. Zurich: Orell, Füssli, 1844–1847.

Tillich, Paul. *Systematic Theology*. 3 vols. Chicago: Chicago University Press, 1957.

Torrance, Thomas. *Space, Time and Resurrection*. Edinburgh: T&T Clark, 1976.

————. *Theology in Reconciliation*. Eugene, OR: Wipf and Stock, 1996.

Secondary Literature

Allen, Michael. "Jonathan Edwards and the Lapsarian Debate." *Scottish Journal of Theology* 62, no. 3 (2009): 299–315.

Amemiya, Eiichi (雨宮栄一), Keiji Ogawa (小川圭治), and Heita Mori (森平太), eds. *Yoshio Inoue Studies* (井上良雄研究). Tokyo: Protestant Press (新教出版社), 2006.

Ameriks, Karl. *Kant and the Historical Turn*. Oxford: Oxford University Press, 2006.

Anderson, Clifford. "A Theology of Experience? Karl Barth and the Transcendental Argument." In *Karl Barth and American Evangelicalism*, edited by Bruce McCormack and Clifford Anderson. Grand Rapids: Eerdmans, 2010.

Baark, Sigurd. *The Affirmations of Reason: On Karl Barth's Speculative Theology*. Cham, Switzerland: Palgrave Macmillan, 2018.

Balthasar, Hans Urs von. *The Theology of Karl Barth: Exposition and Interpretation*. Translated by Edward T. Oakes. San Francisco: Ignatius Press, 1992.

Barrett, William. *Irrational Man: A Study in Existential Philosophy*. Garden City, NY: Doubleday, 1962.

Becker, Dieter. *Karl Barth und Martin Buber, Denker in dialogischer Nachbarschaft? Zur Bedeutung Martin Bubers für die Anthropologie Karl Barths*. Göttingen: Vandenhoeck & Ruprecht, 1986.

Beeke, Joel, and Mark Jones. *A Puritan Theology: Doctrine for Life*. Grand Rapids: Reformation Heritage Books, 2012.

Beintker, Michael. *Die Dialektik in der "dialektischen Theologie" Karl Barths*. Munich: Chr. Kaiser, 1987.

———. "Unterricht in der christlichen Religion." *Verkündigung und Forschung* 30, no. 2 (1985): 45–49.

Berkouwer, Gerrit. *The Triumph of Grace in the Theology of Karl Barth*. Translated by Harry Boer. London: Paternoster, 1956.

Bertram, Robert. "'Faith Alone Justifies': Luther on *Iustia Fidei*." In *Justification by Faith: Lutherans and Catholics in Dialogue*, vol. 7, edited by H. George Anderson, T. Austin Murphy, and Joseph A. Burgess. Minneapolis: Augsburg, 1985.

Boersma, Hans. *Nouvelle Théologie and Sacramental Ontology: A Return to Mystery*. Oxford: Oxford University Press, 2009.

———. *Violence, Hospitality, and the Cross: Reappropriating the Atonement Tradition*. Grand Rapids: Baker Academics, 2004.

Bolt, John. "Exploring Barth's Eschatology: A Salutary Exercise for Evangelicals." In *Karl Barth and Evangelical Theology: Convergences and Divergences*, edited by Sung Wook Chung. Grand Rapids: Baker Academic, 2006.

———. *A Free Church, A Holy Nation: Abraham Kuyper's American Public Theology*. Grand Rapids: Eerdmans, 2001.

Bouillard, Henri. *Karl Barth*. 2 vols. Paris: Aubier, 1957.

Bradshaw, Timothy. "Karl Barth on the Trinity: A Family Resemblance." *Scottish Journal of Theology* 39, no. 2 (1986): 145–64.

Brock, Cory. *Orthodox Yet Modern: Herman Bavinck's Use of Friedrich Schleiermacher*. Bellingham, WA: Lexham Press, 2020.

Brock, Cory, and Nathaniel Gray Sutanto. "Herman Bavinck's Reformed Eclecticism: On Catholicity, Consciousness, and Theological Epistemology." *Scottish Journal of Theology* 70, no. 3 (2017): 310–32.

Bromiley, Geoffrey. "Karl Barth's Doctrine of Inspiration." *Journal of the Transactions of the Victoria Institute* 87 (1955): 66–80.

Buckley, James. "Barth and Rahner." In *The Wiley-Blackwell Companion to Karl Barth*, edited by George Hunsinger and Keith Johnson, 607–17. Oxford: Wiley-Blackwell, 2020.

Busch, Eberhard. *Die Anfänge des Theologen Karl Barth in seinen Göttingen Jahren*. Göttingen: Vandenhoek & Ruprecht, 1987.

———. *Barth*. Nashville: Abingdon, 2008.

———. *Karl Barth: His Life from Letters and Autobiographical Texts*. Translated by John Bowden. London: SCM, 1975.

———. *Meine Zeit mit Karl Barth*. Göttingen: Vandenhoeck & Ruprecht, 2011.

Chao, Tzu-ch'en (趙紫宸). *Barth's Religious Thought* (巴德的宗教思想). Shanghai: Youth Association Press (青年協會書局), 1939.

Chung, Sung Wook, ed. *Karl Barth and Evangelical Theology: Convergences and Divergences*. Grand Rapids: Baker, 2006.

Clark, Gordon. *Karl Barth's Theological Method*. Philadelphia: P&R, 1963.

Collins, Paul. *Trinitarian Theology, West and East: Karl Barth, the Cappadocian Fathers, and John Zizioulas*. Oxford: Oxford University Press, 2001.

Congdon, David. "*Apokatastasis* and Apostolicity: A Response to Oliver Crisp on the Question of Barth's Universalism." *Scottish Journal of Theology* 67, no. 4 (2014): 464–80.

Cortez, Marc. "What Does It Mean to Call Karl Barth a 'Christocentric' Theologian?" *Scottish Journal of Theology* 60, no. 2 (2007): 127–43.

Crisp, Oliver. *Divinity and Humanity.* Cambridge: Cambridge University Press, 2007.

———. "Karl Barth and Jonathan Edwards on Reprobation (and Hell)." In *Engaging with Barth: Contemporary Evangelical Critiques*, edited by David Gibson and Daniel Strange. Nottingham: Apollos, 2008.

———. "Karl Barth on Creation." In *Karl Barth and Evangelical Theology: Convergences and Divergences*, edited by Sung Wook Chung. Grand Rapids: Baker Academic, 2006.

Dalferth, Ingolf. "Karl Barth's Eschatological Realism." In *Karl Barth: Centenary Essays*, edited by Stephen Sykes. Cambridge: Cambridge University Press, 1989.

DeVries, Dawn. "Does Faith Save? Calvin, Schleiermacher and Barth on the Nature of Faith." In *The Reality of Faith in Theology: Studies on Karl Barth—Princeton-Kampen Consultation 2005*, edited by Bruce McCormack and Gerrit Neven. Bern: Peter Lang, 2007.

Diller, Kevin. *Theology's Epistemological Dilemma: How Karl Barth and Alvin Plantinga Provide a Unified Response.* Downers Grove, IL: IVP Academic, 2014.

Dulles, Avery. "Two Languages of Salvation: The Lutheran-Catholic Joint Declaration." *First Things* 98, no. 12 (1999): 25–30.

Ebeling, Gerhard. "Glaube und Liebe." In *Martin Luther: 450 Jahre Reformation*, edited by Helmut Gollwitzer. Köln: Dumont, 1967.

Erickson, Millard. *Christian Theology.* Grand Rapids: Baker Academic, 2013.

Fesko, John. *The Covenant of Redemption: Origins, Development, and Reception.* Göttingen: Vandenhoeck & Ruprecht, 2016.

———. *Reformed Apologetics: Retrieving the Classical Reformed Approach to Defending the Faith.* Grand Rapids: Baker, 2019.

Fiddes, Paul. *The Creative Suffering of God.* Oxford: Oxford University Press, 1988.

Ford, David. *Barth and God's Story.* Eugene, OR: Wipf and Stock, 1985.

Frei, Hans. "The Doctrine of Revelation in the Thought of Karl Barth, 1909 to 1922." Ph.D. diss., Yale University, 1956.

———. "Scripture as Realistic Narrative: Karl Barth as Critic of Historical Criticism." In *Thy Word Is Truth: Barth on Scripture,* edited by George Hunsinger. Grand Rapids: Eerdmans, 2012.

———. *Theology and Narrative.* Edited by G. Hunsinger and W. Placher. Oxford: Oxford University Press, 1993.

Furry, Timothy. "Analogous Analogies? Thomas Aquinas and Karl Barth." *Scottish Journal of Theology* 63, no. 3 (2010): 318–30.

Gaffin, Richard. "Old Amsterdam and Inerrancy?" *Westminster Theological Journal* 44, no. 2 (1982): 250–89.

Garcia, Mark. *Life in Christ: Union with Christ and Twofold Grace in Calvin's Theology.* Milton Keynes, UK: Paternoster, 2008.

Gavrilyuk, Paul. "The Retrieval of Deification: How a Once-Despised Archaism Became an Ecumenical Desideratum." *Modern Theology* 25, no. 4 (2009): 647–59.

———. *The Suffering of the Impassible God: The Dialectics of Patristic Thought.* Oxford: Oxford University Press, 2004.

Gibson, David, and Daniel Strange, eds. *Engaging with Barth: Contemporary Evangelical Critiques.* Nottingham: Apollos, 2008.

Glomsrud, Ryan. "Karl Barth as Historical Theologian." In *Engaging with Barth: Contemporary Evangelical Critiques,* edited by David Gibson and Daniel Strange. Nottingham: Apollos, 2008.

———. "Karl Barth between Pietism and Orthodoxy: A Post-Enlightenment Ressourcement of Classical Protestantism." D.Phil. thesis, University of Oxford, 2009.

Gockel, Matthias. *Barth and Schleiermacher on the Doctrine of Election: A Systematic-Theological Comparison.* Oxford: Oxford University Press, 2006.

———. "How to Read Karl Barth with Charity: A Critical Reply to George Hunsinger," *Modern Theology* 32, no. 2 (2016): 259–67.

Green, Bradley. *Colin Gunton and the Failure of Augustine.* Eugene, OR: Pickwick, 2011.

Green, Christopher. *Doxological Theology: Karl Barth on Divine Providence, Evil, and the Angels.* London: Bloomsbury, 2011.

Greggs, Tom. *Barth, Origen, and Universal Salvation: Restoring Particularity.* Oxford: Oxford University Press, 2009.

———. "'Jesus Is Victor': Passing the Impasse of Barth on Universalism." *Scottish Journal of Theology* 60, no. 2 (2007):196–212.

Gruchy, John De. "Reflections on 'Doing Theology' in South Africa after Sixty Years in Conversation with Barth." *Stellenbosch Theological Journal* 5, no. 1 (2019): 11–28.

Gunton, Colin. *The Barth Lectures.* New York: T&T Clark, 2007.

———. *Being and Becoming: The Doctrine of God in Charles Hartshorne and Karl Barth.* Oxford: Oxford University Press, 1978.

Gutiérrez, Gustavo. *A Theology of Liberation.* New York: Orbis, 2012.

Harinck, George. "How Can an Elephant Understand a Whale and Vice Versa?" In *Karl Barth and American Evangelicalism,* edited by Bruce McCormack and Clifford Anderson. Grand Rapids: Eerdmans, 2011.

Hart, Trevor. "Barth and Küng on Justification: 'Imaginary Differences'?" *Irish Theological Quarterly* 59, no. 2 (1993): 94–113.

Hastings, Ross. "Discerning the Spirit: Ambivalent Assurance in the Soteriology of Jonathan Edwards and Barthian Correctives." *Scottish Journal of Theology* 63, no. 4 (2010): 437–55.

He, Guanghu (何光滬), and Daniel Yeung (楊熙楠), eds. *Sino-Christian Theology Reader* (漢語神學讀本). 2 vols. Hong Kong: Logos and Pneuma (道風), 2009.

Hector, Kevin. "Immutability, Necessity and Triunity: Towards a Resolution of the Trinity and Election Controversy." *Scottish Journal of Theology* 65, no. 1 (2012): 64–81.

Hendry, George. "The Transcendental Method in the Theology of Karl Barth." *Scottish Journal of Theology* 37, no. 2 (1984): 213–27.

Hitchcock, Nathan. *Karl Barth and the Resurrection of the Flesh: The Loss of the Body in Participatory Eschatology.* Eugene, OR: Wipf and Stock, 2013.

Hollweg, Walter. *Heinrich Bullingers Hausbuch: Eine Untersuchung über die Anfänge der reformierten Predigtliteratur.* Gießen: Münchowsche Universitätsdruckerei, 1956.

Hong, Liang (洪亮). *Six Studies in the Theology of Karl Barth and Jürgen Moltmann* (巴特與莫特曼神學管窺). Hong Kong: VW Link (德慧文化), 2020.

Horton, Michael. "A Stony Jar: The Legacy of Karl Barth for Evangelical Theology." In *Engaging with Barth: Contemporary Evangelical Critiques,* edited by David Gibson and Daniel Strange. Nottingham: Apollos, 2008.

Hunsinger, George. *Disruptive Grace: Studies in the Theology of Karl Barth.* Grand Rapids: Eerdmans, 2000.

———. "Election and the Trinity: Twenty-Five Theses on the Theology of Karl Barth." *Modern Theology* 24, no. 2 (2008): 179–98.

———. "*Fides Christo Formata*: Luther, Barth and the Joint Declaration." In *The Gospel of Justification in Christ: Where Does the Church Stand Today?*. edited by Wayne Stumme. Grand Rapids: Eerdmans, 2006.

———. *How to Read Karl Barth: The Shape of His Theology*. Oxford: Oxford University Press, 1991.

———. "Karl Barth's Christology: Its Basic Chalcedonian Character." In *The Cambridge Companion to Karl Barth*, edited by John Webster. Cambridge: Cambridge University Press, 2000.

———. "Karl Barth's *The Göttingen Dogmatics*." *Scottish Journal of Theology* 46, no. 3 (1993): 371–82.

———. *Philippians*. Grand Rapids: Brazos, 2020.

———. "Postliberal Theology." In *The Cambridge Companion to Postmodern Theology*, edited by Kevin Vanhoozer. Cambridge: Cambridge University Press, 2003.

———. *Reading Barth with Charity: A Hermeneutical Proposal*. Grand Rapids: Baker Academic, 2015.

———. "Review of *Barth, Origen, and Universalism: Restoring Particularity*, by Tom Greggs." *Modern Theology* 28, no. 2 (2012): 356–58.

———. "A Tale of Two Simultaneities: Justification and Sanctification in Calvin and Barth." In *Conversing with Barth*, edited by John C. McDowell and Mike Higton. Aldershot, UK: Ashgate, 2004.

———, ed. *Thy Word Is Truth: Barth on Scripture*. Grand Rapids: Eerdmans, 2012.

Hunsinger, George, and Keith Johnson, eds. *The Wiley-Blackwell Companion to Karl Barth*. Oxford: Wiley-Blackwell, 2020.

Jenson, Matt. *The Gravity of Sin: Augustine, Luther and Barth on homo incurvatus in se*. London: T&T Clark, 2006.

Jenson, Robert. *God after God: The God of the Past and the God of the Future as Seen in the Works of Karl Barth*. Minneapolis: Fortress, 2010.

Johnson, Keith. *Karl Barth and the Analogia Entis*. London: T&T Clark, 2010.

Johnson, William Stacy. *The Mystery of God: Karl Barth and the Postmodern Foundations of Theology*. Louisville: Westminster John Knox, 1997.

Jones, Mark. *Why Heaven Kissed Earth: The Christology of the Puritan Reformed Orthodox Theologian, Thomas Goodwin (1600–1680)*. Göttingen: Vandenhoeck & Ruprecht, 2010.

Jones, Paul Dafydd. *The Humanity of Christ: Christology in Karl Barth's Church Dogmatics*. London: T&T Clark, 2008.

Jones, Paul Dafydd, and Paul Nimmo, eds. *The Oxford Handbook of Karl Barth*. Oxford: Oxford University Press, 2020.

Jüngel, Eberhard. *God's Being Is in Becoming: The Trinitarian Being of God in the Theology of Karl Barth*. Translated by John Webster. Grand Rapids: Eerdmans, 2001.

———. *Gottes Sein ist im Werden*. Tübingen: Mohr, 1965.

———. *Justification: The Heart of the Christian Faith*. Edinburgh: T&T Clark, 2001.

———. "Von der Dialektik zur Analogie: Die Schule Kierkegaards und der Einspruch Petersons." In *Barth-Studien*. Zurich: Benziger, 1982.

Kim, Young-Gwan. *Karl Barth's Reception in Korea*. New York: Peter Lang, 2003.

Kitamori, Kazoh. *Theologie des Schmerzes Gottes*. Translated by Tsuneaki Kato and Paul Schneiss. Göttingen: Vandenhoeck & Ruprecht, 1972.

———. *Theology of the Pain of God*. Translated. Eugene, OR: Wipf and Stock, 2005.

Krötke, Wolf. *Sin and Nothingness in the Theology of Karl Barth*. Edited and translated by Philip Ziegler and Christina-Maria Bammel. Princeton: Princeton Theological Seminary, 2005.

Küng, Hans. *Justification: The Doctrine of Karl Barth and a Catholic Reflection*. Philadelphia: Westminster, 1981.

La Montagne, D. Paul. *Barth and Rationality: Critical Realism in Theology*. Eugene, OR: Wipf and Stock, 2012.

Letham, Robert. "Theodore Beza: A Reassessment." *Scottish Journal of Theology* 40, no. 1 (1987): 25–40.

Liao, Chin-Ping. "Tanabe Hajime's Religious Philosophy." *NCCU Philosophical Journal* 32 (2014): 57–91.

Lin, Hong-Hsin (林鴻信). *Systematic Theology* (系統神學). 2 vols. Taipei: Campus (校園), 2017.

Lindbeck, George. "Barth and Textuality." *Theology Today* 43, no. 3 (1986): 361–76.

Lohmann, Johann. *Karl Barth und der Neukantianismus.* Berlin: Walter de Gruyter, 1995.

Malloy, Christopher. *Engrafted into Christ: A Critique of the Joint Declaration.* New York: Peter Lang, 2005.

Mangina, Joseph. *Karl Barth: Theologian of Christian Witness.* London: Westminster John Knox, 2004.

Marga, Amy. "Jesus Christ and the Modern Sinner: Karl Barth's Retrieval of Luther's Substantive Christology." *Currents in Theology and Mission* 34, no. 4 (2007): 260–70.

———. *Karl Barth's Dialogue with Catholicism in Göttingen and Münster: Its Significance for His Doctrine of God.* Tübingen: Mohr Siebeck, 2010.

Marshall, Bruce. *Christology in Conflict: The Identity of a Saviour in Rahner and Barth.* Oxford: Blackwell, 1987.

McCormack, Bruce, ed. "The Being of Holy Scripture Is in Becoming." In *Evangelicals and Scripture: Tradition, Authority and Hermeneutics,* edited by Vincent Bacote, Laura Miguelez, and Dennis Okholm. Downers Grove, IL: IVP Academic, 2004.

———. "Election and the Trinity, Theses in Response to George Hunsinger." *Scottish Journal of Theology* 63, no. 2 (2010): 203–24.

———. *Engaging the Doctrine of God: Contemporary Protestant Perspectives.* Grand Rapids: Baker, 2008.

———. *For Us and Our Salvation.* Princeton: Princeton Theological Seminary, 1993.

————. "Grace and Being: The Role of God's Gracious Election in Karl Barth's Theological Ontology." In *The Cambridge Companion to Karl Barth,* edited by John Webster. Cambridge: Cambridge University Press, 2000.

————, ed. *Justification in Perspective: Historical Developments and Contemporary Challenges.* Grand Rapids: Baker Academic, 2006.

————. "Karl Barth's Christology as Resource for a Reformed Version of Kenoticism." *International Journal of Systematic Theology* 8, no. 3 (2006): 243–51.

————. *Karl Barth's Critically Realistic Dialectical Theology: Its Genesis and Development 1909–1936.* Oxford: Clarendon Press, 1995.

————. "The Ontological Presuppositions of Barth's Doctrine of the Atonement." In *The Glory of the Atonement: Biblical, Theological and Practical Perspectives,* edited by Charles E. Hill and Frank A. James III. Downers Grove, IL: IVP, 2004.

————. *Orthodox and Modern: Studies in the Theology of Karl Barth.* Grand Rapids: Baker Academic, 2008.

————, ed. *The Reality of Faith in Theology: Studies on Karl Barth.* Bern: Peter Lang, 2005.

————. "Revelation and History in Transfoundationalist Perspective: Karl Barth's Theological Epistemology in Conversation with a Schleiermacherian Tradition." *Journal of Religion* 78, no. 1 (1998): 18–37.

————. "Seek God Where He May Be Found: A Response to Edwin Chr. Van Driel." *Scottish Journal of Theology* 60, no. 1 (2007): 62–79.

————. "So That He May Be Merciful to All: Karl Barth and the Problem of Universalism." In *Karl Barth and American Evangelicalism,* edited by Bruce McCormack and Clifford Anderson. Grand Rapids: Eerdmans, 2011.

————. "The Sum of the Gospel: The Doctrine of Election in

the Theologies of Alexander Schweizer and Karl Barth." In *Toward the Future of Reformed Theology: Tasks, Topics, Traditions*, edited by David Willis and Michael Welker. Grand Rapids: Eerdmans, 1999.

McDonald, Nathan. "The *Imago Dei* and Election: Reading Genesis 1:26–28 and Old Testament Scholarship with Karl Barth." *International Journal of Systematic Theology* 10, no. 3 (2008): 303–27.

McDonald, Suzanne. "Barth's 'Other' Doctrine of Election in the *Church Dogmatics.*" *International Journal of Systematic Theology* 9, no. 2 (2007): 134–47.

———. "Evangelical Questioning of Election in Barth: A Pneumatological Perspective from the Reformed Heritage." In *Karl Barth and American Evangelicalism*, edited by Bruce McCormack and Clifford Anderson. Grand Rapids: Eerdmans, 2010.

———. *Re-Imaging Election: Divine Election as Representing God to Others and Others to God*. Grand Rapids: Eerdmans, 2010.

McDowell, John. "Learning Where to Place One's Hope: The Eschatological Significance of Election in Barth." *Scottish Journal of Theology* 53, no. 3 (2000): 316–38.

———. "'Mend Your Speech a Little': Reading Karl Barth's *das Nichtige* through Donald MacKinnon's Tragic Vision." In *Conversing with Barth*, edited by John C. McDowell and Mike Higton. Aldershot, UK: Ashgate, 2004.

———. "Much Ado about Nothing: Karl Barth's Being Unable to Do Nothing about Nothingness." *International Journal of Systematic Theology* 4, no. 3 (2002): 319–35.

McGrath, Alister. "Justification: Barth, Trent and Küng." *Scottish Journal of Theology* 34, no. 6 (1981): 517–29.

———. "Karl Barth's Doctrine of Justification from an Evangelical Perspective." In *Karl Barth and Evangelical Theology: Convergences and Divergences*, edited by Sung Woo Chung. Grand Rapids: Baker Academic, 2006.

McKenny, Gerald. *The Analogy of Grace: Karl Barth's Moral Theology*. Oxford: Oxford University Press, 2013.

McMaken, W. Travis. "Election and the Pattern of Exchange in Karl Barth's Doctrine of the Atonement." *Journal of Reformed Theology* 3, no. 2 (2009): 202–18.

Migliore, Daniel, ed. *Reading the Gospels with Karl Barth*. Grand Rapids: Eerdmans, 2017.

Molnar, Paul. "The Function of the Immanent Trinity in Karl Barth: Implications for Today." *Scottish Journal of Theology* 42, no. 3 (1989): 367–99.

———. "'Thy Word Is Truth': The Role of Faith in Reading Scripture Theologically with Karl Barth." *Scottish Journal of Theology* 63, no. 1 (2010): 70–92.

———. "The Trinity and the Freedom of God." *Journal for Christian Theological Research* 8 (2003): 59–66.

———. "The Trinity, Election and God's Ontological Freedom: A Response to Kevin Hector." *International Journal of Systematic Theology* 8, no. 3 (2006): 294–306.

Mouw, Richard. *He Shines in All That's Fair: Culture and Common Grace*. Grand Rapids: Eerdmans, 2001.

———. "Some Reflections on Sphere Sovereignty." In *Religion, Pluralism, and Public Life: Abraham Kuyper's Legacy for the Twenty-First Century*, edited by Luis Lugo. Grand Rapids: Eerdmans, 2000.

Muller, Richard. *Christ and the Decree: Christology and Predestination in Reformed Theology from Calvin to Perkins*. Grand Rapids: Baker, 1986.

———. *Dictionary of Latin and Greek Theological Terms Drawn Principally from Protestant Scholastic Theology*. Grand Rapids: Baker Academic, 1985.

———. *Post-Reformation Reformed Dogmatics*. Volume 1. Grand Rapids: Baker Academic, 2003.

Murphy, Francesca Aran. *God Is Not a Story: Realism Revisited*. Oxford: Oxford University Press, 2007.

Neder, Adam. *Participation in Christ: An Entry into Karl Barth's Church Dogmatics.* Louisville: Westminster John Knox, 2009.

Ng Yu-Kwan (吳汝鈞). *Phenomenology of Pure Vitality: Second Volume* (純粹力動現象學：續篇). Taipei: Commercial Press (台灣商務), 2008.

Nimmo, Paul. *Being in Action: The Theological Shape of Barth's Ethical Vision.* London: T&T Clark, 2007.

———. "Karl Barth and the *concursus Dei*—A Chalcedonianism Too Far?" *International Journal of Systematic Theolgy* 9, no. 1 (2007): 58–72.

Oliphint, Scott. "Is There a Reformed Objection to Natural Theology?" *Westminster Theological Journal* 74, no. 1 (2012): 169–203.

Packer, James. *Knowing God.* Downers Grove, IL: InterVarsity Press, 1993.

Pattison, George. *God and Being: An Enquiry.* Oxford: Oxford University Press, 2011.

Penner, Myron. "Calvin, Barth, and the Subject of Atonement." In *Calvin, Barth and Reformed Theology*, edited by Neil McDonald and Carl Trueman. Eugene, OR: Wipf and Stock, 2008.

Poythress, Vern. *The Mystery of the Trinity: A Trinitarian Approach to the Attributes of God.* Phillipsburg, NJ: P&R, 2020.

Price, Daniel. *Karl Barth's Anthropology in Light of Modern Thought.* Grand Rapids: Eerdmans, 2002.

Qu, Thomas. "After Nietzsche: How Could We Do Sino-Christian Theology Today?" *Logos and Pneuma* 50, no. 1 (2019): 155–82.

Qu, Thomas, and Paulos Huang, eds. *Yearbook of Chinese Theology 2019.* Leiden: Brill, 2019.

Rasmussen, Joel. *Between Irony and Witness: Kierkegaard's Poetics of Faith, Hope and Love.* London: T&T Clark, 2005.

———. "The Transformation of Metaphysics." In *The Oxford Handbook of Nineteenth-Century Christian Thought*, edited by Joel Rasmussen, Judith Wolfe, and Johannes Zachhuber. Oxford: Oxford University Press, 2017.

Rasmussen, Joel, Judith Wolfe, and Johannes Zachhuber, eds. *The Oxford Handbook of Nineteenth-Century Christian Thought.* Oxford: Oxford University Press, 2017.

Rehnman, Sebastian. *Divine Discourse: The Theological Methodology of John Owen.* Grand Rapids: Baker Academic, 2002.

———. "Does It Matter If Christian Theology Is Contradictory? Barth on Logic and Theology." In *Engaging with Barth: Contemporary Evangelical Critiques,* edited by David Gibson and Daniel Strange. Nottingham: Apollos, 2008.

Reymond, Robert. "Calvin's Doctrine of Holy Scripture (1.6–10)." In *A Theological Guide to Calvin's Institutes,* edited by Peter Lillback and David Hall. Phillipsburg, NJ: P&R, 2008.

———. *The Justification of Knowledge: An Introductory Study in Christian Apologetic Methodology.* Phillipsburg, NJ: Presbyterian and Reformed, 1979.

———. *A New Systematic Theology of the Christian Faith.* Nashville: Thomas Nelson, 1998.

Richardson, Kurt Anders. "*Christus Praesens*: Barth's Radically Realist Christology and Its Necessity for Theological Method." In *Karl Barth and Evangelical Theology: Convergences and Divergences,* edited by Sung Wook Chung. Grand Rapids: Baker, 2006.

———. *Reading Karl Barth: New Directions for North American Theology.* Grand Rapids: Baker, 2004.

Rigsby, Curtis. "Nishida on God, Barth and Christianity." *Asian Philosophy* 19, no. 2 (2009): 119–57.

Rodin, R. Scott. *Evil and Theodicy in the Theology of Karl Barth.* New York: Peter Lang, 1997.

Rodríguez, Rubén Rosario. *Dogmatics after Babel: Beyond Theologies of Word and Culture.* Louisville: Westminster John Knox, 2018.

Rogers, Jack. "Biblical Authority and Confessional Change." *Journal of Presbyterian History* 58, no. 2 (1981): 131–60.

Rogers, Jack, and Donald McKim. *The Authority and Interpretation of the Bible.* San Francisco: Harper & Row, 1979.

Ruschke, Werner. *Entstehung und Ausführung der Diastasentheologie in Karl Barths zweitem Römerbrief.* Neukirchen: Neukirchener Verlag, 1987.

Ryken, Leland. *Worldly Saints: The Puritans as They Really Were.* Grand Rapids: Zondervan, 1986.

Sánchez, Leopoldo. "What Does Japan Have to Do with Either Latin America or U.S. Hispanics? Reading Kazoh Kitamori's 'Theology of the Pain of God' from a Latino Perspective." *Missio Apostolica* 12, no. 1 (2004): 36–47.

Sanks, Howland. "David Tracy's Theological Project: An Overview and Some Implications." *Theological Studies* 54, no. 4 (1993): 698–727.

Schulweis, Harold. "Karl Barth's Job: Morality and Theodicy." *The Jewish Quarterly Review* 65, no. 3 (1975): 156–67.

Smith, Aaron. "God's Self-Specification: His Being Is His Electing." *Scottish Journal of Theology* 62, no. 1 (2009): 1–25.

Sonderegger, Katherine. "The Doctrine of Inspiration and the Reliability of Scripture." In *Thy Word Is Truth: Barth on Scripture,* edited by George Hunsinger. Grand Rapids: Eerdmans, 2012.

Song, Choan-Seng. "The Relation of Divine Revelation and Man's Religion in the Theologies of Karl Barth and Paul Tillich." Ph.D. diss., Union Theological Seminary, 1964.

Spencer, Archie. *The Analogy of Faith: The Quest for God's Speakability.* Downers Grove, IL: IVP Academic, 2015.

Spiekermann, Ingrid. *Gotteserkenntnis: Ein Beitrag zur Grundfrage der neuen Theologie Karl Barths.* Munich: Chr. Kaiser, 1985.

Stumme, Wayne, ed. *The Gospel of Justification in Christ: Where Does the Church Stand Today?* Grand Rapids: Eerdmans, 2006.

Sumner, Darren. *Karl Barth and the Incarnation: Christology and the Humanity of God*. London: Bloomsbury, 2014.

Sutanto, Nathaniel Gray. *God and Knowledge: Herman Bavinck's Theological Epistemology*. London: T&T Clark, 2020.

Takizawa, Katsumi. "Über die Möglichkeit des Glaubens." *Evangelische Theologie* 10 (1935): 376–402.

Tanner, Kathryn. "Creation and Providence." In *The Cambridge Companion to Karl Barth*, edited by John Webster. Cambridge: Cambridge University Press, 2000.

Teske, Ronald. "Augustine's Use of 'Substantia' in Speaking about God." *Modern Schoolman* 62, no. 3 (1985): 147–63.

Tietz, Christiane. *Karl Barth: A Life in Conflict*. Translated by Victoria Barnett. Oxford: Oxford University Press, 2021.

———. "Karl Barth and Charlotte von Kirschbaum." *Theology Today* 74, no. 2 (2017): 86–111.

———. *Karl Barth: Ein Leben im Widerspruch*. Munich: C. H. Beck, 2019.

Torrance, Thomas. *Karl Barth: An Introduction to His Early Theology 1910–1931*. Edinburgh: T&T Clark, 1962.

Tracy, David. *The Analogical Imagination: Christian Theology and the Culture of Pluralism*. New York: Crossroad, 1981.

———. "Lindbeck's New Program for Theology: A Reflection." *The Thomist* 49, no. 3 (1985): 460–72.

Trueman, Carl R. "Calvin, Barth, and Reformed Theology: Historical Prolegomena." In *Calvin, Barth and Reformed Theology*, edited by Neil MacDonald and Carl Trueman. Eugene, OR: Wipf and Stock, 2008.

———. *The Claims of Truth: John Owen's Trinitarian Theology*. Carlisle: Paternoster, 1998.

———. *John Owen: Reformed Catholic, Renaissance Man*. Burlington, VT: Ashgate, 2007.

———. "John Owen's *Dissertation on Divine Justice*: An Exercise in Christocentric Scholasticism." *Calvin Theological Journal* 33, no. 1 (1998): 87–103.

Tseng, Shao Kai. "Barth on Actualistic Ontology." In *The Wiley-Blackwell Companion to Karl Barth*, edited by George Hunsinger and Keith Johnson. Oxford: Wiley-Blackwell, 2020.

———. *Barth's Ontology of Sin and Grace: Variations on a Theme of Augustine*. London: Routledge, 2019.

———. "Church." In *The Oxford Handbook of Nineteenth-Century Christian Thought*, edited by Joel Rasmussen, Judith Wolfe, and Johannes Zachhuber. Oxford: Oxford University Press, 2017.

———. "Condemnation and Universal Salvation: Karl Barth's 'Reverent Agnosticism' revisited." *Scottish Journal of Theology* 71, no. 3 (2018): 324–38.

———. *Immanuel Kant*. Phillipsburg, NJ: P&R, 2020.

———. "Karl Barths aktualistische Ontologie: Ihre Substanzgrammatik des Seins und Prozessgrammatik des Werdens." *Neue Zeitschrift für Systematische Theologie und Religionsphilosophie* 61, no. 1 (2019): 32–50.

———. *Karl Barth's Infralapsarian Theology: Origins and Development, 1920–1953*. Downers Grove, IL: IVP Academic, 2016.

———. *"Non Potest Non Peccare:* Karl Barth on Original Sin and the Bondage of the Will." *Neue Zeitschrift für Systematische Theologies und Religionsphilosophie* 60, no. 2 (2018): 185–207.

Turchin, Sean. "Kierkegaard's Echo in the Early Theology of Karl Barth." *Kierkegaard Studies Yearbook* 2012, no. 1 (2012): 323–36.

Van Asselt, Willem. *The Federal Theology of Johannes Cocceius (1603–1669)*. Translated by Raymond A. Blacketer. Leiden: Brill, 2001.

———. "On the Maccovius Affair." In *Revisiting the Synod of Dordt*, edited by Aza Goudriaan and Fred van Lieburg. Leiden: Brill, 2006.

Van Driel, Edwin. *Incarnation Anyway: Arguments for Supralapsarian Christology*. Oxford: Oxford University Press, 2008.

———. "Karl Barth on the Eternal Existence of Jesus Christ." *Scottish Journal of Theology* 60, no. 1 (2007): 45–61.

Van Kuiken, Jerome. *Christ's Humanity in Current and Ancient Controversy: Fallen or Not?* London: Bloomsbury, 2017.

Van Til, Cornelius. *Christianity and Barthianism*. Philadelphia: P&R, 1962.

———. "Has Karl Barth Become Orthodox?" *Westminster Theological Journal* 16, no. 2 (1954): 135–81.

———. *The New Modernism*. Philadelphia: P&R, 1946.

Vanhoozer, Kevin, ed. *The Cambridge Companion to Postmodern Theology*. Cambridge: Cambridge University Press, 2003.

———. "A Person of the Book? Barth on Biblical Authority and Interpretation." In *Karl Barth and Evangelical Theology: Convergences and Divergences*, edited by Sung Wook Chung. Grand Rapids: Baker, 2006.

Veenhof, Jan. *Revelatie en inspiratie*. Amsterdam: Buijten & Schipperheijin, 1968.

Walker, Ralph. "Kant and Transcendental Arguments." In *The Cambridge Companion to Kant and Modern Philosophy*, edited by Paul Guyer. Cambridge: Cambridge University Press, 2006.

Wan, Milton. "Authentic Humanity in the Theology of Paul Tillich and Karl Barth." D.Phil. diss., University of Oxford, 1984.

Ward, Graham. "Barth, Hegel and the Possibility for Christian Apologetics." In *Conversing with Barth*, edited by John C. McDowell and Mike Higton. Aldershot, UK: Ashgate, 2004.

———. "Barth, Modernity, and Postmodernity." In *The Cambridge Companion to Karl Barth*, edited by John Webster. Cambridge: Cambridge University Press, 2000.

Watson, Gordon. "Karl Barth and St. Anselm's Theological Programme." *Scottish Journal of Theology* 30, no. 1 (1977): 31–45.

Weber, Otto. *Karl Barths Kirchliche Dogmatik: Ein einführender Bericht*. Düsseldorf: Neukirchener Verlag, 1975.

Webster, John. *Barth's Earlier Theology*. London: T&T Clark, 2005.

———. *Barth's Moral Theology: Human Action in Barth's Thought*. London: T&T Clark, 1998.

———, ed. *The Cambridge Companion to Karl Barth*. Cambridge: Cambridge University Press, 2000.

———. *Karl Barth*. 2nd edition. New York: Continuum, 2004.

———. "'There is no past in the Church, so there is no past in theology': Barth on the History of Modern Protestant Theology." In *Conversing with Barth*, edited by John McDowell and Mike Higton. Aldershot, UK: Ashgate, 2004.

Weinrich, Michael. "Bund." In *Barth-Handbuch*, edited by Michael Beintker. Tübingen: Mohr Siebeck, 2016.

Wigley, Stephen. "The von Balthasar Thesis: A Re-examination of von Balthasar's Study of Barth in the Light of Bruce McCormack." *Scottish Journal of Theology* 56, no. 3 (2003): 345–59.

Wolterstorff, Nicholas. "Barth on Evil." *Faith and Philosophy* 13, no. 4 (1996): 584–604.

Wübbenhorst, Karla. "Calvin's Doctrine of Justification: Variations on a Lutheran Theme." In *Justification in Perspective: Historical Perspectives and Contemporary Challenges*, edited by Bruce McCormack. Grand Rapids: Baker, 2006.

Xu, Ximian. "Karl Barth's Ontology of Holy Scripture Revisited." *Scottish Journal of Theology* 74, no. 2 (2021): 26–40.

Yeung Arnold (楊牧谷). *Theology of Reconciliation and Church Renewal* (復和神學與教會更新). Hong Kong: Seed Press (種籽出版), 1987.

Yu, Carver. "The Contrast of Two Ontological Models as a Clue to Indigenous Theology." D.Phil. diss., University of Oxford, 1981.

RECOMMENDED READING

It is a well-known fact that varying interpretations of Barth abound, and that there are contradictory accounts of his theology even among his followers. A few typical responses to this phenomenon have ensued on the evangelical side. Some are simply discouraged by this fact from seriously engaging with Barth, thinking that his writings are characteristically, if not intentionally, ambiguous. Others take this fact to imply that Barth programmatically contradicts himself. As we saw in chapter 2, however, these attitudes are mostly based on unfounded myths about the Swiss theologian. The most heated controversy in contemporary Barth studies is in fact a debate on whether the substantive aspect of Barth's doctrine of God contradicts its methodological aspect. Traditionalists have shown that, textually, there is no such contradiction. Revisionists, however, contend that Barth's theological method must be understood against the background of his intellectual biography and the broader history of modern philosophy and theology. Once this interpretive framework is established, revisionists aver, one can easily identify a fundamental contradiction between the substantive aspect of

Barth's doctrine of God (the affirmation of the immanent Trinity as God's immutable essence) and its methodological aspect (the programmatic insistence on understanding "being" as a function of "becoming").

This situation should sound familiar to evangelical defenders of biblical authority. There sometimes seem as many biblical interpretations as there are Christians (to borrow a quip on Barth from Professor Carl Trueman). This fact, however, has not discouraged evangelicals from seeking objective meaning in the biblical texts. We do not deduce from this fact that the Bible lacks perspicuity. According to historic Protestantism, as succinctly expressed in the Westminster Confession (1.4, 1.7, and 1.9), the *authority* of Scripture is part and parcel of its textual *perspicuity*. Not all parts of Scripture are "alike plain in themselves," of course, but we still affirm that there is an "infallible rule of interpretation of Scripture" within Scripture that is perspicuous.

As a general rule of thumb, evangelical hermeneutics teaches us that when we approach the writings of any author, we should first assume that there are plain meanings and intents in the text, and that a perspicuous *rule of interpretation* of the text is to be found in the text itself. Why, then, should this not also be—why has this not been—our first step in attempting to understand Barth? In the present volume, I have been at pains to suggest that we should avoid jumping to the conclusion that Barth's text lacks perspicuity or programmatically contradicts itself and making this conclusion the point of departure in our interpretation of his writings. Evangelical readers who are suspicious of the type of hermeneutics, which gives priority to historical criticism over the text itself, should resonate with George Hunsinger, *Reading Barth with Charity: A Hermeneutical Proposal* (Grand Rapids: Baker Academic, 2015).

With the foregoing considerations in mind, I suggest that the texts recommended below be read in the order they are listed.

This list of recommended readings is intended to establish a rule of interpretation of Barth's text from the text itself, before proceeding to methodological, historical-analytical, and intellectual-biographical considerations.

(1) Hunsinger, George. *How to Read Karl Barth: The Shape of His Theology.* Oxford: Oxford University Press, 1991. This book establishes a perspicuous rule of interpretation of the text from the text for readers of Barth. Both novices and experts can benefit immensely from this book. It was published well before the traditionalist-revisionist debate, and most of its contents are uncontroversial, so the reader would not have to be worried about possible biases that might arise from reading it. There are other good introductory texts that may be read alongside *How to Read Karl Barth.* These include: John Webster, *Karl Barth,* 2nd edition (New York: Continuum, 2004), and Eberhard Busch, *Barth* (Nashville: Abingdon, 2008). A biographical sketch can also serve as a helpful complement: Eberhard Busch, *Karl Barth: His Life from Letters and Autobiographical Texts,* trans. John Bowden (London: SCM, 1975).

(2) Johnson, Keith L. *The Essential Karl Barth: A Reader and Commentary.* Grand Rapids: Baker Academic, 2019. This is a masterful selection of Barth's writings with authoritative annotations from one of the leading voices in contemporary Barth studies. The commentary does not engage in controversy directly and is suitable for readers looking to gain a comprehensive overview of Barth's theology. Such an overview is important for the development of a rule of interpretation of the text from the text.

(3) *CD* II/1, §28, "The Being of God Who Loves in Freedom"; *CD* II/1, §33, "The Election of Jesus Christ." Not all of Barth's writings are "alike plain in themselves." For a "rule of

interpretation" of the text from the text, I recommend these two paragraphs. I suggest that the reader begin the dive into Barth's writings with these two paragraphs, before proceeding to any other part of the *Church Dogmatics* or, for that matter, any other work by the theologian. Both traditionalists and revisionists would agree that these paragraphs are foundational to Barth's mature theology, and much of the controversy has revolved around the themes set forth in them. Treating *Romans* II or *CD* I/1–2 as the source of the rule of interpretation has led to some of the most popular myths about Barth in evangelicalism and beyond, and so it is not advisable to begin with these earlier texts.

(4) *Anselm: Fides Quaerens Intellectum.* One of revisionism's central intellectual-biographical contentions is that *Anselm* plays no important role in Barth's mature theology. However, Sigurd Baark has shown that Barth's basically Anselmian mode of reflection is the most fundamental aspect of his mature theological method, which finally allowed him to break through the impasse of (neo-) Kantian positivism and idealist-metaphysical historicism. I have introduced Barth's basically Anselmian method at some length in the present volume. After having read *CD* II/1–2, §§ 28 and 33, the reader will be in a position to decide whether the Anselmian spirit manifests itself in the consciousness of Barth.

(5) Webster, John, ed. *The Cambridge Companion to Karl Barth.* Cambridge: Cambridge University Press, 2000. This volume marks the beginning of some of the most important debates in contemporary Barth studies, including the aforementioned one between traditionalism and revisionism (see "Grace and Being: The Role of God's Gracious Election in Karl Barth's Theological Ontology" and "Karl Barth's Christology: Its Basic Chalcedonian Character"). All the chapters in this volume are heavyweights, each representing one central area of contemporary Barth studies.

(6) McCormack, Bruce. *Karl Barth's Critically Realistic Dialectical Theology: Its Genesis and Development 1909–1936.* Oxford: Clarendon Press, 1995. This intellectual-biographical monograph is the most significant game changer in both Anglophone and German Barth studies since the publication of the 1951 paradigm-setting volume by Hans Urs von Balthasar, *The Theology of Karl Barth: Exposition and Interpretation,* trans. Edward T. Oakes (San Francisco: Ignatius Press, 1992). Professor McCormack's thesis that *Anselm* has no significant bearing on Barth's mature theology has dominated much of Barth studies in recent decades. This thesis was seriously challenged in 2018 (see the recommended monograph by Sigurd Baark below), though many remain unconvinced by it. The other thesis of McCormack's volume is an important contribution that is widely accepted among Barth scholars today, namely, that the Christocentric reorientation of the doctrine of election, which began in 1936, represents the culmination of Barth's theological development. Professor McCormack would later revise his thesis and contend that the identification of Jesus Christ as the electing God in *CD* II/2 (1942) is where Barth developed a truly and thoroughly Christocentric ontology. Whether this later revision of the thesis is true has been at the heart of the debate between traditionalism and revisionism.

(7) Jones, Paul Dafydd, and Paul Nimmo, eds. *The Oxford Handbook of Karl Barth.* Oxford: Oxford University Press, 2020. Published just a week later than *The Wiley-Blackwell Companion to Karl Barth* (see below), this is the most authoritative reference volume on Barth in the English language to date. The intellectual-biographical sketch by multiple authors in the first part of the volume offers the most up-to-date information in this area, though regrettably there is no contribution from Christiane Tietz. The volume has an obvious revisionist leaning, with

traditionalist authors being assigned topics less central to the current debates. Almost all the authors are established authorities in Barth studies, except a few younger pioneers of new areas within the field. The contributors are exclusively American, British, and European, who have dominated Barth studies until recent decades. Conservative evangelical voices are not represented in the volume. Still, this handbook gives the reader a helpful survey of Barth studies, led by those whom I like to call "establishment Barthians."

(8) Hunsinger, George, and Keith Johnson, eds. *The Wiley-Blackwell Companion to Karl Barth*. Oxford: Wiley-Blackwell, 2020. Published almost concurrently with *The Oxford Handbook of Karl Barth*, this work provides a more balanced representation of established authorities in the field and younger pioneers at the frontiers of contemporary Barth studies. It features authors from non-Western ethno-cultural backgrounds, of non-Barthian convictions, and with areas of expertise outside of conventional Barth studies. Even hard-line Reformed and evangelical authors like Ryan Glomsrud are represented in this volume. The biographical dimension of the *Companion* is much thinner than that of the *Oxford Handbook*. The contribution by Christiane Tietz at the beginning of the volume, however, helps to avoid the suspicion of a hagiography. The doctrinal part of the *Companion* has a traditionalist tilt, with Professor Paul Molnar opening up the first main section of the first volume with a chapter on the Trinity. The second volume of the *Companion* brings Barth into dialogue with major figures and themes, with contributions from a wide variety of authors within and outside the field of Barth studies.

(9) Tietz, Christiane. *Karl Barth: A Life in Conflict*. Translated by Victoria Barnett. Oxford: Oxford University Press, 2021. This is

presently the most academically up-to-date biography of Barth. While the older biography by Eberhard Busch relies primarily on Barth's letters and autobiographical texts, which Busch reads in the light of his own personal knowledge of his Swiss mentor, Professor Tietz offers a more robust view of Barth's life as a theologian by drawing on a much wider variety of sources. This new biography focuses on the theological theme of *Widerspruch*, rendered in the title of the English translation as "conflict." The German word can be variously translated as "antithesis," "contradiction," "protest," etc. Barth is portrayed in this biography as a witness of Jesus Christ protesting against the spirit of the age, as the "red pastor" revolting against the economic order of the West, as a theological rebel challenging the established order of liberal theology that dominated much of academic theology in Europe during his early career, and as an other-worldly citizen who defied the political order of the Third Reich. The term *Widerspruch* also encapsulates the dialectical characteristics of Barth's own theology. Professor Tietz boldly highlights the actualistic correspondences, as it were, between Barth's theological dialectics and some contradictions in his personal life. This dimension of the *Widerspruch* becomes especially provocative in Professor Tietz's candid account of Barth's three-way relationship with his wife, Nelly, and Charlotte von Kirschbaum. This topic was previously untouchable in Barth studies under the dominance of establishment Barthians, but Professor Tietz brings it to the foreground in a constructive and scholarly way. Without discrediting Barth's theology, this biography serves to remind his followers, as well as those who critically draw on his insights, that there are genuinely problematic aspects of his theology that beg for correction and revision.

(10) Baark, Sigurd. *The Affirmations of Reason: On Karl Barth's Speculative Theology*. Cham, Switzerland: Palgrave Macmillan,

2018. Ever since the publication of Professor Bruce McCormack's *Barth's Critically Realistic Dialectical Theology* in 1995, attempts to interpret Barth's mature theology in the light of an Anselmian program of *credo ut intelligam* have generally been dismissed by establishment Barthians as academically outdated and indefensible. Professor McCormack rightly brings to our attention the post-Kantian dimension of Barth's development as a theologian. What the McCormack paradigm misses is the other dimension, in which Barth reacts against the idealist-metaphysical strain of liberal theology represented chiefly by Schleiermacher, Hegel, and Schelling. Sigurd Baark, Professor McCormack's erstwhile *Doktorsohn* at Princeton Theological Seminary, brings this dimension to light to demonstrate the key role that *Anselm* played in Barth's theological development. This monograph offers the most erudite and sophisticated intellectual-biographical and historical-philosophical paradigm to date, shedding light on aspects of Barth's theological development previously neglected by Hans Urs von Balthasar, Hans Frei, T. F. Torrance, and Bruce McCormack. Although Baark does not directly cite the works of the leading proponents of the traditionalist school of Barth interpretation, he demonstrates in this monograph that, with the Anselmian-Barthian method of reflective *Nachdenken*, Barth's affirmation of the immutability of the immanent Trinity is consistent with his theology as a whole. If this monograph is given the attention that it deserves, it may give rise to the next dominant paradigm in Barth studies.

INDEX OF SCRIPTURE

INDEX OF SUBJECTS AND NAMES

110–11, 115, 122, 125,
127–28, 132–33
revisionism (interpretation of
Barth), 50, 64
Reymond, Robert L., 9, 89,
101–2, 107
Ritchlian School, 20, 38, 44
Rutherford, Samuel, 116

saga, biblical narratives as, 77–78,
125–28, 132
Schelling, Friedrich, 4, 44
Schilder, Klaas, 37, 39–40
Schleiermacher, Friedrich, 3,
18, 34, 38, 44–45, 48–49,
56–57, 59, 65, 81, 88, 121,
138
Scripture
as Word of God, 66, 68–69,
109–10, 113, 122
inspiration of, 8–9, 28, 31,
43, 101, 107, 109–11,
114, 125, 127, 133
sublation (*Aufhebung*), 57, 82,
86, 88

Takizawa, Katsumi, 28
Tanabe, Hajime, 27, 28
Thomas Aquinas, 23, 103, 105
Tillich, Paul, 3, 19–20, 22, 24

Torrance, Thomas F., 14, 17,
21–24, 64, 134–35
Tracy, David, 12, 16
traditionalism (interpretation
of Barth), 10, 12, 24, 45,
64–65, 96
transcendence, 3, 5, 102
Trinity, immanent, 13, 75, 88,
91–93, 104–5, 108
Troeltsch, Ernst, 44, 81

univocity, 101–2, 124–25, 133
unsublatable subjectivity, Godus,
52, 55, 65

Van Til, Cornelius, 1, 3–4, 18,
36–41, 43, 74–75, 79–80,
88–89, 91, 93, 131
Vos, Geerhardus, 34, 115–19,
121, 125

Westminster Standards,
100–101, 107–8, 113, 143
witness, 10, 12, 60, 64–66, 68–69,
77–79, 113, 131, 137, 142
Wolf, Christian, 17, 50
Word of God
essential (hypostatic), 68, 110
implanted, 109–10, 117
written, 110

Shao Kai ("Alex") Tseng (DPhil, Oxford) is research professor in the Department of Philosophy at Zhejiang University, China. His research publications have covered areas including modern theology, Continental philosophy, Reformed orthodoxy, Song-Ming Confucianism, and philosophy of music. He is the author of *G. W. F. Hegel* (2018) in the P&R Great Thinkers series, *Barth's Ontology of Sin and Grace: Variations on a Theme of Augustine* (2019), and *Karl Barth's Infralapsarian Theology: Origins and Development 1920–1953* (2016), and a contributor to the *Oxford Handbook of Nineteenth-Century Christian Thought* (2017) and *Blackwell Companion to Karl Barth* (2020).

Did you find this book helpful?
Consider leaving a review online.
The author appreciates your feedback!

Or write to P&R at editorial@prpbooks.com
with your comments. We'd love to hear from you.